MARKET, PLAN, & STATE

MARKET, PLAN, & STATE

The Strengths and Weaknesses of the Two World Economic Systems

ADAM ZWASS

M. E. SHARPE, INC.
Armonk, New York
London, England

Available in the United Kingdom and Europe from M. E. Sharpe, Publishers, 3 Henrietta Street, London WC2E 8LU.

Translated from the German, *Zwei Weltsysteme: Ihre Stärken und Schwächen*

Translated by Michel Vale

Library of Congress Cataloging-in-Publication Data

Zwass, Adam.
 Market, plan, and state.

 Translation of: Zwei Weltsysteme.
 1. Capitalism. 2. Socialism. I. Title.
HB501.Z9313 1987   330.9′04   86-15581
ISBN 0-87332-396-3

Printed in the United States of America

*To my very young grandson, Joshua Jonathan,
with love and affection*

Contents

Preface to the American Edition

The present study, I feel, has been long overdue. For quite some time, the market economies have been searching for a role that planning might play in their economic management. At the same time, the planned economies have been trying, in many disparate ways, to fit market mechanisms into their centrally managed systems. New developments within both economic worlds lend renewed urgency to the analysis of their convergence and divergence.

Crisis phenomena in both world systems are discussed in the first chapter of this work. In the market economies the specificity of these developments in the era of the new revolution in science and technology consists in ever longer periods of recession, accompanied by ever greater technological unemployment that cannot be justified by the low growth rate only, and an uneven course of adjustment to the worldwide market competition induced by the great industrial powers. The systemic weakness of the planned economies, namely deficient mechanisms for economic steering, geared toward autarky, results in these countries' backwardness in economic competition with the developed industrial countries, as a direct consequence of low productivity and poor quality of production.

The second chapter compares economic and social structural changes in the West, in the East, and in the Third World, and considers the moving forces of social evolution, productivity, and work ethics as well as the economic potential of the three world regions. The effects of the new revolution in science and technology are contrasted with the effects of the socialist revolution.

Chapters three through six confront conservative and liberal theory with practice in the East and in the West. Recent reform experiments in traditionally conservative Soviet economic management, particularly since the accession of the more dynamic Gorbachev leadership, and broad modifications of the economic model in reform-oriented Hungary are analyzed. In the industrialized countries of the West, a tendency toward state intervention is gaining. In this context, an investigation is also made of the economic and social effects of nationalization in several industrialized countries of the West, particularly in Austria, France, and Great Britain. Finally, the seventh chapter analyzes the interdependence between crisis phenomena in the economy and ideology.

The first main conclusion arrived at in this comparison is that progress in social relations occurs faster in the Western industrialized countries, with their more extensive industrial and technological base, than in the countries that have labeled their system socialist, which have an underdeveloped state-owned and state-controlled production base. Another conclusion is that human beings overrate their capacities when they undertake to run a complex, diversified modern economy with directives from a central body rather than with the wisdom accumulated in economic mechanisms shaped by centuries of human economic activity.

* * *

I wish to express my thanks to the Board of the Austrian National Bank for its material and moral support, and to the Bank's Study Group on the Soviet Union and Eastern Europe for providing a stimulating environment and a sounding board for some of these ideas. I am also grateful to my wife Friederike for her multifaceted help, and to Gertrude Czipke for a careful reading of the manuscript. Michel Vale was a skilled translator. David B. Biesel provided an editorial environment for which I am grateful.

ADAM ZWASS

MARKET, PLAN, & STATE

1. Signs of crisis in the East and in the West

In the 1930s, while the market economies of Europe and the United States were experiencing the most serious economic crisis in their history, the Soviet Union was enjoying unprecedented rates of growth which astonished the world. The boldest projects of the ambitious first Five-Year Plan were completed; huge factories, power plants, and a transport network stretching far and wide were put into operation in an astonishingly short time.

It was the pioneer spirit of the great October Revolution that provided the inspiration for this most dynamic period of development in the history of Russia, the goal of which was to overcome centuries of backwardness relative to Western civilization within a few decades. No one anticipated that that ambitious Five-Year Plan would initiate a completely new stage in the history of the Soviet Union. This was far removed from the sublime ideas of the Revolution, which had augured liberty, fraternity, and equality but had in fact established an unprecedentedly rigorous rule of force and a command economy devised to industrialize Russia, pulling it out of its extreme backwardness at the most rapid possible rate. No one dreamed that the number of victims of forced collectivization and death through starvation would be almost as large as the number of unemployed in the market economies, immersed in crisis.

The movement in whose behalf the October Revolution was carried out had passed the death sentence on capitalism as far back as 1848. Many of the symptoms observed at that time had become more acute while others had been eliminated. But one point had definitely not been vindicated: the workers did not become poorer—either relatively or absolutely—as history progressed. Nowhere was prosperity shared by so many as in the industrial states of the West. And one other point had been decisively proven: the market economies were not able to guarantee continuous production, uninterrupted by crisis. This applies even to the period after World War II, when the boom lasted longer than ever before; and it applies today.

The Soviet Union and the nations of Southern and Eastern Europe that came under Soviet influence in the aftermath of World War II were able to maintain a dynamic economic growth for many years after the war. But the economic system that had taken shape under the conditions specific to backward Russia at that time was based on a concept of growth that stressed heavy industry at the expense of consumption. This came to constitute a serious obstacle to further development.

The state—the interventionist state—which is the bogeyman of the competitive market, became the general caretaker of an economy caught up in a dynamic growth. Self-regulating factors were replaced by the subjective commands of the hierarchically structured administrative bureaucracy and the competitive market gave way to the seller's market, certainly no promoter of quality. Market mechanisms, downgraded to a technical tool of accounting, and, above all, prices, now set by central authorities, lost their economic significance and consequently their parametric function as well. The planned economies no longer generated any warning signals of approaching malaise. As Jozef Pajestka, the former chief planner of Poland, once so trenchantly observed, plans were drawn up carefully, but growth was hardly systematic. It is no exaggeration to say that the planned economies give rise to greater disproportionalities than other economic systems.

The stormy enthusiasm of the pioneers of the October Revolution gradually waned. The revolutionaries of yesterday grew fat and became the ruling elite of a totalitarian state. The ideologues fell victim to Stalin's reign of terror, their moral and intellectual potential suppressed by the mentality of the state bureaucracy: self-complacent, greedy, domineering, and obsessed with maintaining the status quo.

The factors stimulating growth soon flagged. During the boom years from 1960 to 1973 the annual average growth rate in the Council for Mutual Economic Assistance (CMEA) countries was much higher (7.2 percent) than in the Organization for Economic Cooperation and Development (OECD) countries (5.0 percent), and only 1.3 percent lower than the growth rate in the newly industrializing countries (NIC) in the period between 1968 and 1972. The recession triggered by the oil crisis reduced the OECD growth rate to 0.3 percent in the years 1973 to 1975, while the planned economies still showed an above average (5.6 percent) growth, higher even than that of the NICs (4.9 percent). However, in 1975–1979, the five years of recovery, the OECD countries grew at a rate (annual average 4 percent) only 0.6 percent lower than did the CMEA countries, where the rate was already 2.1 percent lower than in the NICs. In the recession years 1979 to 1981 the annual average growth rate in the Eastern bloc was higher (3.2 percent) than in the OECD (1.3 percent) but 1.6 percent lower than that in the NICs.[1] In 1981, the gross national product in the CMEA rose by 1.2 percent; in 1982 by only 0.6 percent; in 1983 it recovered to 3.1 percent; in 1984 it rose by 3.8; and in 1985 by 3.2 percent.

When the economic recession began in the Western industrial countries after the years of boom, the planned economies found that they were no longer shielded from it.

The characteristics of the economic crisis varied just as much as the social systems in the respective blocs. The growth rate of the market economies has been relatively lower than that of the planned economies, but even in time of crisis they have maintained their high performance and are still able to maintain a maximum level of productivity and commodity quality, the most advanced technology, and for some, a maximum measure of prosperity. Yet the handicap that plagued them a century previously remains—namely, their cyclic, irregular growth, for which, unfortunately, no effective remedy has yet been found.

Paradoxically, it is the high productivity and the flexibility of the competitive market which constitute the principal cause of economic cycles. Rapid growth in production capacities during a time of boom leads to oversaturation and overproduction. Unrestrained demand increases the cost of labor, which, as a consequence, is replaced by ever more advanced technology. In the current period, electronics and microprocessors have done the rest. In 1972, twenty-nine hours of work were necessary to produce 1,000 marks' worth of industrial goods in the Federal Republic of Germany. In 1978, the same value required only fourteen hours to produce. In the printing industry, new electronic machinery typeset 800,000 letters per hour; the rate for lead typesetters was only 18,000.[2] If one applies the Marxist criterion for assessing a social system—namely, the productivity of labor of which it is potentially capable of achieving—a market economy is superior to a planned economy. It is not only more productive, it is also more advanced, more creative, and more conducive to prosperity; and, most importantly, it alone has proven compatible with a democratic, and thus pluralistic, ruling system.

A planned economy is the youngest economic system in the world. Yet, despite its youthfulness, sclerosis has already set in. The symptoms are familiar enough; the succession of Kremlin leaders has named them by name. No one, however, has ventured to attempt a cure, since that would entail reducing the power of the omnipotent bureaucracy which embraces the whole of political, economic, cultural, and social life. Khrushchev tried but was overthrown by the paladins. The crisis of the planned economies is not a cyclical crisis; it is a consequence of flaws intrinsic to the system. The symptoms are discernible to varying degrees in every planned economy, and recent developments in Poland show how deep the abyss can be in real socialism. The belief that a planned economy is a favorable alternative to a crisis-prone market economy has been dissipated. Both world systems are in a crisis. In the planned economies, however, the crisis is manifested not in overproduction and oversaturation of the market, but in an acute shortage of goods and an undersupplied population; not in an open unemployment, but in underemployment behind factory walls. A planned economy is no alternative to a competitive market economy, because its ailments are more serious. Indeed, it has shown clearly what must be avoided to prevent an evil of even greater magnitude: the all-embracing intervention of the state and a hypertrophied ruling bureaucracy with powers beyond rational measure, paralyzing initiative and innovativeness and driving the specific cost of labor, capital, and raw materials to unprecedented heights. Unemployment hidden behind factory walls merely reduces the productivity of labor to an intolerably low level.

A market economy is more adaptable

In the planned economies, traditional steering mechanisms have lost or greatly depleted their economic content. There are no reliable warning signals and no self-regulating factors for the growing disproportionalities, which can only be remedied by commands from the state bureaucracy; the parameters that are available are established, unfortunately, on the basis of deficient information.

But the laissez-faire stage of early capitalism is also long past. The invisible hand of the market suffers from arthritis. Still, it is too early to condemn the self-regulating mechanisms to oblivion. During the deepest recession so far, they were still able to force the Organization of Petroleum Exporting Countries (OPEC), the mightiest cartel of modern times, to its knees. In 1973 OPEC was the source of one-third of the West's fuel consumption; by mid-1982 this figure was only 28.5 percent.[3] A fourfold increase in the price of oil restored the competitive value of sources of energy that had earlier been unprofitable, alternative sources of energy were tapped, and economizing measures were instituted. The monopolistic practices of OPEC were brought to a halt: in 1980, the official oil price indicator was 302.9 (100 = 1951), and the spot price was 381.2. In 1982 these figures were 388.1 and 271.6.[4]

The planned economies lack adaptability; their main headache is not so much unused production capacities as unbounded waste of those capacities. Time and time again, reports to the party congresses and plenary sessions show how little the administrative bureaucracy is concerned with the rational utilization of production capacities, built at so great a cost. Scarce and expensive resources are wasted more indiscriminately now than in times when labor power, fuels, and raw materials were available in abundance.

The steering system used in the East was never equally appropriate to all countries. Now this is understood. The October Revolution evolved into a social system that was the only system possible given the conditions of backward Russia at the time, namely a system designed to initiate a fast industrialization. But while a regime named ''bourgeois democracy'' could be passed over, a whole stage in human civilization cannot.

The sublime theories of philosophical socialism led ineluctably to the praxis of real socialism, which probably fit into the traditions and habits of mind of the population and of the ruling elite of old Russia. This evolution certainly was more befitting the possibilities of this backward state than the establishment of a postindustrial society in a semifeudal country. So far so good. But the same system was forced upon the countries of Eastern and Southeastern Europe, which differed radically from one another and even more from Russia.

It would be very easy to draw the conclusion that Stalin, in using the all-powerful state as an instrument to overcome centuries of backwardness, was not embracing a philosophical paradigm, but rather was simply following in the footsteps of his powerful predecessor, Peter the Great, or of Sergei Witte, the Finance Minister of the last Tsar. Later, when he incorporated the countries of Eastern and Southeastern Europe into the sphere of influence of the Soviet Union and forced the Soviet social system upon them, he was acting in the spirit of the great Russian Empire as well as in accordance with the principle of Westphalia, *Cuius regio eius religio.*

Of course, real socialism is even less adapted even to the situation in Eastern and Southeastern Europe than it is to the Soviet Union. The East German ruling party's theses on the Karl Marx anniversary, celebrated in 1983, proclaimed: "his theory is omnipotent, because it is true." Let it be noted that Marx never said that a proletarian revolution should be carried from an economically backward country into an industrially developed country in such an unusual way. As we know, the proletarians of the German Democratic Republic rebelled against this unconventional proletarian revolution—indeed they were the first in the East bloc to do so—thereby causing deep disappointment to their government, which, as Berthold Brecht so aptly put it, was faithful to the Party line.

The practical experience of the planned economies shows clearly that Marxian theory is not as effective in the industrially developed GDR and Czechoslovakia as it is in the economically underdeveloped countries of Eastern Europe, and further shows that the rule of the bureaucracy bears the same fruits everywhere. The economically underdeveloped countries have not been raised to the level of those that were economically advanced; rather, as planned economies the latter are in fact in the process of falling to the level of performance of the former. No less a person than the head of the GDR's Socialist Unity Party, Erich Honecker, noted at the Fifth Conclave of the Central Committee (November 1982) that the labor productivity in the GDR was 30 percent lower than in the Federal Republic of Germany or in France. Indeed, the party leader needed only to take a few examples from agriculture to show to what extent the GDR economy, once so highly disciplined, had declined in performance: in 1982, 1.7 million hogs and 182,000 cattle died in their stalls.

In Czechoslovakia—which was one of the highly industrialized countries of Europe between the wars—this social system, transplanted from a situation of backwardness, has had an unfavorable impact. In its annual report for 1980, the Economic Commission for Europe observed: "Czechoslovakia shows the highest ore and steel consumption per capita in the world; it consumes 30 percent more metal per industrial unit than the other industrially developed countries of the world."[5] Only three-fourths of the amount of metal consumed ends in the finished product; one-fourth is wasted. Only 70 percent of wood material is productively used, compared with a normal figure of 90 percent. In 1979 the per capita income of Czechoslovakia was no more than 47.5 percent of the per capita income of France, 40.6 percent of that of the GDR, and only 55 percent of that of Austria.[6]

In Hungary, where, thanks to a successful reform of the steering system, some considerable progress has been made in improving efficiency, only a third of the products of heavy industry are of good enough quality to be exported to the industrial countries of the West. Another third can be used only domestically or in the CMEA, and finally one-third require a quality change.[7] The wastefulness of the economies of Poland, Romania, or the Soviet Union is described much more thoroughly in the reports of their top officials than in the research reports of the harshest Western critics.

The planned economies lack far more than the self-regulating mechanisms of the traditional market; there is no pluralism, and the workforce has no authentic representation for its interests. The interests of the workers are equated with the interests of the state, although their class structures diverge and the state, moreover, is under the strict control of an omnipotent ruling bureaucracy preeminently concerned with maintaining its privileged position, and hence disinclined to reforms that might undermine that position.

The steady succession of conflicts is not counterbalanced by any potential for functional resolution. Emancipatory impulses from the smaller nations have not made enough inroads to bring the traditional steering system into closer accord with existing conditions. And it is not surprising that there are outbreaks, frequently uncontrollable, of mass discontent. However, these fall short of achieving any lasting change. From the revolutionary uprising in the GDR in June 1953 and the mass movements in Hungary and Poland in October 1956, to the Prague Spring of 1968, to the unprecedented and valiant struggle of the Polish people in 1980–82, no lasting changes in the existing regime have been achieved. The geopolitical factor, directly or indirectly, has had a decisive influence on the course of events, and the legitimate aspiration to forge a radically reformed economic and political system has been doomed to failure.

The recent events in Poland have shown once again that the traditional centrally administered economy is an organic component of a one-party regime, and that an effective economic reform is a real possibility only if it is preceded by a radical reform of the political regime.

It has become clear as well that Joseph Schumpeter's postulate for a successful reform, namely "to preserve order in the midst of change, and to maintain change in the midst of order," is applicable only in a pluralistic social system. Despite devastating crises, the market economy has demonstrated its ability to maintain order while comprehensive structural changes are effected and to ensure steady progress.

Both world systems are class societies; they both have their workers and their ruling elites, although the latter may be differently structured in the two cases. In both, the way class conflicts are resolved is in need of reform. In the countries of real socialism, the theory of a classless society and the *de facto* subordination of the trade unions to the leading role of the party have long been in need of reexamination. The authority of the state is supreme; the interests of consumers are subordinate to the interests of the state, which the state itself interprets arbitrarily.

On the other hand, the Western social systems have never been able to coordinate demands with the existing means for meeting those demands, to dampen the tendency to live beyond existing means, to orchestrate divergent class interests, and to ascertain and then institutionalize the limits of permissible state intervention. They have always been profit oriented, but over time they have seen a steady and quite impressive increase in the workers' share of the pie as well as improved social services, by virtue of their organic embeddedness in a democratic state system and the role of the trade unions in economic decision-making.

The credibility gap

The market economy suffers from an incurable disease. It is subject to crises, and, thus far, no remedy has been able to eliminate this problem. However, the fading of the belief that a solution can be found within the framework of the existing system is having a devastating effect on the minds of political and economic leaders. This is all the more depressing when it is assumed that any alternative would be worse than the present market economy. This system, however devastating it may sometimes be in its effects, is still, to paraphrase Churchill, "the worst form of government except for all the others that have been tried from time to time." The pervasive skepticism, pessimism, and lethargy in the West stands in sharp contrast to the optimism of purpose trumpeted in the East by the Party leadership: "The way of social progress is hard, sometimes even painful," said Brezhnev to the Twenty-sixth Party Congress (1981). "There will be great and complicated tasks to solve," he continued, but "We will solve them, we will solve them without fail," he assured his audience. This optimism is dutifully conveyed by the mass media, despite the heavy burdens borne by those living under really existing socialism as compared to the citizens of the Western democracies.

To what extent is the economic crisis in the East and in the West a systemic crisis?

Although the market economies are still capable of maximizing efficiency and the planned economies, even with their declining growth rates, still guarantee full employment, the current symptoms of crisis in the two world systems have features indicative of a structural crisis in economic policy. Unemployment in the OECD countries is higher than the economic recession would warrant; the environment is under assault and material resources are strained; the international credit system has been put severely to the test by the growing indebtedness of the developing countries and the Eastern bloc; and the lack of international cooperation among the Western industrial countries hinders the development of a viable plan to promote growth worldwide. Economic theory has clearly failed. Neither supply-side or demand-side economics has been able to overcome the symptoms of crisis. To be sure, inflation has been curbed to some extent, but unemployment, budget deficits, and government indebtedness have soared. Forecasts continue to be grim and contradictory, but they do not contain answers. "As we are unable to explain and grasp the present very well," said Blaise Pascal, "we endeavor ingeniously to obtain an insight into the future."

By all appearances, it is not so much that the traditional market mechanisms have failed, as that the state has distorted their workings. State intervention, although too slipshod and feeble to promote economic growth and combat unemployment, has nevertheless been forceful enough to dampen the effects of the self-regulating factors of the market.

The symptoms of malaise in the planned economies are different, but no less grave and immanent to the system. Economic growth has declined, but still remains higher than in the market economies; stagnation does not seriously increase unemployment or reduce the living standard. However, the consequences of the unmistakeable decline in economic performance are by no means unproblematic. The pervasive shortage of mass consumer goods and the under-supply of the population are certainly neither easier to bear nor easier to bring under control than overproduction. The unemployed behind the factory walls are unable to produce more products and overcome the ever-growing goods shortage, just as the unemployed in the OECD countries aggravate, rather than diminish, overproduction because of their declining buying power.

In Eastern Europe, where ecology is not taken so seriously and where the "greens" are not permitted to be active, the environment is more polluted than almost anywhere else. This is especially true of the large population centers of Poland and the Soviet Union. In Poland, the lack of unpolluted water threatens to become the number one problem in the very near future. Gone forever are the days when the entire Eastern bloc could benefit from the abundance of the nearby and easily tapped fuel and raw material resources of the Soviet Union. New sources are being opened up in Siberia and the Far East, where exploration and extraction are expensive and conveyance requires gas and oil pipelines stretching for thousands of miles. Increased supplies to meet increased demands are reserved for those Eastern countries who participate in the tapping of deposits and the construction of pipelines.

But the term "economic crisis" is too vague to describe the economic difficulties plaguing the East.

The planned economies have never had an economic and political system adequate to a developed industrial society. Although it is certainly true that the social system that evolved in the Soviet Union in the 1930s was aimed at overcoming centuries of backwardness by means of exploitative "primitive accumulation" to accelerate industrialization, it is also true that, after this indispensible historical mission was completed, a qualitatively new steering system more in alignment with the conditions of a modern industrial society had to be developed. It is interesting that the planned economies have never been able to find a good alternative to such market mechanisms as real prices, profit, interest, exchange rates, or an effective money and capital market. The imitations of these alien mechanisms have functioned worse than the originals. On the other hand, the mechanisms inherent to the planned economies also proved inadequate to the need.

The planned economies have no more understood and practically used market mechanisms than market economies have practically implemented planning in the area of employment. Resource allocation has suffered most from the concept of rapid industrialization (everything for heavy industry, and what is left over for consumption) and from the ineffectual steering parameters. The extent of human hardship in the market economies guided by profit and demand is smaller than in the centrally planned economies. In no other social system is the proportion of heavy industry in the total economy as high as in the planned economies (in the Soviet Union it is more than 70 percent). The economic structure in the Eastern countries is more disproportioned and the ratio of supply to demand more out of balance than in the Western industrial countries.

If worldwide economic cooperation among the market economies suffers from lack of coordination, intrabloc cooperation of the Eastern countries suffers from a lack of steering mechanisms. The Eastern substitutes for market mechanisms, which are ineffective domestically, are even less effective in intra-CMEA trade, and are outright unusable in relations with the Western industrial states. The resolutions on integration of the CMEA, developed years ago, are still unfulfilled because prices, shielded from the international markets, are not comparable, currencies cannot be exchanged, and there are no economically grounded exchange rates. Despite innumerable decisions, it has been impossible to coordinate the national economic plans and to form effective joint firms. The International Bank for Economic Cooperation, established in 1964, is still a clearing house, and the International Investment Bank, established in 1971, has no functioning capital of its own that would enable it to finance investments. The CMEA banks and all the CMEA countries are forced to turn to international money and capital markets, where they are borrowers, not lenders. Despite many efforts, they have still not been able to create a price basis grounded in the internal cost ratios of the participating countries. In intra-CMEA trade, world market prices, borrowed from the West and adjusted appropriately, are still used; in trade with the industrial countries of the West, not only the prices but also the currencies of the partner countries are used.

Can the crisis be overcome?

The market economies have experienced and survived many seemingly incurable crises, admittedly not without some considerable derailments that led to self-destruction, to totalitarianism, and to two world wars. However, they were also able to bring about a unique economic boom with democracy and prosperity after the Second World War. The peoples of Eastern and Southeastern Europe have made many attempts to bring about structural change but have been driven back into the traditional real socialist conditions by their own ruling hierarchy or by the geopolitical factor. The Soviet Union and a few of the Eastern countries are still trying to cope with their accumulating economic problems by perfecting the instruments of planning and the organizational structure of administration within the framework of the existing system. It is still taboo to hold the system responsible for economic deficiencies; rather, it is always mistakes on the part of those who carry out the administrative directives that are blamed.

The persistent symptoms of malaise were called by their right names by Yuri Andropov in his inauguration speech on November 22, 1982: "The leading indicator of economic efficiency, namely, the productivity of labor, is growing at a rate that cannot be satisfactory to us; an asymmetry still persists in the respective growth of the raw materials sectors and the processing industries; the material intensity of production remains practically unchanged at its same high level."[8] But, as Andropov candidly admitted, he had no pat recipes, and in any case his rule was too short to enable him to come to grips with the accumulated problems.

The unresolved problems are showing a tendency to escalate. While there may be no hope that the self-regulating forces of the market will cure the malaise of the industrial countries of the West, there is also no hope that the party leadership of the Eastern countries—should they wish to cure the problems of the system—will accept the risk entailed in a radical, and now seemingly unavoidable, liberalization of the state system, i.e., the relinquishing of a considerable portion of their power.

Mikhail Gorbachev has been in power for two years. Young and dynamic, he rid the country of the mighty gerontocracy, including the 80-year old prime minister Nikolai Tikhonov. Only three of the Brezhnev-era members of the Politburo have remained in place. About one-third of the 157 first secretaries of the regional party committees, 10 out of 24 department chiefs of the Central Committee, and one-third of the members of the Council of Ministers have been removed.

The new generation that has risen to power with Gorbachev replaced long-time office holders who had lost all sense of reality. Most of the new appointees are, like Gorbachev, too young to have experienced the romance of Lenin's revolution, or Stalin's terror, or the horrors of the Second World War. This is the best educated generation of power holders the Soviet Union has ever known—pragmatic and free of ideological ballast. Gorbachev has begun a pitiless campaign against corruption and against the country's oldest enemy, alcoholism, which threatened the health of the population and had caused a drop in labor productivity to a level unacceptable for the second economic power in the world. The new leader has initiated radical measures aimed at modernization of the obsolete technical base of Soviet industry and at joining in the new revolution in science and technology taking place in the Western industrialized countries.

Gorbachev has submitted the lengthy rule of Leonid Brezhnev to harsh criticism, labeling the 1970s and the early '80s as "a period of inertia and stagnation." The new version of the Third Party Program, adopted by the 27th Party Congress on March 5, 1986, stated: "There appeared difficulties and unfavorable tendencies. Negative signals in the economy were not recognized in time, and the necessary structural changes were either not envisaged, or not implemented."

Gorbachev wishes to be regarded as the direct heir of the leader of the October Revolution and founder of the Soviet state: "It is not my own personal style," he told *Time* on September 9, 1985, "this is something we all learned from Lenin." But observers who translated that phrase into a hope that Gorbachev could return to Lenin's strategy of the New Economic Policy (NEP) of 1921 will be disappointed. Respects paid to Lenin and his economic policy do not mean a reimplementation of the policy of the 1920s in the 1980s. At the time of Lenin's New Economic Policy only the "commanding heights," the key industries, were in the hands of the state, while approximately half of the agricultural sector and about half of retail trade were still in private hands. A few years after Lenin's death, Stalin abolished the principles of NEP, nationalized all industry, trade, and services, collectivized agriculture, and created a powerful bureaucracy which fully controls the economic life of the country.

Can and would Gorbachev rock the foundations of the system and risk his leadership position? Who would support him in such a noble endeavor? Khrushchev tried to decentralize the management of the economy, with well known results; Gorbachev is certainly not interested in sharing his fate. The present leader wants to find a solution within the existing system rather than radically change the system itself. Seweryn Bialer and Joan Afferica are right in their appreciation of Gorbachev: "The quintessential technocrat offers a reforming regime, technological expertise, managerial experience and political skills" (*The New York Times*, February 11, 1986), but not much more.

Those who expect privatization of some of the sectors of economic activity will not be satisfied. The new version of the Third Party Program states that "the strengthening and enlarging of the social ownership of the means of production are the basic objectives of the socialist system." The illusions of those who expected an extensive decentralization of economic management have been shattered by the statement, made by Prime Minister Nikolai Ryzhkov on March 3, 1986, to the 27th Party Congress: "We have not and will not fulfill the hopes of the bourgeois ideologues regarding our rejection of the principles of the democratic centralism, central management, and economic planning."

Although there is no reason for optimism, especially considering the increasingly bitter confrontation between the two world systems, which is leading them into a costly and devastating arms race, the breakdown theories now so popular can not stand up to scrutiny. The spectre of the world economic crisis of the 1930s is now often unfairly evoked to portray the impending danger for the industrial countries of the West. But a few figures will show the essential difference between those days and now. Before the Wall Street stock market crash of October 24, 1929, U.S. Steel shares were quoted at $375; in July 1932 they were only $22. General Motors shares fell from $92 to $4.50. Montgomery Ward fell from $138 to $3, and General Electric from $220 to $20.[9] The number of unemployed in the United States increased within a short time from 400,000 to 15 million (the number of gainfully employed was one-third lower than today).

In economically weak countries the unemployment was even more acute. In 1929 the number of unemployed in Poland was 70,000 and the number of gainfully employed 2,400,000, but in 1934 the number of unemployed increased to 740,000 and the number of employed decreased to 1,830,000; the share of part-time employed increased to 36 percent (1932).[10] At the depth of the depression no less than one-third of Austria's workforce were unemployed. Measures designed to shift domestic difficulties to neighboring countries by currency devaluations, the beggar-my-neighbor policy, bore poisoned fruit: the difference between the exchange rate and the parity (determined by its gold content) of the British pound increased from 7 percent in September 1931 to 20.1 percent in October, 23.6 percent in November, and 30.7 percent in December. The value of the dollar plunged after the United States left the gold standard on April 19, 1933: by 12.5 percent in April 1933, 18.4 percent in May, 32.6 percent in September, and 36 percent in December 1933.[11]

The present economic crisis has produced severe strains. In the West, it has caused excessively high unemployment considering the relatively moderate decline in business, especially in the United States but also in most of the countries of Western Europe. Budget deficits and government debt have soared, and many banks and businesses, both large and small, have been driven into insolvency. In the East, it has sharpened the disproportionalities between heavy industry, which is still growing, a lagging agriculture, and the foods and consumer goods industries, as well as between the sectors producing raw materials and the processing industries. It has made the chronic crisis in supply more acute, driven Poland and Romania to the point of bankruptcy, and has led to major payment problems in the GDR and Hungary, which have had an impact on the entire Western banking world. Still, the consequences of this crisis cannot be compared with those of the 1930s. So far at least, there have been no spectacular crashes with worldwide repercussions. The insolvent countries such as Mexico, Poland, Romania, etc. have been able to reschedule their debt and the international credit network, of which the Eastern bloc countries have also made liberal use, continues to function. Further, the market economies of today are more firmly rooted in the ways of democracy than in the period between the wars, the role of the trade unions is much stronger than in the prewar period, and there are at present no dictatorships that could imperil the liberal traditions of the market economies. The Western world is more immune to extremist movements of the right or the left than in the period between the wars, and in the East a reversion to a Stalinist-type dictatorship does not appear to be in the offing. The Western democracies have been spared social and economic shocks. However, the same cannot be said about the Eastern countries and the situation in Poland still displays the unmistakeable signs of a deep social, economic, and political crisis.

While it may be said with some justification that not much was learned from the worldwide economic crisis of the 1930s, nonetheless, today we have quite sophisticated economic theories both in the East and in the West, in particular the undisputed and still indispensable theory of John Maynard Keynes. In those days, as Henry S. Wallich recalls, German Chancellor Hans Luther had to travel around in a plane to gather money together. Today the world has a well-functioning network of issuing banks, an International Monetary Fund, and a World Bank (to which three Eastern European countries, Romania, Poland, and Hungary, belong). Other international coordinating institutions, a European currency system, and many other supporting networks are functioning and, while they do not yet accomplish everything that is necessary, they are able to prevent the worst from occurring.

The geopolitical situation is different

The two world wars of this century have considerably changed the political landscape. The aftermath of World War I saw the establishment of the Soviet Union, the first communist superpower, in the East, fascist Italy in Southern Europe, and the end of the Austro-Hungarian monarchy. The aftermath of World War II saw the countries of Eastern and Southeastern Europe drawn into the Soviet sphere of influence and the partitioning of Germany. The division of the world into two political blocs operating at cross purposes has assumed distinct contours. Still, it would not be farfetched to say that the geopolitical situation today offers more favorable conditions for economic relations than did the interwar period. The treaties of Versailles had more grievous consequences for developments in Europe than did the Yalta agreement. After World War I, Germany, Austria, and Hungary were strained to the breaking point by the burden of war reparations, and the consequences of the economic crisis were much more severe in those countries than elsewhere. In crisis-wracked Germany, the forces which would later trigger World War II were breeding. The social and political structures of the countries of Europe were not yet sufficiently defined, and the play of pluralistic forces was bedevilled by controversy. Eastern and Southeastern Europe (with the exception of Czechoslovakia) were ruled by dictatorships or semidictatorships.

Today, Western Europe has been united in the European Community, and although the Community contains many contradictions, it has resolved many of the controversies between nations and eliminated customs barriers. The consolidation of the democratic system has had a stabilizing effect. With the passing of Franco's fascist regime in Spain, the Salazar regime in Portugal, and the military junta in Greece, all the countries of Western Europe are now governed by democratic or social democratic parties. West Germany functions better than the undivided country of the period between the wars, and East Germany is economically the most advanced country of Eastern Europe.

Although protectionist measures complicate economic cooperation, so far the conditions do not exist for a devastating economic war with an infamous beggar-my-neighbor policy.

The balance of power between the American economic power and the countries of Europe has a more positive countenance than in the period prior to World War II. Indeed, the European countries have shown themselves able to compete with the oppressive preponderance of the United States in economic growth and, in part, in scientific and technical progress as well, and in many sectors they are now on a par. In 1929 U.S. industrial production was 75 percent higher than in 1913, the French showed a 38.5 percent improvement, the Germans only 10 percent, and Great Britain only 9 percent improvement. In the boom period between 1960 and 1973, the average annual growth rate in Western Europe (4.8 percent) was 0.7 percent higher than in the United States; in the recession years 1973 to 1975, the American economy showed 0.8 percent negative growth, while the economy of Western Europe grew by 0.8 percent.

In the recovery phase between 1975 and 1979, U.S. economic growth was 4.5 percent, somewhat higher than Western Europe, which showed an average rate of 3.4 percent. But in the recession years 1979 to 1981, the average annual U.S. growth rate was 0.9 percent, which was only 0.1 percent higher than the growth rate of Western Europe.

Japan's growth rate is still outstanding: 4.9 percent in the boom period from 1960 to 1973, and in the recovery phase 1975 to 1979, 1.2 percent higher than the OECD average.[12]

The fact that Western Europe has kept pace with the United States may be seen as a proof that these countries did indeed learn something from the world crisis of the 1930s. The undeniable progress of Western Europe would have been impossible without the generous Marshall Plan.

The economic and political situation in Eastern Europe has a different impact now than between the wars

The Soviet Union was isolated from the world community of nations in the interwar period. The structural upheavals it was undergoing in the economic and political spheres were largely unknown to the rest of the world. Stalin's dictatorship was one of the cruelest in world history. The Soviet economy was focused more on autarky than on cooperation. The state monopoly over foreign trade and over the currency was an organic component of the steering system that evolved in the 1930s and paralyzed the mechanisms of economic intercourse with the world outside.

The ruble, reduced to an instrument of economic accounting and cut off from the world markets, had no economically grounded exchange rate and was nonconvertible throughout the entire interwar period, as it still is today. Soviet foreign trade was reduced to almost nothing. In not one year in the interwar period did it reach the volume of 1913 (10,090 million rubles at 1950 exchange rates). It had picked up somewhat in the NEP period, but after peaking in 1930 (7302 million rubles) it decreased steadily to 1207 million rubles in 1939. In 1940 it rose again to 2157 million rubles as a consequence of the agreement with Germany, but this was only the level of 1924.[13]

Today the world has to cope with the fact of an Eastern bloc led by the Soviet Union. The political consequences of the division of the world into two blocs are familiar enough. Our main interest here is to assess the impact of the new geopolitical situation on the world economy. The following considerations are therefore of relevance.

The countries of Eastern and Southeastern Europe, which currently conduct a considerable share of their foreign trade among themselves and with the Soviet Union, had almost no economic ties with each other or with the Soviet Union in the interwar period. In 1938, the foreign trade of Czechoslovakia with the Soviet Union (total exports and imports) was only 6.3 million rubles; Poland's was 1.6 million rubles; Romania's, 0.2 million rubles; Bulgaria's, 0.2 million rubles; and Hungary's, 0; the share of these countries in the Soviet Union's total trade was a meager 1.7 percent.[14]

The countries of Eastern and Southeastern Europe were part of the world market. They were, however, the most backward countries of the continent and were always borrowers, never lenders. Their situation is the same today; although their economic level is much higher than in the interwar period, they still suffer from the same difficulties. What a historian's pen might have described for the interwar period would apply almost equally well today.

At the West German Thirty-fourth Congress of Historians, held in mid-October 1982 with the theme "Margins of Action in History," the prewar situation of Eastern and Southeastern Europe was described as follows: "Industry urgently needed capital and know-how which could only be gotten in the West. Economic ties to Vienna, Budapest, and Berlin had been loosened, and those to London, Paris, and New York strengthened. But this merely created new dependencies, especially as not only industry, but the governments themselves were in the market for foreign loans to boost their currencies which (with the exception of Czechoslovakia's) had become highly inflated after the War."[15]

At that time it was the world economic crisis that barred the way to Western credits; today it is the insolvency of Poland and Romania. Further—and this is still true today—in many cases the industries of these countries were not competitive and too small a share of foreign loans had found its way into productive investment projects, having been used instead to reschedule old debts.

However, the situation in the interwar period was much worse if one considers that the debtors in Eastern Europe were forced to pledge their national patrimony, their monopolies, and even some of their tax revenues to secure new loans from the League of Nations, and like Germany were compelled to accept the supervision of a commissioner, appointed by the League of Nations.[16] Poland's payments situation was poor at that time and has remained poor. Poland would offer foreign creditors extraordinary financial advances to be able to obtain foreign credits at all. Today Poland has this phase behind it and it is compelled to apply for a rescheduling of due loans.

The countries of Eastern and Southeastern Europe have made some major progress in economic development in the postwar period. But their steering system does not provide a viable basis for developing a range of competitive export goods. In the 1970s, they imported in such large volume because they wanted to take advantage of modern Western technology as a vehicle of technical progress. This goal has remained unachieved because, to be effective, advanced technology must have an advanced steering system and management, and this the countries of Eastern Europe do not have. The consequence of this wrong economic strategy was a mountain of debt which these countries would like now to reduce, not by additional exports, but by cutting back on imports. This is no easy task if one considers that a cutback in imports means a fall in production and in exports and a further deepening of the crisis in supply.

The root of the problems lies in the steering system, which is so in need of reform, and in the geopolitical confrontation which entails enormous costs and makes an advantageous economic cooperation more difficult for both sides. In the brief period of detente, however, it became clear that the geopolitical constellations of the postwar period need not be an obstacle to a beneficial division of labor between the systems: whereas in the interwar period, the Soviet Union's foreign trade had been reduced nearly to the vanishing point, and the countries of Eastern and Southeastern Europe had been a heavy burden on the world economy, in the 1970s, the OECD countries sold goods amounting to about $290 billion on the Eastern markets and imported goods to an amount of $230 billion from the East. Further, in 1981 the exports of the OECD countries to the East were 50 billion dollars compared with only 7.8 billion dollars in 1970.

However unfavorable the conditions for business as usual between the market economies and the planned economies may be, experience has shown that under certain conditions economic cooperation with advantage to both sides does have chances for success. The differences in social systems need not necessarily have a destabilizing influence on the world economy. Quite the contrary, a rich division of labor would be able not only to promote detente but also to alleviate the symptoms of crisis in both East and West.

Nothing indicates that the present economic crisis, however disturbing its symptoms may be, has reached the depths of the 1930s, or even could do so. Both national and international means of prevention are now more effective and other conditions are more favorable than they were then. Still, the signs of crisis are grave enough and the danger of their escalation too great a risk to rely exclusively on the free play of the market to eliminate them.

It becomes increasingly clear that the market economies will not be able to eliminate their escalating economic problems without extensive state intervention, while the planned economies will have to undertake a radical dismantling of their ruling bureaucracies. But to date, neither theory nor practice has brought forth an answer as to how far either of these two measures can go without necessitating alteration of the intrinsic steering mechanisms as well.

It is not only the Soviet leaders who lack panaceas. None are forthcoming in the market economies either. But the search for solutions is still worth the effort.

Even the profound crisis of the 1930s was brought under control

On January 30, 1933, at the peak of the world economic crisis, Hitler came to power; a few months later, on April 19, the newly elected President of the United States, Franklin Delano Roosevelt, announced his New Deal. Hitler's way led to self-destruction of the traditional system in fascism and world war; Roosevelt's way was supposed to lead to the salvation of human civilization. The escalation of the world economic crisis led ineluctably to the collapse of the established order: growing unemployment and poverty, social unrest, an endless chain of bankruptcies, devaluation of the currency, and a worldwide economic war marked the situation in Europe and America; more than a fourth of the employable population in the United States was unemployed; shares fell to a fraction of their value prior to the stock market crash of October 24, 1929; automobile production fell by a half, construction declined by a third, and the capacities of the steel industry were only 12 percent utilized.

The situation in the other countries of the world was similar or worse. The hope that the self-regulating mechanisms of the market would restore the disrupted equilibrium was in vain. Three years had lapsed between Wall Street's "Black Tuesday" of October 24, 1929, and the October elections of 1932, in which the hapless President Herbert Hoover went down to a severe defeat. President Franklin Roosevelt did not rely on the mechanisms of the market but intervened in the market with the full might of the state. The measures he adopted differed very little from the economic policy which President Wilson had pursued during World War I.

If we find these measures, undertaken more than fifty years ago in an incomparably more difficult situation, still worthy of mention today, it is because they still have not lost their character as a guideline. Roosevelt's New Deal contained all the ingredients of the options being discussed today, and in particular one of the most important of them, a few years later destined to acquire a permanent place in economic history—the theory of John Maynard Keynes.

The National Industrial Recovery Act (NIRA) which came into force in June 1933 was an ambitious program for creating jobs. To this end the Public Works Administration disposed tremendous financial resources, the equivalent today of about a hundred billion dollars. Four million unemployed were to be given jobs in public works projects. To finance this huge program, it was wealthy Americans who were to pay.

Of course, other measures were taken which were tailored to the particular emergency of the time, e.g., the Emergency Banking Act, which transferred control of the banking system to the Treasury Department and the compendious contracts system to regulate prices, wages, and conditions of competition.

These measures, designed for an emergency, showed how far state intervention must go when economic structures and the institutions and mechanisms holding them together break down in an escalating crisis. They also showed that the necessary therapy, if applied, is painful but can be successful even in the advanced stages of economic crisis. In view of the success of the New Deal in combating an economic crisis heading for disaster, it is warranted to ask whether a crisis must develop so far as to make such painful emergency measures necessary and whether economic crisis must lead to the suicide of the free world in fascism and world war, as was the case in the 1930s? It is illuminating that the expression "crisis of the system"—which was used at that time as it is today—reflects less a crisis of a social system than the paralysis of the moral and intellectual forces of the ruling elite and the failure of economic theoreticians.

Although the innocuous term "recession" is often used to describe the current economic situation and the effects of the crisis are still a far cry from those of the 1930s, it would be both dangerous and irresponsible to abandon them to the free play of spontaneous forces.

The revolution in science and technology hurt full employment

Today's economic crisis is marked not so much by declining growth and economic stagnation as by the excessive number of unemployed which is much higher than mere economic recession would warrant. Indeed, it is not just the economic recession which is forcing workers out of production, but increasingly the scientific and technical revolution and the use of automation and robots in production. This is clearly a postindustrial unemployment, whose causes are more complicated and more difficult to combat than in earlier periods of development.

Whereas in the earlier stages of industrialization, agriculture, highly overmanned, furnished its surplus labor to industry, today the problem lies with industry, which, equipped with microprocessors and robots, is driving a growing portion of its labor force into redundancy. At the turn of the century labor time per year was about 3,000 hours per employed person. Today the level is 1,700 to 1,800 depending on the country. Moreover, although the actual labor expended has been reduced by almost half, three to five times as much is produced.[17] However, industry cannot funnel its excess labor power into other economic sectors as agriculture had done earlier. The advance of the scientific and technical revolution has wrought fundamental changes in economic structures. Not only has the share of agriculture in the creation of the gross national product been reduced to a negligible quantity, the share of industry itself is declining steadily, as evidenced by the following figures.

Structure of gross national product in 1960 and 1980 (share in percent)

	Agriculture		Total industry		Processing industries		Service sector	
	1960	1980	1960	1980	1960	1980	1960	1980
OECD	6	4	40	37	30	27	54	62
USA	4	3	38	34	29	24	58	63
Japan	—	4	45	41	34	29	42	55

Source: "The World Economy," in *Financial Times*, July 9, 1982.

The share of services in the total product of the OECD countries is currently much greater than the combined share of the crucial economic sectors in early capitalism, i.e., agriculture and industry. It goes without saying that the sectors included in the aggregate category, "services," are not able to employ all the labor force set free by industry. Other qualifications and training are necessary.

The figures in the table above also clearly show why unemployment is relatively higher in the United States and relatively lower in Japan than elsewhere: the share of industry in the Gross National Product of the United States is 34 percent, while in Japan it is still as high as 41 percent.

The economic structures of the planned economies are still relatively unaffected by the revolution in science and technology

If unemployment in the planned economies is still insignificantly low, this is not only because the right to work is guaranteed in the constitution of the Eastern countries but also because the advance of the scientific and technical revolution has been slower and its impact on economic structures weaker than in the industrial countries of the West. A comparison of the economic structures of East and West will demonstrate this claim:

Share of different economic sectors in creation of the national product in the East and West in 1980, in percent

	Industry and construction	Agriculture and forestry	Transportation and services
Bulgaria	60.8	16.7	22.5
Czechoslovakia	75.5	7.3	17.2
GDR	68.8	9.1	22.1
Poland	60.9	14.2	24.9
Romania	68.6	15.2	16.2
Hungary	60.1	15.8	24.1
USSR	61.4	15.2	24.4
Austria (1979)	48.2	6.1	45.7
Belgium	38.0	2.8	59.2
France	40.1	5.4	54.5
FRG	50.1	2.9	47.0
Great Britain	39.5	2.2	58.3
USA	34.0	3.0	63.0

Sources: Poland's *Statistical Yearbook 1982*, p. 504; for the United States, *Financial Times*, July 9, 1982.

Although the national product is calculated and aggregated in a somewhat different way than in the West, the figures nevertheless clearly show that the economic structures of the highly industrialized countries of Eastern Europe, such as the GDR and Czechoslovakia, are still a long way from those of the industrial countries of the West. Further, the difference between the levels of development of the USSR and the United States is enormous.

The obvious conclusion is that it has been the scientific and technical revolution, rather than the October Revolution, which has had such a decisive influence on the shaping of the economy and on consumption patterns. Labor is much cheaper than machinery in the East, as indeed is necessarily the case in the early stages of industrialization. Hence, rationalization of the labor process moves forward slowly and the share of manual work is much higher in the East than in the West. The ratio of unskilled labor to skilled labor in the Soviet Union (85:100) is almost twice as high as in the United States (38:100).[18]

The fluctuation in the labor force has already reached unsupportable dimensions: in the Soviet Union, 20 million persons change their jobs each year and each change of job means an average loss of twenty-six work days. Nevertheless, this unemployment is not reflected in the statistics since it is "internalized in the factories," to use Bruno Frisch's expression.[19]

Nor has there been any lack of attempts in the Eastern countries to raise productivity and hence generate higher wages by reducing the amount of labor expended. However, the preference throughout is still to fulfill plan targets by employing more labor. There has been no interest in reproducing the experiment of a machinery factory near Tula which was able to triple the productivity of labor in ten years by pruning the excess work force.

Only 2 percent of Soviet factories followed the example. The Hungarian railroad car and machinery company Raba fared no better. The state-owned enterprises, chronically undersupplied, require a reserve work force so that gaps in production can be made up when the supplies, impatiently awaited, finally arrive. Then plan targets are met through febrile efforts in the last days of the month.

The rising costs of wages are no incentive to rationalize the labor process in the Eastern countries. Other factors are necessary over which factory managers have no influence. The West Germans complain, for instance, that as late as 1970 firms used 50 percent of their invested funds to expand existing plants, but in 1980 only one mark in every four was invested for the same purpose and 75 percent of industrial investments was for rationalization.[20] The Eastern countries, on the other hand, complain that the greater part of their investment capital is rendered inactive in construction concrete. In the Soviet Union, the share of machinery and equipment in the total amount invested in 1980 was only 38 percent, while the portion invested in construction and assembly works was 52 percent.[21] In a planned economy it is still easier to obtain a place in the state plan for a new investment project with a relatively low cost estimate, for which financing, work force, machinery and equipment are then centrally allocated, than to undertake rationalizations on one's own initiative and hence thereby assume the entire risk and responsibility oneself.

There is no conflict between modern technology and unemployment in the East because chronic supply problems make hoarding a necessity and because Party officials are opposed to allowing unemployment.

On the other hand, in the industrial countries of the West no realistic growth rate could reduce the unemployment rate to an acceptable level of 3–5 percent. West German experts have calculated that to achieve full employment by 1990 an annual average growth rate of 6 percent would be required. But such dynamic growth would not only be impossible, it would also scarcely be desirable, since production would have to double within a decade. Abundance is suffocating the nation, writes the sociologist Michael Jungblut.[22]

Two distinct sets of problems must therefore be addressed: bringing under control the recession and the unemployment it has caused, and combating the unemployment resulting from the scientific and technical revolution.

More or less state intervention?

> "Anyone who believes that we can reduce the state to a minimum is a dreamer."   —John Kenneth Galbraith
> interviewed in Der Spiegel

The free market is no divine command, to be sure. However, it may legitimately be asked where the limits of the state should be drawn. The basic (Bad Godesberg) program of the West German Socialist Party (SPD) coined the slogan "competition as far as possible, planning as far as necessary."[23]

It would, of course, be better for the economy if the state bureaucracy could be suppressed. All the countries of real socialism, whose economies creak under the omnipotent dominion of the state bureaucracy and show the disastrous consequences of a total nationalization of the means of production (both real and human capital), seek salvation in "less planning and more market." Indeed Hungary has opted for this path and has become the envy of the liberals of all the Eastern countries.

But the times of a laissez-faire market are gone forever, and there is now virtually no country on earth that is free of interventionism. Occasionally, conservative governments call themselves advocates of a free market, unhindered by the state. A Kohl government cabinet minister, Dr. Stoltenberg, published in the *Handelsblatt* of 31 December 1982 an article titled "The state must be kept within its limits." Stoltenberg wrote: "The state must provide a clear framework within the political system; firms must keep their production capacities competitive and adapt flexibly to market conditions; and the social partners must reach wage and labor agreements that accord with market conditions."[24] Neither the Kohl government in West Germany nor the Reagan government in the United States shies away from state intervention. Galbraith has called the latter "one of the most interventionist governments we have ever had," which has even decreed "regulations on the import of automobiles and steel."

State intervention is increasing, not decreasing. The figures in the following table on the rising share of public expenditure in the gross national product of the major countries of Western Europe are only one of many demonstrations of this.

Total public expenditures (including transfer) in percent of GNP

	1958/67	1968/77	1978/80
FRG	35.2	41.6	46.5
Denmark	27.9	43.9	54.2
France	36.0	40.6	45.9
Ireland	29.4	41.5	51.2
Italy	33.1	41.1	46.2
Netherlands	36.5	48.6	58.0
Belgium	31.1	40.3	51.3
Great Britain	34.1	42.6	43.0
Luxembourg	33.3	41.9	54.4
European Community	34.8	41.9	46.9

Source: *Kommission der Europäischen Gemeinschaften* and Prof. P. Bernholz, "Der Wohlstaat auf dem falschen Weg," in *N.Z.Z.*, November 28–29, 1982.

The tendency is clear enough, though the initial and 1978–1980 levels vary depending on the country. The share of state expenditure in the GNP increased more sharply in Belgium, Denmark, Ireland, and the Netherlands than in the other countries listed and somewhat more slowly in the Federal Republic of Germany, France, Great Britain, and Italy. Public expenditures are much above average in the Netherlands and Denmark.

Growing state expenditures are financed with increased tax revenues and social security in-payments, as is evident from the following data.

Proportion of tax revenues and social security payments (in percent GNP)

	Tax revenues	Social security payments	Total
Sweden	34.6	15.1	49.7
Netherlands	28.7	19.3	48.0
Denmark	44.2	0.5	44.7
France	24.3	18.2	42.5
Belgium	29.6	12.8	42.4
Austria	26.3	15.8	42.1
Great Britain	39.4	15.1	44.5
FRG	24.3	14.1	38.4
Italy	22.8	12.5	35.3
Canada	31.1	3.7	34.8
USA	22.1	8.2	30.3
Switzerland	19.4	9.4	28.8
Japan	18.4	7.9	26.3

Source: *Handelsblatt*, November 5–6, 1982.

These data on tax revenues and social security in-payments showed that the redistribution mechanisms are more pronounced in Europe than in America or Japan. But even in Europe, appreciable differences are discernible. The burden is lowest in Switzerland, followed by Italy and the FRG, and greatest in Sweden and the Netherlands. Austria is in an intermediate position. Nevertheless, there is no unequivocal proof that the principal cause of the present recession is the growing role of redistributive measures, as is often alleged. In the United States, the state redistributes much less than in Europe, but the economic recession between 1980 and 1982 was deeper and unemployment was higher than in the Western European countries. In 1983 and 1984 these indicators changed to the benefit of the United States.

The growth of industrial societies into welfare states has been hallmarked by a veritable explosion in social services and rapidly rising wages, although the rises have not been equal everywhere. Workers in the United States have profited less than the workers of Western Europe. In 1981, the average wage per hour was lower than ten years previously, and there has been no net wage increase since 1967.[25] The cost of labor is lower in the United States than in the Federal Republic of Germany. Further, labor productivity is growing more slowly in the United States than in most of the OECD countries.

Cost of wages and labor productivity

	FRG	USA	France	Italy	Japan	Great Britain
Cost of labor per hour 1981 in DM	25.03	24.97	19.81	19.32	16.32	16.00
Labor productivity per hour, average growth 1973 to 1980 in %	4.8	1.7	4.9	3.5	7.2	1.4

Source: "World Economy," in *Financial Times*, July 9, 1982.

The cost of labor was lowest in 1981 in Japan and Great Britain. The rise in the Italian level to the level of France is interesting. Great Britain, where wages are stagnating, also shows the lowest growth in the productivity of labor. Only Japan has been able to achieve an above average increase in productivity of 2 percent while keeping its wage costs lower than the other OECD countries. The productivity of labor increased at an above average rate in the Federal Republic of Germany and France. In the early 1970s, labor productivity in the United States increased by an annual average of 3 percent, but most recently it has increased by only 0.3 percent.

Falling profits, declining capital formation, and decreasing willingness to invest as causes of the 1980–1982 recession

Increasing taxes and social security payments, the discrepancy between the cost of wages and labor productivity, and unused production capacities have caused a perceptible fall in profits, as is evident from the figures (top of p. 27).

The utilization of production capacities was much lower in 1981 and 1982. The rate of profit declined from about a third to one-fourth of the national product between 1965 and 1980. However, considerable differences exist among the individual countries (see second table, p. 27).

The figures show that the sharpest decrease in the rate of profit was in West Germany and Great Britain; in Austria it declined from 42 percent in 1960 to 32 percent in 1982.[26]

In the second half of the 1950s the rate of profit in West Germany was 10

Utilization of production capacity and rate of profit in the principal OECD countries (between 1965 and 1980)

	Utilization of production capacities in percent	Profit in percent of gross national product
1965	87.7	33.5
1970	83.1	30.3
1975	74.0	25.5
1977	81.2	25.5
1979	84.7	25.7
1980	80.0	24.9

Source: *Financial Times*, July 9, 1982.

Rate of profit in the processing industries in percent of constant capital

	United States	FRG	Great Britain
1955–1959	28	38	17
1960–1962	27	29	15
1963–1967	36	21	14
1968–1971	26	22	11
1972–1975	21	16	8
1976–1979	22	17	6

Source: *Financial Times*, July 9, 1982.

percent higher, but in the second half of the 1970s it was 5 percent lower than in the United States. Great Britain is the hardest hit, however: its rate of profit has declined to almost a third of the 1955–59 level.

The decline in the rate of profit has a negative effect on capital formation, but the discrepancy among the individual OECD countries differs considerably in this respect.

Capital formation between 1965 and 1981 prices and exchange rates of 1975 (in billions of U.S. dollars)

	United States	EEC (9)	Japan	FRG	France
1965	247.7	224.1	61.4	76.2	48.3
1970	262.5	288.4	137.5	91.6	66.2
1975	261.6	247.5	161.8	87.2	78.8
1979	331.1	334.7	203.7	108.1	85.2
1980	307.5	342.7	203.7	112.1	86.9
1981	309.0	329.7	208.0	108.2	84.9

Source: *Financial Times*, July 9, 1982.

Whereas in the United States capital formation was 6.7 percent lower in 1981 than in 1979, in the countries of Western Europe it remained more or less stable and in Japan it even rose. Compared with 1965, capital formation in Europe and Japan was much more dynamic than in the United States, as may be seen from the following comparative figures:

Capital formation in Europe and Japan (U.S. = 100)

	USA	EEC (9)	Japan	FRG	France
1965	100	0.90	0.247	0.307	0.201
1981	100	106.7	0.67	0.349	0.274

The gap between Japan and the United States decreased from almost 75 percent in 1965 to 23 percent in 1981; the countries of the European Economic Community (EEC), which were still 10 percent behind in 1965, formed 6.7 percent more capital in 1981 than the United States, which is clearly losing out in its competition with the other industrial countries of the West. The decline in investments is one of the principal causes of the economic recession. But, as we mentioned earlier, the unemployment rate is considerably higher than can be explained by the economic recession alone. This discrepancy is indeed a consequence of the distinctive features of the present phase of development, which has been defined as the scientific and technical revolution. Competition for markets is fiercer. The firm which is able to undercut costs and prices by automation and robotization of the labor process will be successful. This is the response of business to the explosion in wages and social services.

Even with all its adaptative devices the competitive market is no longer able to cope with this problem. Both conservatives, who would like to maintain the rules of laissez-faire capitalism, and the liberals, who regard state intervention as desirable, have concluded that the free market no longer exists and that the difficult problems of the current period cannot be resolved without state intervention. But neither economic theory nor economic practice is able to say what the state should do to come to terms with the mounting problems.

Economic theory goes begging

A side effect of the economic upswing of 1975 to 1979 was an above average inflation rate. Combating inflation with a stringently applied monetarist policy became the prime goal of economic strategy, especially in the United States. But restricting the money inflow drove interest rates up. Credits and investments became more expensive. Monetarism has its roots in the United States, but its effects are perceptible in other countries as well. Money flows in where interest rates are high. No country has been spared rising interest rates. In each, domestic causes may be found for the economic recession. However, the whole Western world is affected by an upswing or downswing in the American economy and by American economic policy. A close examination of Reagan's economic policy confirms Galbraith's allegation that this government, which aimed at allowing laws of the market free play, has been less hesitant of state intervention than any U.S. government before it. It is likewise true that economic theory has been more of a hindrance than a help to Reagan's economic policy, that is to say monetarist theory and the supply-side school, which are the principal ingredients of Reagan-omics. The core idea of this school is that the arch enemy of world stagnation is not an overall decline in demand, but a supply that has become too expensive, and that a reduction in costs will bring about a revival in investments and a resumption of economic growth; consequently, Reagan pushed through considerable tax reductions, even though the U.S. tax rate is already one of the lowest in the world. The consequence was a rapidly growing budget deficit.

Success has a hundred fathers, failure is an orphan

Economists argue among themselves, each blaming the other for failure. They invite the conclusion that Reagan adviser Edwin Harper best put into words: "The U.S. economy is too complicated and too dependent on many individual decisions to be able to be explained by any one single theory."[27]

The 1980 Nobel Prize laureate and former White House economic adviser Lawrence Klein, a Keynesian, called supply-side theory "pure nonsense." "This theory," he said, "deceives public opinion. . . . If we were to have a Nuremberg trial for economists, the supply siders would be on the bench of the accused."[28]

Michael Evans, chief economist of the Wall Street investment firm McMahan, Brafman, Morgan and Co., dealt with the monetarists no more kindly: "These people," he said, "have proven that they are idiots." Monetary policy was misleading because it reduced the money supply without considering the harm it would do to the economy. As the U.S. inflation rate decreased (from 12.4 percent in 1980), joblessness increased. "This aspect of monetarism," concludes Evans, "belongs in the rubbish bin of economic theory."

The 1976 Nobel Prize laureate Milton Friedman defended monetarism in his criticism of Federal Reserve practice: "If Federal Reserve practice is monetarism, I am no monetarist," said Friedman.

The failure of monetarism and the supply-side school has brought the Keynesians back into the picture. One of their spokesmen, Lester Thurow of the Massachusetts Institute of Technology, said: "In the next four to five years we'll have to combat unemployment, and in that situation old-fashioned Keynesianism could again be helpful."

In the meantime, the authority of economic theory has declined to a new low.

Felix Rohatyn, of the banking house Lazard Freres and Co., observed: "The Keynesians fueled inflation, and now the monetarists and supply siders, as well as Reaganomics, are well on the way toward plunging the economy into a depression. People are becoming more and more skeptical of economic theory, and indeed they have good reason to be skeptical."[29]

But the leader in the White House seems to go his own way, independent of economic theories, and declares that he would like above all to bring the budget deficit under control. A one-year wage freeze was decreed for government employees and inflation adjustments for pensions and social security were delayed; a tax on call, i.e., a 1 percent supplementary tax on taxable assets and earnings, was planned for 1986, as well as a consumer tax for petroleum products if the deficit predictions for this fiscal year exceed 2.5 percent of the GNP; and 55 billion dollars will be cut from the military arms program from the 160 billion dollars budgeted over the coming five years.[30]

The U.S. economy grew in 1985 at the rate of 2.7 percent—slower growth than in the previous year—but the unemployment rate was held at a relatively low 7.2 percent. Economic growth continues and no recession is to be expected in the near future. A significant concern remains the current account deficit ($26.1 billion in 1985).

Great Britain and West Germany, under conservative governments, also adopted supply-side policies. Britain under Thatcher opted for monetarism, with rigorous control of the money supply, a cutback in public expenditures, and a reduction in domestic borrowing. But there were also tax reductions, targeted to stimulate investment and a willingness to accept risk in the private sector. However, no breakthroughs were achieved. Industrial output declined to the level of a decade before while the number of unemployed increased; 44 percent of part-time workers in the European Community were in England.[31]

The Christian Democratic Union–Free Democratic Party coalition government in West Germany also followed supply-side policies. As the Council of Experts formulated the question: "At core the issue is one of adaptation rather than a general crisis in demand owing to generally disrupted expectations. However much importance one ascribes to the decline of demand, . . . it cannot be combated simply by issuing money when the public coffers are empty; confidence is lacking in a state saddled with an enormous debt."

Helmut Kohl's economic policy is anti-inflationary. He and his finance minister Stoltenberg created the environment of stable but low economic growth. The unemployment has remained static. During the entire term of the Kohl government it has been no lower than 2 million people. This policy does not bode well for Kohl or for his coalition in the January 1987 elections.

The Kohl government adopted a package of economizing measures: rents were to be raised; scheduled pension increases were postponed and family subsidies reduced; scholarships were to be paid back after completion of study; and persons earning more than 50,000 marks per year were called upon to pay in a supplementary 5 percent to stimulate investment. However, the government also wanted to create a more favorable climate for investment. The annual economic report published on January 26, 1984, reads: "To resume growth, a fundamental reorientation in economic, finance, and social policy is necessary." In particular, the "investment power and competitiveness" of firms must be reinforced. "More to investments" must have priority over "more for demand."

Social democratic governments staked their policy on an expansion of demand, with the deficit in private investment to be made up by increased state activities. However, growing budget deficits and the growing government debt placed certain limits on this economic policy and those limits could not be transgressed. The Social Democrats, with their slogan of fueling the economy by implementing a new edition of Keynesian policies aimed at lowering unemployment, could be the winners of the upcoming January 1987 elections.

The planned economies have long years of experience but no theory adequate to explain their system

Marxism is still the official theory and ideology of "real socialism." However, the proletarian revolution was neither begun nor carried out in consistency with Marxism. According to the fundamental postulates of Marxism, a postcapitalist proletarian revolution should begin where the economy has reached an adequate level of maturity and where capitalism has already exhausted its creative potential. The Russia of 1919, in which the rural population made up more than 80 percent of the total population and industrialization was only beginning, had neither a mature economy, a well-established class of capitalists, nor a mature proletariat capable of exercising power. The proletariat first had to be created and developed into a powerful social class.

Nonetheless, the attempt was made to realize the slogans of the October Revolution. Factories were placed under workers' control, and money, reduced to paper because of the terrible inflation, was abolished. The nationalized state bank was dissolved and a war economy *in natura* was established. The consequences were devastating. After a brief experiment with a mixed economy (the New Economic Policy or NEP), the social system and the concept of growth were assimilated into the traditional cultural setting of Russia. Once again, as had ever been the case in the history of this country, the attempt was made to realize the ardently desired but elusive dream of overcoming centuries of backwardness through the instrumentality of an omnipresent and omnipotent state. The precondition for a postcapitalist revolution, i.e., industrialization, and a forced restructuring of the country's backward economic and social structures, no matter the price, became the prime objectives of the revolution begun in 1917.

But let one thing be clear: the economic system established in the early 1930s and enduring essentially unchanged to this day had very little to do with the theory and ideology that inspired the great October Revolution. A connection between yesterday's ideology and today's practice may be postulated only on the assumption that a state economy steered by a hierarchically structured planning and administrative bureaucracy is identical with a system in which the living labor, freed of alienation, is itself the ruling factor in the units of production. The gap between the ideal of a society emancipated from every constraint and the grim reality of an omnipotent and omnipresent state is not, however, the only reason for the deficiency of the official theory. Economic theory, especially, has gone begging. Although value categories such as money, prices, profits, and credit are applicable in a planned economy, they bear little similarity with those economic categories that inspired Marxist value categories; yet Marxism still remains the dominant theory of official economics in the planned economies.

The prices for commodities and money in the planned economies are equivalent to traditional price and exchange rates in form but not in content. They are established autonomously and are not part of the international price and exchange rate structure. Their functions both as economic factors and as parameters are limited. Thus they do not function as allocation factors. The state places no trust in the traditional mechanisms of the invisible hand, but decides itself where investments are most needed. Value categories are therefore merely technical instruments of accounting rather than economic mechanisms for steering the economy.

Official theory exists to justify practice by portraying it as the best possible option for achieving the desired social system or by proclaiming the present reality to just that. But it is a very poor guidepost when the symptoms of crisis have become patent as well as unsurmountable. To quote the late Italian Communist leader Lucio Lombardo Radice: "The despotism which has industrialized the society so dynamically, and brought it up to the standards of modern science, has become a procrustean bed for its further development, an 'iron maiden'; in the authoritarian and centralist phase of real socialism, Marxist-Leninist doctrine has become a genuine 'state religion.'"[32]

Every one of the planned economies is attempting to find a way out of its troubles, but so far none has met with success. The official theory may help the ruling elite keep the people obedient, but it is useless to a society that requires reform from stem to stern if it is to cope with its problems.

To be effective, any reform would have to begin by reducing the power of the state. But the ruling elites have no desire to destroy the state. They want to keep it as it is, for it is, after all, *their* state, a tangible instrument of their dominion. The elite research team in Novosibirsk which in mid-1983 completed an analysis of the Soviet economy, was quite aware of the state of affairs: "The existing system could only be changed by social groups who occupy a high position and consequently are bound to this system through their personal interests," it stated.[33] Meanwhile, apologists use hybrid theories to justify the reality of real socialism, effectively obstructing the way to a new conception of the future that takes into account the specific conditions of the Eastern countries. The planned economies have more difficulties in doing this than the market economies, since self-regulating forces no longer operate in them.

One thing is clear: the theory of convergence, which postulated that the two world systems would become more alike, through the use of more planning in the one and more market in the other, is out of the picture. Any economic system must perfect the mechanisms intrinsic to it, if it is to function efficiently.

The economic situation has eased somewhat, but the symptoms of crisis remain

An upswing in economic activity has been noticeable in the United States since the second half of 1982; in 1983 the indicators of economic performance improved further, and in 1984 many sectors of the economy were experiencing a boom. The 1984 growth rate of 6.8 percent was the best showing since 1951. In 1983, the signs of recovery began to appear in Europe as well. In Eastern Europe, the growth rate in 1983 was 0.2 percent lower than in the period between 1976 and 1980, but 1.1 percent higher than in the preceding year. Recovery in the countries of Eastern and Southern Europe has been more conspicuous than in the Soviet Union; in these countries, after zero growth in 1980 and declines of 2.1 percent and 0.1 percent in 1981 and 1982, respectively, there was an increase of 3.1 percent in the national product in 1983 and 3.9 percent in 1984.

According to the ECE data, the net material product in the Eastern bloc grew in 1985 at an average rate of 3.2 percent. The highest growth rate was achieved in Rumania and GDR (5.9 and 4.8 percent, respectively); the lowest, in Hungary and Bulgaria (1.4 and 1.8 percent, respectively). The economies of the Soviet Union and of Poland grew at the average rate of 3 percent.

Despite the importance of this economic revival after the recession, which was the longest in postwar history, it may be fair to say that the flaws inherent to the system may have receded somewhat into the background, but they have not been overcome. Unemployment is above average in almost all the industrial countries of the West. The adaptation of economic structures to the requirements of the scientific and technical revolution has come up against major difficulties as declining basic industries release more workers than the technologically advanced industries can absorb. The social conflicts in the Federal Republic of Germany, in France, and in Great Britain do not make the process of adjustment easier.

In the East, the administrative bureaucracy is still powerful and stifles creative initiative. These countries are behind in the development of modern technologies and do not have a broad range of exportable goods; their productivity is low and the specific expenditure of capital and labor is excessively high.

The gap in the level of development of the two world systems has diminished over the last thirty years, although the performance of the Eastern countries is still about half that of the Western countries:

Gross national product total and per capita
(GNP in billions of dollars, per capita in dollars, population in millions)

	GNP 1950	GNP 1960	GNP 1970	GNP 1980	Population 1980	Per capita GNP 1980
Countries of the Warsaw Pact, total	457.12	795.71	1,269.34	1,745.47	375.00	4.655
including:						
Soviet Union	323.12	573.48	945.44	1,280.14	265.50	4.822
Southern and Eastern Europe	134.00	222.23	323.90	465.32	109.50	4.250
NATO total	1,622.84	2,419.14	3,687.44	4,951.90	578.50	8.560
including:						
USA	958.99	1,318.62	1,925.05	2,556.71	227.64	11.231
Western Europe	602.37	1,004.74	1,601.74	2,158.31	326.87	6.603
Japan	91.90	216.48	595.16	955.31	117.03	8.163

Source: Edward N. Lutwak, *The Grand Strategy of the Soviet Union*. New York: St. Martins' Press, 1983, p. 170.

There are major differences in potential among the countries in each group. In an evaluation of the competitiveness of twenty-two industrial countries published by the European Management Forum, Japan and Switzerland ranked first and second, with 70.31 and 70.10 points, respectively, followed at some distance by the United States with 64.38 and Federal Republic of Germany with 62.63. Austria moved up from tenth to seventh place with 57.74 points, and a few other countries (Sweden, Finland, and Italy) also improved their ranking. Great Britain, with 51.55 points, had fallen one place to number fourteen.[34] The economic revival has been feebler and decline in the periods of recession greater in Britain than elsewhere, and the country continues to lose ground to the other industrial countries. In 1983 its economic performance was one-third lower than that of the Federal Republic, although it has only 10 percent less population.[35] Both labor productivity and hourly wages are considerably lower than elsewhere: in 1981 the wage index was 65 (U.S. = 100), but in 1983 it was only 53; in the auto industry the wage index decreased from 45 to 39, and in the steel industry from 45 to 36.[36] Adjustment difficulties are also considerable in France, which has not yet assimilated the extensive restructuring of property relations that has taken place in the last few years. The economic situation is extremely critical in the countries of the Western European periphery which rank last (with 41.31 and 38.07 points) on the competitive list of the twenty-two industrial countries.

The Eastern countries have also been unable to surmount the problems immanent to their system. The crisis in agriculture is especially acute in the Soviet Union. Although the grain harvest was 190 million tons in 1983, an improvement over preceding years, it was still about 50 million tons below the plan target; the harvest of 1984 was not more than 180 million tons and 1985 (the data are not officially published), not more than 190 million tons. With 39 percent of the total employed population working in industry and 20 percent working in agriculture,[37] the economic and social structures of the Soviet Union resembled the OECD structures of 1960. In the OECD countries, agriculture accounted for only 9.4 percent of the total number of employed in 1983, while industry and commerce accounted for 31.5 percent.[38]

Poland continues to be the problem child not only of the Eastern bloc but of 500 creditor banks throughout the world. After an economic decline with negative growth rates of –6 percent, –12 percent, and –5 percent, positive growth of 6.0 percent were achieved in 1983, 5.6 and 3.0 percent in 1984 and 1985. However, the per capita national product is still 13 percent and labor productivity 17 percent lower than in 1978. By the end of 1985, Poland's indebtedness to the West, at $31.0 billion, was equivalent to five years of exports (Poland also owed $7.0 billion to the CMEA countries). Romania was forced to apply for a rescheduling of its debt, estimated at 6.0 billion dollars.

The German Democratic Republic and Czechoslovakia, which after the war were able to supply advanced technologies to the other members of the Eastern bloc, are now themselves forced to import advanced technology. The GDR and Hungary are struggling to regain creditworthiness.

East-West economic relations are sensitive to political developments, which nowadays tend more to confrontation than to coexistence. Confrontation means enormous arms expenditures. The major part of the $600 billion spent yearly on weapons is a consequence of East-West confrontation. Nearly $150 billion are the costs of the Warsaw Pact. The cost is a burden to the peoples of both hemispheres. The growing armaments industry puts strains on energy and raw materials resources, which are growing steadily scarcer, and on the environment, already extremely polluted. War is not the only means of suicide for the human race. The arms build-up, even without war, is slowly and ineluctably leading mankind to its grave. It wastes the best human and material resources and makes the environment intolerable. Although orders to the weapons industry stimulate business in the West, this is a very shortsighted solution. Over the long term, an unremitting arms race means, if not mankind's last war, quite definitely the depletion of all raw material resources and a total pollution of the environment, i.e., the total destruction of the means of existence for generations to come.

No easy cures

The advocates of state intervention justly claim that the "invisible hand of the market" is suffering from arthritis and cannot cope with the acute problems of the present. However, they must accept the reproach that, with the exception of Keynes's deficit spending, no other economic policy has been able to restore economic growth and that budget deficits and government debt cannot be extended beyond bearable limits. An even more serious objection is that Keynes's remedy, conceived in a time of depressed demand due to a shortage of money, has become obsolete in the quite different situation we have today. Nonetheless, had it not been for Roosevelt's New Deal, the competitive market as a component of a pluralistic society would have been doomed to total collapse even as fascism and world war loomed. And today as well, we face not only an economic challenge; "the survival of our free society is at stake."[39]

Of course, the world of today is different from the world of the 1930s. But one way it is different is that the threat of unemployment has become greater: it seems that there is no growth rate high enough to restore full employment. Unemployment today is not merely temporary, a product of recession; it is chronic, a consequence of the revolution in science and technology. The conclusion is obvious that full employment will not be restored by anti-recession policies. The director of the International Labor Organisation (ILO), Francis Blanchard, forecast that by mid-1984 about 35 million or 9.5 percent of the active population in the twenty-four countries of the OECD would be unemployed.[40]

Not one but two problems must be solved to restore social equilibrium. The recession and the unemployment linked to it must be combated, and workers who have been made permanently redundant by the scientific and technical revolution must be provided with a way back into the production process.

Of course, for the worker himself it makes no difference if he has been expelled from the production process by economic recession or by robotics and microprocessors. But economic policymakers cannot be indifferent to this issue. After all, the correct therapy depends on a correct diagnosis of the ailment.

Shorter workdays?

Eventually, the workday will have to be shortened, in the interest of combating the unemployment that has resulted from the scientific and technical revolution. The forty-hour week will certainly be replaced by a thirty-five-hour week. The question is whether this social and economic measure is justified at the present time.

If combating the recession is accepted as the prime task of the current economic policy (there is no doubt that it has the highest priority), the answer to this question must be negative. A condition for economic revival is the prospect of growing profits and investment incentives. But shortening working hours will reduce the prospects of profits and thus the desire to invest. Nevertheless, no one doubts that a competitive economy can be revived only by means compatible with the market, not by means that go against it. Shorter work hours in times of recession will not achieve the goal desired; rather, businessmen would be forced to resort even more to rationalization and automation of the production process to maintain their competitiveness. The additional jobs created by shorter work hours will sooner or later be rationalized out of existence and the problem will crop up again after apparently having been solved.

Not only the advocates of state intervention, but also the proponents of a free market are prepared to burden the economy with a larger labor force than is justified by economic performance. While President Reagan would like to place the task of creating jobs for some of the 8.4 million unemployed in the hands of the 14.7 million American firms, the British Treasury Office has calculated that 75 percent of the effect of a two-hour reduction in work hours could be eliminated by overtime and growing productivity.[41]

Total time on the job varies broadly throughout the world. In 1983 it was shortest in Belgium (1,748 hours per year) and in France (1,780 hours per year), but longest in Japan (2,096 hours per year), followed by the United States (1,904 hours per year).[42] The age of retirement also varies. More people between the ages of sixty and sixty-four are working in Great Britain (75.8 percent), Sweden (69 percent), and the United States (61.8 percent) than in the other countries. Austria is at the bottom of the list with 26.1 percent; Belgium has 33 percent and West Germany 39.5 percent.[43] It is apparent that a reduction in total work time and in the age of retirement would only be possible as a result of an international agreement. France, which wanted to move to a thirty-five hour work week by 1985, now declares that it would be impossible for France to do this in isolation.

But while no country can reduce work hours on its own, there has been an increasing number of agreements between firms and their work forces and between the state and trade unions concerning reductions in the work week or in the retirement age. Many agreements between work forces and their firms have been concluded in Austria and in other industrial countries. The Belgian government is attempting to induce employers and employees to reduce work time by 5 percent while reducing real wages by 3 percent; SAB of Sweden has already introduced a 35-hour week and reduced real wages by 5 percent. In Great Britain the machinery industry has reduced the work week from 40 to 39 hours. Royal Dutch Airlines (KLM) has recently implemented a similar measure.

Agreements moving up the age of retirement in return for a reduction in pensions have been even more common. In Sweden, part-time work with semi-retirement is widespread, with income being reduced to 65 percent. Four out of every five workers in the Federal Republic retire with a pension of 65–75 percent of their wage before they reach the legal age of retirement (sixty-three years). A labor institute in Nuremberg calculated that 440,000 jobs could be created by reducing the retirement age to fifty-five years. Since April 1, 1983, every worker in France has been able to retire at the age of sixty. The new agreement provides for 50 percent of the pension to be financed by the general social security system. The difference between this 50 percent and the normal 70 percent pension after the age of 65, i.e., the increment of 20 percent, will be covered by a fund of 30 billion francs created for seven years, consisting of 20 billion francs from the social partners and 10 billion francs from the state.

A reduction in the work week in a few sectors of the economy or a lowering of the retirement age would cut unemployment, but it could not cure the recession. Measures which promoted investment and export would have to be more consistent than those undertaken so far. The issue is not to replace the market, but to adjust it where it has failed and eliminate vicissitudes that impair performance, and to undertake measures that could restore the market's intrinsic dynamic. More economizing is needed in these times. If measures to reduce demand are not just as dangerous as depriving the market of its "social" attribute (which it has never completely deserved), nevertheless it seems more asocial than social to maintain the same social services for rich and poor.

Full employment and underemployment in the planned economies
No employment solution for a functional market economy

Unemployment should be discussed in the context of the state's custodial and organizational activities. The experiences of the last few years, including the planned economies' experiments with reform, clearly show that the best solution would be to reduce the state's custodial function, but to expand its organizational function to include the creation of jobs. The planned economies are not to be envied the consequences of their employment situation, and certainly it should not be emulated. Underemployment is precisely the phenomenon which causes a decline in productivity, with inevitable effects on the standard of living.

Unemployment is a social illness which affects a growing portion of the active population—more than a tenth in times of crisis. No appropriate means have yet been found to both meet the requirements of economic efficiency and to do justice to the social aspect of this problem. Dismissing redundant workers and paying them assistance out of the state budget is not an adequate solution, but neither is financing underemployment in the factories at the expense of company profits and state subsidies.

Experimental or reformed factories in the Soviet Union and in Hungary have made the resolution of this problem part of the overall modernization program. The experiments at the Shchekino factory in the Soviet Union and the Raba factory in Hungary, and the large-scale reform experiment begun early in 1984 by five Soviet economic ministries (on the basis of a Party and government resolution of July 26, 1983), advocate dismissal of the underemployed, the savings to benefit the wages fund for factory employees, in order to increase labor productivity.

A private factory that wants to be competitive internationally cannot allow itself to employ more people than are needed for the production process. Also, the cost of labor must be proportional to the costs of the machinery that would replace it. The reduction in work time should be discussed in this context as well. The choice between living labor and the machinery that would make it redundant must be left to the factory to decide. A prospering economy is in the interest of employers and the employees alike, regardless of whether the employer is the state, as in the planned economies, or the state and private businessmen in the market economies. An appropriate ratio between the cost of labor and profit is independent of the system. So far, private enterprise has proven itself more efficient and more conducive to prosperity than a state economy steered by a state bureaucracy. Moreover, a private enterprise economy appears to be the *conditio sine qua non* of a pluralistic society, the greatest achievement of which has been the authentic representation of workers' interests by trade unions.

Experience clearly shows that a partnership between employee and employer organizations is much more conducive to the interests of both sides than a social policy based on the conflict or identification of these interests. In Austria such partnership has been able to solve economic and labor problems to the good of both the economy and the work force; this in contrast to the endless hostile conflicts between labor and capital in a number of other countries.

The social aspect of the unemployment problem cannot be disregarded in a pluralistic society. But the economically and socially appropriate solution is not underemployment as in the planned economies but full employment within the context of a suitable program of a growth that is friendly to the environment. However, if a growth rate ensuring full employment is not achievable, then measures to create jobs are to be preferred to lines of unemployed and state intervention to alleviate their social distress.

There is work enough: the expansion of the infrastructure, measures to protect the environment, etc., could employ many persons. What is lacking is money. The question then arises whether it would not be more expedient to use a major share of the unemployment fund for creating jobs rather than for direct aid. West Germany spends about 50 billion DM yearly for support to the unemployed while another 43 billion DM is lost because of absenteeism. The problem is not a purely economic one: it is a problem of social policy. The principle of work for everyone remains an important task of the modern state.

The steering systems existing in East and West are to blame for their seemingly insurmountable difficulties. However, although there is no lack of notions about fantastic social systems, there are in fact only two real, existing world systems, namely, really existing socialism and the market economy, social or not. *Tertium non datur*. The American Nobel Prize laureate Paul Samuelson rightfully observes: "Either we learn to control depressions and inflations better than before World War II, or we set the entire political structure of our society at risk."[44]

Notes

1. "World Economy, Statistical Trends," *Financial Times*, 7 September 1982.
2. According to DGB calculations in *Der Spiegel*, 49/1982, p. 37.
3. *Financial Times*, 7 September 1982.
4. Ibid.
5. *Economic Survey for Europe*, 1980, p. 130
6. *Handbook of Economic Statistics*, National Foreign Assessment Center.
7. Klaus Reinhard and Inge Santner Cyrus-Bericht, *Der Spiegel*, 52/1982, 1980, pp. 10 and 11.
8. *Pravda* (Moscow), 23 November 1982.
9. V. Singer, "Weltwirtschafstkrise," in *Wirtschaftswoche*, 47/1982.
10. Lucjan Kieszczynski, "Die grosse Wirtschaftskrise 1929–1935," in *Trybuna Ludu*, 4 January 1983.
11. I. Trachtenberg, *Währungskrisen*, Moscow, 1963, pp. 608–636.
12. *Financial Times*, 7 September 1982.
13. *Aussenhandel in den Jahren 1918 to 1940*, Moscow, 1960, p. 14.
14. W. Zolotarev, *Aussenhandel der Sozialistischen Länder*, Moscow, 1964, p. 169.
15. Prof. Dr. W. Fisher, "Lehren aus der Geschichte," *FAZ*, 21 October 1982.
16. Ibid.
17. Prof. Bruno Frisch, "Arbeitslosigkeit als Geburtswehen der Automation," in *Neue Zürcher Zeitung*, 27 November 1982.
18. *The Economist*, 24 June 1978, p. 83.
19. *Neue Zürcher Zeitung*, 27 November 1982.
20. *Der Spiegel*, 49/1982, p. 37.
21. *Narodnoe khoziaistvo SSSR* for 1980, p. 334.
22. The period before 29 October 1981.
23. P. 14.
24. *Handelsblatt*, 31 December 1982.
25. Samuel Brittan, "Clues to World Stagnation in Financial Times," 22 July 1982.
26. *Die Presse* (Vienna), 4 November 1982.
27. "Where have all the answers gone," *Time*, 17 January 1983.
28. Ibid.
29. Ibid..
30. State of the Union address, 26 January 1983.
31. Jan Hargreaves, "Unemployment in Europe," *Financial Times*, 24 January 1983.
32. Lucio Lombardo Radice: "Die DDR—'despotischer Staatssozialismus,'" in *Der Spiegel*, 42/1978.
33. Quoted in *FAZ*, 10 August 1983.
34. European Management Forum (17 February 1984).
35. "Weights in EEC," *Salzburger Nachrichten*, 1 May 1984.
36. *The Wall Street Journal*, 26 April 1984.
37. *Narodnoe khoziaistvo SSSR 1922–1982*, p. 317.
38. *OGB-ND*, 22–26 March 1984.
39. According to Henry Kissinger as reported in *Newsweek*, 21 January 1983.
40. *Die Presse*, 25 January 1982.

41. Jan Hargreaves, "Why shorter hours are here to stay," *Financial Times*, 24 January 1983.

42. "Arbeitszeit international," *Salzburger Nachrichten*, 7 April 1984.

43. Jan Hargreaves, op. cit.

44. On this point see also Prof. Bruno Frisch: "Arbeitslosigkeit als Geburtswehen der Automation," in *Neue Zürcher Zeitung*, 27 November 1982.

2. The West, the East, and the Third World are at a structural turning point

No one doubts any longer that the 1979–1982 recession was something more than one of the cyclical cooling-off periods of the economy. It continued longer than normal in some countries, and the unemployment rate has been considerably greater than a cyclical recession would warrant. Whereas the number of unemployed in the Federal Republic of Germany was 0.6 million in 1967 and about 1.7 million in the recession of 1975, in 1981–1983 it rose to 2.4 million.[1] The situation was even worse in the United States and Great Britain. And although there has been a revival of sorts in the United States, it has been very slow in making itself felt on the European continent and, what is even more important for evaluating the situation, the economic revival has not led to any perceptible reduction in the number of unemployed. Though the growth rate reached 2.7 percent in 1985, the unemployment rate in the United States was still 7.2 percent in early 1985.

The marked decline in economic growth in the Eastern bloc has left its mark on international developments over the last few years. Growing foreign trade but also the considerable growth in debt to the West are conspicuous. The influence of the developing countries and threshold countries on economic events has grown steadily stronger; their debt to the West has grown to gigantic proportions, and they have had an impact on the leading banks of the world and at the same time have driven the Western industrial countries out of the world market in many economic sectors.

Against this dismal background we must also cope with rampant pollution of the environment and an escalating arms race that is absorbing an increasing share of natural resources, many of which have now become quite scarce, and a growing share of the national product. Thus the question is posed more and more frequently, and indeed now even by conservative circles in the West, whether we are perhaps in the throes of collapse, since no recovery is in sight. Marx and Engels signed the death warrant of capitalism as long ago as 1848 and in every economic crisis since that time, we hear that it is the last one, the one that must ineluctably lead to the collapse of the social order.

Yet it is generally recognized that no social system—and this includes the real socialism established in the East—has caused such a dynamic development of technology and increase in the standard of living and social services or such thoroughly modernized social structures as the competitive market economy of the modern era.

But the situation is now much different than it may have appeared in the early 1970s, and given that fact, the question arises whether perhaps Yuri Andropov was correct when he said that "we are now witnessing a significant deepening of the general crisis of [the capitalist] social system."[2] Of course, the difficulties are now greater than they were before, and the desire for a more efficient social system which can eliminate economic crises, unemployment, inflation, and environmental pollution is thoroughly justified. But it would be equally justified to ask whether in historical terms the new system of real socialism might not offer a suitable alternative to the capitalist system, which is four times as old, and whether the difficulties this relatively young system is experiencing are truly greater and more compromising of the system than are the difficulties with which the West has had to cope.

It is unclear whether the crisis symptoms in the East may be defined as a cyclic breakdown. No economist in either East or West can demonstrate that Kondratiev's cyclic law is also applicable to a planned economy. Just as the market economies do not create suitable conditions for full employment, the planned economies are unable to create the right conditions for an efficient utilization of work force. The stifling effect of the state bureaucracy, which the planned economies can no longer tolerate, as well as the inadequate satisfaction of the needs of the population are the principal causes for the decline in economic activity in the East.

Thanks to the pioneer achievements of the revolutionary elite, who were able to convey their belief in the emancipatory effect of the socialist revolution and later backed it up with direct force applied by the state, the transition from an agricultural economy to an industrial economy was more rapid in the Soviet Union than elsewhere in the world, and further gave rise to a mass production industry that was able to manufacture standardized products to satisfy the most elementary needs of the population. But the distortions in economic proportions were discernible from the very outset, and these would have serious consequences for the economy and the society at large. First, to defend the achievements of the revolution and later for other reasons as well, a military industrial complex was created which absorbed the best of the population, the natural resources, and an excessively high proportion of the national product. An education to obedience and to patriotism in the spirit of the greatest leaders of all time was able to replace the ideology of utopian socialism for a while, but the ideological motivation, which was supposed to play such an important role in promoting performance, progressively crumbled.

Common traits of the management era
in the East and in the West

Despite unbridgeable differences in the question of property and in steering methods, both economic systems show unmistakeable features of the so-called management era, at least in the first phase of industrialization. First there is the mass production of standardized commodities, the breakdown of the production process into simplified special functions, and a functional set of organizational principles that creates a layer of professional managers. The principal sectors of the economy at this stage were the food and textile industries, the steel and petrochemical industries, machinery construction, the auto industry (especially in the West), and, of course, the armaments sector.

The management era, with its mass production, huge firms, and large plants, reached especially high growth rates in the East, but in the United States it has been approaching its end since the early 1970s. In Japan and Western Europe, this process set in a few years later. In the East, the economic structure, as well as the system of steering and organization, all bear the unmistakeable markings of the first phase of industrialization. But in the Western industrial countries, the old steering system has gradually been replaced by a more flexible system intended to pave the way to a more modern economic formation, i.e., a production structure in which the information sciences play the prominent role. It has revolutionized society, because most of industrial production is in the hands of the workers whose performance approached that of the intellectual workers. It has also revolutionized the economic structure insofar as microprocessors, computers, robots, semiconductors, telecommunications, etc., have assumed a growing role alongside mass production. New production centers have been formed; modern production is steadily shifting its locus from the Atlantic to the Pacific. This true social revolution seems to have realized the dream of socialist movements of all epochs, namely, to at least partially bringing manual labor up to par with intellectual labor. But this did not take place where these solutions were components of the state ideology, but where the material conditions were ripe, namely, in the highly industrialized and democratic countries of this world.

It was easier to adopt the exploitative
methods of early capitalism, but more difficult
to carry the pioneering achievements of
mature capitalism to completion

The impressive growth of the planned economy in the first phase of industrialization was due first and foremost to its adoption of the exploitative methods of early capitalism. Its backwardness in its later phase of development is due to the lack of those dynamic forces which have been responsible for the stormy technical progress of the modern market economy: a business community willing to take risks, competition, functioning money, parametric prices, an effective incentive system, and integration into the international division of labor with modern steering mechanisms. But above all, the backwardness of the East is due principally to the inflated ruling bureaucracy which discourages any creative effort.

In an article entitled "The First Tasks of Soviet Power," published on April 26, 1918, Lenin, the founder of the Soviet state, called the Taylor system "the last word of capitalism, which like all the advances of capitalism, unites the fine bestiality of bourgeois exploitation with a number of the most valuable scientific achievements."[3] A few lines later he writes: "In Russia we must thoroughly study, systematically test, and evaluate the Taylor system."[4] But at the time Lenin wrote these words, the Taylor system had already been tested and was being used. On April 25, 1918, the Menshevik organ *Vpered* (which for the time being was still legal) published an article which asserted: "A policy of chastisement of the industrial trust is being carried out under the banner of the nationalization of industry, and under the banner of restoring the country's forces of production, attempts are being made to eliminate the eight-hour work day, and to introduce piecework, the Taylor system and even blacklisting."[5]

The progress achieved through the Taylor system and similar work methods in the initial stages of both economic systems is no longer possible once creativity, initiative, and a commensurate motivation of those involved in the production process have become prime conditions for the continued growth of the economy and society. Although the industrial countries of the West have been unable to eliminate the fundamental flaws of the system, such as cyclical depressions and unemployment, they have succeeded in gradually abandoning the exploitative work methods of their past and moving toward more humane and more effective relationships between capital and labor. They have accepted the trade unions as a responsible social force, and of the three principal factors of the production process—capital, machinery, and human beings—it is human beings and their needs that are increasingly being given prime consideration.

In the planned economies, on the other hand, unemployment, no longer an acute social problem, is still relevant as an economic problem. Although a social minimum is guaranteed, the needs of the population are not met to a degree befitting the present level of development, while the overall relationship between the state-owned factory and the worker is still adapted more to the beginning stage rather than the late stage of the management era.

Piecework, strict discipline, subordination to a massive administrative hierarchy, commands and rigorous compliance, and exclusion of the trade unions as authentic representatives of the work force are still the defining attributes of the relationship between the state and the work force. Indeed, the measures recently undertaken to overhaul the Soviet economy placed prime emphasis on discipline and rigorous fulfillment of the directives of the central authorities.

Creativity and initiative, along with a highly qualified, motivated, and effectively united work force are the prime prerequisites for technological and social progress; it is for this reason that the industrial countries of the West still lead in the brain-intensive sectors of industrial production as well as in the restructuring of society in general. The planned economies, on the other hand, are still the most capable in large construction projects and the weakest in computer manufacturing. They are also far behind the industrial countries of the West in reshaping the class structure of society and in meeting social needs.

The proletarian revolution in economically and culturally backward Russia, which broke historical continuity and leapt over a social stage, namely the stage of mature capitalism, did not abolish the country's centuries of backwardness nor did it take the lead in the progress of civilization. The modernization of economic and social structures and the furtherance of prosperity for the many have not been initiated by countries that regard their state ideology as socialist, but by countries that have developed the appropriate economic conditions to do so, have above all maintained a democratic system, and have not violated historical and intellectual continuity. For this reason, the conflicts that have arisen in the two world systems are different: in the West, the rapid rise in wages and social services has led to a dulling of the motivation of the blue-collar workers on the assembly line, with their dreams of vacation houses and new cars, and dampened the will to invest. In the East, the low standard of living has led to a dampening of motivation to improve one's qualifications and performance, while the all-powerful bureaucracy has dulled the innovative spirit of factory managers, who are reduced to the level of civil servants.

Economic growth has declined in both social systems. But while the economic recession in the industrial states of the West has not led to a loss in leadership in technological progress nor, despite the growing technological unemployment, to a decline in the very considerable buying power of the population, the decline of economic activity in the East has taken place at a time when the needs of the population are unmet, the energy and raw materials sources are shrinking, and the burden of armaments and the costly engagement in areas of conflict throughout the world have assumed intolerable dimensions. The dulled motivation to raise efficiency in the Eastern economies with their antiquated steering mechanisms is causing delays in the assimilation of the technological and cultural advances produced in the industrial states of the West and is broadening the gap between the two systems.

Growing interdependence and the shift of economic power

The most important consequence of the recent stage of development is the growing integration of the world market and the reshuffling of power relations within the different regions of the world economy. It is becoming more and more obvious to the general public that, despite inevitable conflicts and differences, despite the increasingly bitter war of competition, and despite protectionism and trade wars in some sectors of the economy, the well-being of every country and every economic region is dependent on the prosperity of the world economy.

The drastic rise in oil prices brought about by the OPEC countries has had repercussions throughout the world and has driven some countries of the Third World to the verge of bankruptcy. The recession in the industrial countries of the West reduces the export possibilities of the Eastern countries and the developing countries. The decline in investments and economic activity in the Eastern countries, and their considerable debt, has resulted in a cutback in imports and a reduction in exports to the West, thereby aggravating the symptoms of recession in the West and driving unemployment even higher.

However, along with this growing interdependence of the national economies which has characterized the most recent phase of development, world trade has grown at a more dynamic pace than the world GNP. United Nations studies have shown that international trade has increased 1.5 times more rapidly than the national product in the postwar period: 20 percent to 22 percent of the total world product is an item of foreign trade and forecasts indicate that by the year 2000 one-third of the gross national product will be intended for trade.[6]

The CMEA countries are much more dynamic on the world market than they were in the 1950s and 1960s, but they have been clearly surpassed in this respect by Third World countries. CMEA exports to the industrial countries of the West increased from 6.7 billion dollars in 1970 to 45 billion dollars in 1983, but their share in world trade, i.e., 10 percent, was three times lower than their share in world industrial output. The share of the Third World in world trade is twice as high as that of the CMEA countries, although their share in world industrial output is only 8 percent.[7]

The growing interdependency of the national economies of all regions of the world has furthered the transfer of technology from the industrial countries to the less developed regions of the world and has played an essential part in the restructuring of economic capacities. The Eastern and the developing countries have been able to import the most productive machinery and equipment along with licenses for their manufacture and the most up-to-date textile, paper, steel-making, and oil-drilling technologies and to perfect the production processes in critical sectors of the economy. This considerable transfer of technology at a time when the highly industrialized countries of the West were in the process of shifting from a standardized mass production to specialized and complicated manufacture of computers, robots, semiconductors, consumer electronics, and synthetic fibers, has shifted the growing portion of mass production into other regions of the world. Cheap labor and the proximity of raw materials and fuel resources have proven to be more beneficial to mass production than the production system itself.

The developing countries profited more than the East did from the shift in mass production

The steadily escalating dislocation of economic structures and the perfecting of the technological base proved to be much more advantageous to the market economies of the developing countries and the threshold countries, whose national economies were more closely linked with the world economy and international steering mechanisms, than to the planned economies of Eastern Europe, functioning with autonomous mechanisms. In a period of only fifteen years, the countries of South America and Asia have not only shown themselves to be promising competitors of the industrial countries of the West in the manufacture of textiles and consumer goods, they have also specialized in capital-intensive industrial sectors and supplied complicated components for the highly sophisticated products of the computer and electronics industries. The transfer of modern technologies has also helped to raise the productivity of labor in standardized mass production in the threshold countries to a level comparable with that existing in these sectors of the industrially developed countries of the West. Brazil, Hong Kong, Taiwan, Singapore, and a number of other threshold countries have achieved considerable progress in the textile, clothing, shoe, and toy industries. In the period between 1970 and 1975, textile exports increased by 436 percent in South Korea, 347 percent in Taiwan, and 191 percent in Hong Kong.[8]

The share of the Third World in world steel-producing capacity increased from 9 percent in 1974 to 15 percent in 1980.[9] By the early 1970s, Third World countries had already developed a diversified automobile industry, a television manufacturing industry, and similar complicated industrial sectors. South Korea, which began shipbuilding much later than Poland, now has one of the largest wharves in the world; multinationals such as Phillips and General Electric have complicated components for a diversified range of products made in South Korea or Hong Kong. By 1990 the share of the Third World in world exports will be 36–38 percent for clothing, 80 percent for textiles, 25–27 percent for leather goods, and 7–10 percent for metal products. The developing countries and threshold countries account for 40 percent of Western exports, and one-third of U.S. exports, while the CMEA countries account for no more than 3.5 percent.[10]

Of course, the payments situation of the CMEA countries is better and their economies are more advanced than those of the Third World: the debt of the Eastern bloc to the West is no more than a tenth that of the developing countries and no greater than Brazil's total debt. While the CMEA countries were able to square their balance of payments in 1981 and 1982 by making dramatic cutbacks in their imports from the West, and by 1983 had reached a surplus of about 3 billion dollars, the developing countries and threshold countries increased their foreign trade deficit from 21 billion dollars in 1974 to 77.5 billion dollars in 1982, and their debt service to 45 percent of their proceeds from exports.[11]

But the planned economies of the Eastern countries have not been able to make the transition from mass production to a more flexible steering system or, as it is defined in the East, from an extensive to an intensive production model, which is the precondition for a highly developed industry. Complicated machinery, usually acquired on the basis of credits, has increased the efficiency of many large factories and brought newly constructed factories up to the latest technical level, but modern factories are not yet an ostensible part of the overall economic picture of the Eastern planned economies (the military-industrial complex excepted). But it is mainly the steering mechanisms that are backward. The founding of two international CMEA banks and the establishment of a collective currency, i.e., the transferable ruble, created the preconditions for a transition from bilateral to multilateral clearing in intra-CMEA trade. In settlements with the Western industrial countries bilateral clearing has been replaced by settlements in hard currency: bilateral clearing of foreign trade has, however, remained, being intrinsic to the system. The CMEA countries increased the share of the Third World in their total trade from 14.2 percent in 1976 to 18.1 percent in 1981 and, moreover, intra-bloc trade is growing perceptibly. Trade increased by 24.7 percent between 1976 and 1980 and by another 10 percent between 1979 and 1982, while imports from the West decreased by 5 percent in 1981 and by 9.5 percent in 1982.[12] The Soviet Union especially has cultivated intensive economic relations with the Third World. Trade turnover increased from 3.3 billion dollars in 1970 to 8.8 billion dollars in 1975, and in 1981 reached a value of 23 billion dollars.[13] The Soviet Union has concluded cooperation agreements with seventy developing countries; 35 percent of the steel-producing capacity of India, 70 percent of that of Iran, and 95 percent of that of Egypt were built with Soviet help. The principal Soviet export item to the developing countries, however, is weapons, which reached a value of about 7 billion dollars in 1981, i.e., about 60 percent of total exports to this region.[14] The principal Soviet import from the Third World is agricultural products, which accounted for 6.4 billion dollars or about 60 percent of total imports from these countries.[15]

The major industrial centers of the world in competition and confrontation with the planned economies

It used to be said that any superpower, regardless of its system, is to some extent autarkic, given its huge domestic market. The Soviet Union and also the United States, with their relatively small shares in world trade, were given as examples. This view is no longer tenable. As late as the mid-1960s, Harvard Professor Robert B. Reich was still asserting that foreign trade had no essential effect on the American economy; only a small portion of the goods manufactured domestically were traded on the international market, and an equally small share of foreign output entered American markets. However, as time passed, the situation changed dramatically. In 1980, 19 percent of goods produced in the United States were exported, compared with 9.3 percent in 1970; more than 22 percent of goods consumed by Americans were imported (in 1970 9.3 percent).[16] In 1980, 70 percent of the goods produced in the United States were actively involved in competition with foreign manufactures. America has become part of the world market,[17] wrote Reich, and he gave statistics to demonstrate that America's position in world competition is not particularly strong. In 1981 the United States imported about 26 percent of its cars, 17 percent of its steel, 60 percent of television, radios, and tape recorders and record players, 35 percent of textile machinery, and 53 percent of computerized machine tools. Twenty years ago these imports accounted for no more than 10 percent of consumption.[18]

Moreover, America's share in world exports of some important capital-intensive goods has declined sharply; in automobiles and industrial machinery the decline has been about a third, in farm equipment, 40 percent, and as much as 50 percent for telecommunications equipment.[19]

The data below clearly show that America's share in industrial output in foreign trade has declined, while Japan's share has risen appreciably. Between 1960 and 1982 the U.S. share in industrial output and foreign trade decreased by 8.5 percent and 5.3 percent respectively, while the corresponding figures for Western Europe were 5.2 percent and 2.4 percent. Japan's share in industrial output has more than doubled, and it has almost tripled in foreign trade.

Share of the United States, Western Europe and Japan in industrial output and foreign trade of the non-socialist world (in %)

	USA	Western Europe	Japan
1960			
Industrial output	39.6	48.5	6.8
Exports	18.2	45.5	3.5
1970			
Industrial output	35.9	45.7	13.3
Exports	15.3	48.8	6.9
1980			
Industrial output	36.1	43.7	15.2
Exports	11.9	44.2	7.1
1982			
Industrial output	31.1	43.6	16.3
Exports	12.1	43.3	8.5

Source: J. Stolarow and F. Chesin, "Drei Kräftezentren in der kapitalistischen Wirtschaft der Gegenwart" in *MEMO*, Moscow, January 1984, p. 42.

Japan and the Soviet Union embarked upon the path toward becoming world industrial powers at the same time, and the Japanese market economy and the Soviet planned economy have much in common. The Soviet Union is a state economy *par excellence*, but state intervention in Japan is also considerable. A Porsche executive made the observation that "The Japanese have a command economy." Competition and functional market mechanisms remain the main pillars of the economy, but Japan owes its economic strength to the close cooperation between the private sector, which has remained intact, and the state, which does not intervene in the organization of firms. In 1960 Japan was still an economic midget, inferior in every respect to the Soviet economy: its share in the industrial output of the nonsocialist world was 6.8 percent, while its share in foreign trade was only 3.5 percent. Japan, a country over 90 percent dependent on oil imports, was hit harder than other industrial countries by the oil shock in 1973, while the Soviet Union, which produces more oil than any other country in the world (1982: 12,200,000 barrels per day, followed by the United States with 855,000 barrels per day[20]) benefited the most. But its work ethic, more patriarchal than modern, enabled Japan to much more strongly motivate its workers to efficient performance than real socialism in the Soviet Union. Between 1967 and 1973 Japan's annual average growth was 10.4 percent, which was far higher than that of the Soviet Union, and in the following years of relative slowdown between 1972 and 1982 its average growth rate was 3.9 percent, about the same as the Soviet Union's and in some years even higher (the Soviet economy, which had an average annual growth rate of 4.4 percent between 1976 and 1980, grew by 3.4 percent, 3.6 percent and 2.8 percent in 1979 to 1981).

Because of the high quality of its products and the relatively low cost (personnel costs in Japan's auto industry were 35 percent lower in 1982 than in the Federal Republic), Japan was able to drive the established major exporters of highly sophisticated products from the world market. Japan's automobile manufacturers were able to reduce the manufacturing time of a car to forty-eight hours compared with 145 hours in the United States, and since 1980 Japan has been the number one automobile manufacturer and exporter in the world. "In video recorders, the great growth sector of the 1980s," complained Bernhard Plettner, Chairman of the Board of Directors and former head of the multinational Siemens Co., "The Japanese have already captured over 90 percent of the world market."[21] Grundig and its partner, Phillips, have decided in the future to build equipment that is compatible with the Japanese systems. The software for the Japanese system has already cornered 63 percent of the market, while the software for the West German video systems has decreased to 14 percent.[22] The Asian countries, with Japan heading the list, followed by Hong Kong, Singapore, Thailand, and Korea, have cornered about 75 percent of the world market in black-and-white televisions. In photographic, phonographic, and radio equipment they stand virtually alone. They also already account for 60 percent of world's shipbuilding.[23] Japan has been able to capture a dominant share of the market not only for the most modern products of our times, but also for standardized mass production: 40 percent of Japan's textile exports are products whose manufacture requires an advanced technology and a highly skilled labor force.

The Soviet Union makes use of advanced Japanese technology in automobile manufacture and in the tapping of gas, oil, and iron ore deposits in the permafrost zones of the Soviet East. Meanwhile raw materials and fuels, rather than finished products, are the Soviet Union's principal export, in some years accounting for 80 percent of the total Soviet exports to the West. The quality of Soviet finished products is too low to find a Western market, and more often than not they are forcibly imposed in so-called compensation transactions. Giant trading concerns have been set up in the Federal Republic of Germany and in France to reprocess these usually unusable goods. Of course, no one has criticized the quality of Soviet goods more sharply than did former party leader Andropov: "The situation has become simply scandalous. The initial material is good, but the product is such that people prefer to pay a little more to get good and tastefully produced products. We need relief from this situation without delay."[24]

Andropov was speaking of consumer goods, but the quality problem is even greater in electronics, genetic engineering, and the computer industry sectors. It is in these very sectors that Japan, because of its ability to adapt to the needs of the world market, has been able to surpass the highly developed countries of the West, including West Germany, at one time the world champion in conventional technology. The Soviet Union is far ahead in the production of raw materials and fuels, but far behind in other important sectors of the processing industries, as will be evident from the following table.

Manufacture of major products in the Soviet Union, United States, Japan and West Germany in 1980

	Soviet Union	United States	Japan	West Germany
(1,000 articles)				
Automobiles	1,327	6,376*	7,038	3,530
Trucks	872	1,667*	3,554	268
Radios	8,478	11,024	15,343	3,707
Televisions	7,528	9,899	16,327	4,425
(1,000 t.)				
Plastics	3,636	12,418	6,422	6,720
Cellulose	6,334	40,650	7,703	432
Paper products	8,733	59,457	18,335	7,580

*Sales figures.
Source: Statistics of the corresponding countries.

Stimulating and inhibiting factors
in the economic systems

The Western industrial countries surpass the Soviet Union, the world's second economic power, in the most important, and particularly in the most modern, sectors of the economy. But in manufacturing technology, quality of goods, and the conquest of markets, Japan is far ahead of the most productive market economies as well as the oldest planned economy.

Is Japan then an aberration which can be classified as neither capitalistic nor socialistic? By no means. Japan is a thoroughly capitalist country, even using Soviet criteria. However, in each social system there are countries that initially play the role of pioneers but later decline, yielding the number one position to other countries which have been able to activate the potential motivation of the population. England rose to dominate the capitalist world in the eighteenth and nineteenth centuries thanks to the revolutionary effects of great technological inventions and the radical changes brought about by democratic reforms in the state. Germany had taken over the top position by the end of the nineteenth century, and later the United States took the lead. Now it is Japan's turn to move into the leading position in the world economy. In a three-year study sponsored by the Aspen Institute, social scientists of six countries found that the attitude toward work had deteriorated throughout the world, but that there were indeed substantial differences in the work ethics of the various Western countries. After so many decades of top-level achievement, the British now showed the poorest performance. Their commitment to work is only half as great as in the United States, only a third that in West Germany, and only a fifth that in Sweden. "The desire to achieve is weaker, and expectations are lower in no other country, and dissatisfaction with work, nowhere greater than in Great Britain," observed the social scientists.[25] Only 17 percent of British employees were regarded as having a "high" work ethic, compared with 57 percent in Israel, 52 percent in the United States, 50 percent in Japan, and 45 percent in Sweden. Interestingly, "contrary to a current prejudice," the social researchers also found a rapid decline in work ethic in West Germany. Only 26 percent of employed Germans had a work ethic that was assessed as "high."[26]

But the work ethic is by no means uniform throughout the Eastern countries. In the initial phase after the October Revolution and once again after the victory in World War II, the work ethic in the Soviet Union was extremely high. However, today, the low work discipline and the pervasive corruption, as well as alcoholism, are the principal headaches of the Soviet Party leadership. In contrast to the West Germans, whose work ethic is declining compared with the other leading countries of the Western world, the work ethic of the East Germans is regarded as "the highest" in the entire Eastern community even though their labor productivity is only half that of West Germany. However, it is neither the Soviet Union nor East Germany nor Czechoslovakia that leads the way in adapting its social and political system to the facts of the new era; rather, it is Hungary, which since 1968, despite all difficulties, has been endeavoring to introduce some of the principles of the market, to raise the country's performance to the level of the most advanced industrial nations.

However, the most important economic indicators show that the leading Western countries, notwithstanding their ever more frequent economic crises and recessions, are far ahead of the industrial countries of the East. Occasionally, attempts are made to look for the causes of the unbridgeable gap between East and West in the secular backwardness of the East. But since the meteoric rise of Japan within but a few decades, this factor can no longer be regarded as determinant. Nor can the discrepancy, which seems to be growing larger, be ascribed exclusively to differences in the social system. More convincing is the view that that country that is able to make best use of the positive properties of its system will be the most successful. But it is also important that the market economies have at their disposal more factors stimulating the economy than have the planned economies of the East.

Japan has placed its reliance on initiative and industry, perfect quality and flawless control, purposeful and production-related training, and employee motivation through a carefully designed wages system and comprehensive cost–benefit analysis. As regards the continuous adaptation of economic structures and organizational forms to the demands of the time, the economy of Japan has been unsurpassed.

Harvard's Robert Reich has this to say: "The transition has been easier for Japan and for some Continental Europeans because they never fully embraced high-volume standardized production and because they have historically linked their economic development with social change."[27] The competitive market economies offer many more prerequisites than a command economy for the development of such qualities and possibilities.

System viability as exemplified by a few components of production relations

No factor is more essential to the performance of an economy than the way it deals with its labor force. In the Soviet Union and the other planned economies the right to work is constitutionally guaranteed. The market economies, on the other hand, permit unemployment, which in times of crisis sometimes exceeds 10 percent. Of course, full employment is the most coveted goal of any society since it provides working people not only with their material existence, but also with active membership in the community. The high worth placed on this social aspect is evident in one Britisher's response to the question of how far he would be willing to go to get a job: "To the Falkland Islands." Full employment brings social tranquility, since it is the unemployed, not the proletariat, of the modern era who "have nothing to lose but their chains." But a 100 percent guarantee of work is possible only in a state which assumes full responsibility for the economic activity of every enterprise and endeavors to prevent bankruptcies through state subsidies, i.e., at the expense of other production units or at the expense of the population. No market economy can afford such an economic policy if it wishes to remain efficient. The planned economies have followed such a policy, but the price they have had to pay is inefficient enterprises and unemployment behind the factory walls. However, recent developments show clearly that a decisive turn is in the making in both social systems.

The times of early capitalism, when the army of unemployed was used as a means of pressure on the employed, have passed. The state defends every job and both trade unions and employees have been showing a steadily growing willingness to enter into compromises. A genuine partnership has developed in Austria and a number of Scandinavian countries. A radical turn is in the making in France and Italy as well; the workers are less and less willing to enter into the classical class struggle as a way to destroy the capitalist system. It is being realized with increasing clarity that only competitive factories in a competitive economy can guarantee full employment over the long term. Even in the United States a willingness to compromise is beginning to show. The desire to strike has been dampened considerably, and the work force is even willing to accept wage decreases. After a long conflict, the employees of Eastern Airlines agreed to as much as a 23 percent reduction in wages, and the work forces of Ford and General Motors made concessions amounting to a total of 3 billion dollars. In addition, in the United States a new expedient has taken shape which could serve as a model at least in times of recession. In many industrial sectors, automatic inflation adjustments have been curtailed, and employees are ready to invest some of their income in the enterprise. In return, the personnel are aspiring to a greater participation in company affairs. At Eastern Airlines, the trade union of pilots, mechanics, and on-board personnel have declared themselves willing to assume 25 percent of company shares and four executive posts in the administrative board; the work force committed itself to investing 25 percent of its wages in the company.[28] What is more, this initiative came from the employers, not from the trade unions.

The growing disinclination to strike, the fading of the classical class struggle and a willingness to compromise on the part of both employers and employees are discernible not only in Austria, a country where partnership has already become a tradition and where there have been no serious strikes for years, but also in other countries of Western Europe. This trend may be seen as an expression of the renunciation by the enlightened work force and by intellectuals of the ideas of subversion and proletarian revolution in the thought that there may be a worthwhile alternative to a market economy, becoming ever more social, in a bourgeois pluralist democracy. A turn is also becoming discernible in the communist movement of Western Europe and Japan under the banner of Eurocommunism; taking the old socialist theory of revolution further, they seek the perfecting of Western democracy and the competitive market economy rather than a Soviet-style dictatorship of the proletariat. But a similar trend is also evident in the traditional social democratic movement and its trade unions, which are attempting to tailor their demands to existing possibilities and are striving for a balance between employer incentive to invest and employee incentive for productive performance in a flourishing economy.

An about-face in the way the labor force is dealt with also seems imminent in the planned economies. Full employment at any price is now being criticized just as sharply as maintaining worn-out factories and enterprises operating at a loss.

Perceptive analysis has shown that what the planned economies have eliminated is not unemployment, but the subsidizing of unemployment. The fluctuation of the work force, mainly as a consequence of the housing shortage, is excessively high in every planned economy. In the Soviet Union, Poland, or Hungary 15–20 percent of the employed are looking for jobs which promise them better living conditions. Usually this quest takes three to six months. But the times where employees could be chained by force of law to their jobs are irrevocably past.

In terms of efficiency alone, full employment as an irrevocable goal cannot be justified. The precondition for an efficient economy is a functioning labor market which provides the employee with the best possible choice of job and enables the employer to structure his work force as efficiently as possible on the hire and fire concept under trade union control. The costs of maintaining full employment, seen as a social goal, are prohibitively high in the planned economies. No other factor in production relations is so abused as this. It gives the resourceful manager a permanent labor reserve and a means for meeting any augmentation of the plan target and of plugging any gaps in the production process. The price of labor is low compared to the price of machines, and value categories play no particular role in a quantity-oriented growth strategy. Bottlenecks in the supply of semifinished products and raw materials in any planned economy can lead to snags in the production process and to treading lightly in the first twenty days of the month, followed by febrile production activity in the last ten days; hence, nothing is more desirable than a silent labor reserve. But conditions for achieving this goal are created only for priority ventures, at the expense of other production units. This practice deepens the disproportionalities in the commodity structure and causes the supply fall-outs that have become routine in the Eastern countries.

It is one of the paradoxes of the planned economies that, even though they are burdened by chronic supply problems, their stores of semifinished products and raw materials are relatively great in relation to the output, and, while there is chronic overemployment in many industrial enterprises, entire economic sectors are plagued by a labor shortage. In an economy in which a paternal state bears full responsibility for economic success or failure and covers losses with state subsidies, full employment entails both underemployment and overemployment, and the latter has a devastating effect on labor productivity and work morale. The realization that one will receive his wage whether or not he performs commensurately is just as damaging as the hire and fire mentality.

Therefore, not only reform-oriented Hungary but also the more conservative Soviet Union are seeking a way out of this untenable situation. One of the results of this uneconomical way of dealing with the labor force is that the performance of the 4.1 million workers in Hungary is 15–20 percent below the norm of 233 workdays. An average of 2.8 million working hours are lost every year through pure wasted time and unexcused absenteeism.[29] The first major attempt to get rid of redundant labor at a stroke, undertaken by the bus and auto factory, Raba, in February 1979 when it dismissed 249 unneeded blue and white collar workers, did not take root and found no imitators. This reticence is all the more noteworthy since in the Hungarian reform the savings resulting from the reduction of the number of employed were used to raise salaries. But a new experiment has been in progress for the past two years: volunteer teams of workers from state-owned factories pool their efforts in a private initiative after working hours or on Saturdays and Sundays and carry out special contracts of various types, sometimes even for the factories where they work. There are signs that the Soviet Union has also come to the realization that full employment as a social goal is economically indefensible over the long term. In 1966, an experiment was undertaken in the nitrogen factory Shchekino which translated savings in labor into higher wages for an efficient work force. Although the experience was thoroughly positive, no attempt was made to extend this system to other factories. The factory managers are evidently not willing to make cutbacks in their work force and the state fears that this measure could lead to mass unemployment.

The tendency rather is to put off dealing with the problem. Indeed, despite the positive results from the Shchekino experiment, the relationship between the number of persons employed and wages is again to be tested in accordance with a government decision of July 26, 1983 "on supplementary measures to broaden the rights of production associations (enterprises) in planning and in economic activity, and to strengthen their responsibility for the results of labor."[30] It states that full employment as a goal of society is not only uneconomical, it is also unsocial: the overemployment that has been produced by this imposition is one of the main causes of the low labor productivity, low gross national product, and low wages.

The CMEA countries, including those that ranked with the industrially developed countries before World War II, are currently behind the industrial countries of the West in their level of development, as is evident from the table (p. 58).

We see that the economically most developed CMEA countries, such as the Soviet Union or Czechoslovakia and the GDR, correspond at best to Italy in their development. The distance from the other Western countries is still great. If one considers that the Eastern countries use more of the produced gross national product for investments and less for consumption than the Western industrial countries, it is not difficult to conclude that the differences in wages are even greater than the differences in the national product.

Gross national product per capita 1979 in East and West in US$

Eastern Europe		Western Europe	
Bulgaria	3,030	FRG	12,400
Czechoslovakia	5,040	France	10,650
GDR	5,340	Great Britain	7,050
Poland	3,380	Italy	5,620
Romania	3,580	Netherlands	10,860
Hungary	3,340		

Source: *Handbook of Economic Statistics 1980*, National Foreign Assessment Center, October 1980, pp. 10 and 11.

The economic recession has had a negative influence on the growth of the per capita income in both world systems. But in contrast to the economic crises of earlier times, the market economies have taken effective measures to buttress the effective buying power of the population, and it was indeed found that these measures helped considerably to alleviate the recession. As regards the CMEA countries, real wages fell only in Poland, where they declined by at least 25 percent as a consequence of the drastic price rises in early 1972. In other countries, there was a modest growth in real wages; in 1980, 2.4 percent in the Soviet Union, 1.4 percent in the GDR, and 2.5 percent in Romania.[31] A slight decline was observed in the other countries: 0.3 percent in Bulgaria, 0.5 percent in Czechoslovakia, and 1.7 percent in Hungary. In the next three years, real wages stagnated or increased but slightly in the CMEA. In Poland and Hungary, on the other hand, they decreased by a few percentage points as a result of the drastic price rises in early 1984.

Of course, the stagnation of the income of the population has had more negative consequences in the East, where wages still border on the subsistence level, as compared with the West where they have reached an optimum level for the majority of the population. The average monthly wage of a worker in the Soviet Union in 1981 was 172 rubles gross[32] and 159 rubles net[33] or, at the official exchange rate, $220; this average wage was no more than 35 percent of the average net wage of white- and blue-collar workers in Austria for 1982 (11,554 shillings).

Of course, in the East everything possible is done to enhance the quality of life of the population. But their concept of development, attuned to heavy industry, their centrally administered economy that goes hand in hand with this concept, and full employment, based on a rigid organization and discipline of the human material, create neither sufficient financial means nor a commodity structure commensurate with the buying power created.

In comparison to this employment policy, which is neither economically nor socially justified, the technological or recession-related unemployment, which in the market economies has been kept within limits, would seem to be thoroughly justified as a precondition for a successful incomes policy. The idea that rising incomes and worker participation in the firm's affairs create the best possible conditions for an efficient economy seems to have made headway in Japan as well. Japanese managers have given the lie to the claim, heard until even quite recently, that Japan owes its high competitiveness to relatively low wages and costs. A recent comparison made of wages in the chemical industry in Japan and West Germany showed the following: the average monthly earnings of a Japanese chemical worker were 3,300 DM in 1982, which was only 430 DM below the German average. What is most striking, however, is that in the difficult times between 1975 and 1982 the monthly earnings of a Japanese chemical worker rose by 71.5 percent, which corresponds to an annual growth of an average of 8 percent, and this growth rate was identical with the rise in labor productivity.[34] This growth rate was greater than elsewhere; in the period between 1960 and 1980 incomes throughout the world increased by 65 percent.[35] However, Japan's competitiveness is too great to be explained solely by the advantages derived in the structuring of costs from the relatively small wage differential. The proverbial application and industry of Japanese workers have contributed to Japan's economic success. The effective labor time of a Japanese chemical worker is 1,970 hours per year, while his counterpart in the West works only 1,670 hours. A similar difference that influences cost may be discerned in the length of vacations. Persons employed for less than a year receive 12 days of paid vacation per year; those employed between one and two years receive 13.5 paid vacation days, and thereafter an average of 0.6 extra days for each additional year of employment. After twelve years in his profession, paid vacations amount to 20 days; in contrast, all chemical workers in Germany have a standard covenanted right to 30 days of paid vacation. The difference between Germany and Japan in the work time in the automobile industry is just as great. The number of actual hours worked—2,000 hours—is 20 percent higher than in West Germany, where the average is only 1,600 hours. The arguments in the current debate in some of the countries of Western Europe on the introduction of the thirty-five-hour week should therefore also mention Japan's competitive advantage.[36]

Technical progress and the practical implementation of the fruits of research as a criterion for assessing the viability of a system

However one measures the contribution made by a country or a community of countries to the advance of human civilization, stress is invariably laid on advances in the development of modern technology and modern products.

The use of this criterion justifies the conclusion that in the second half of this decade some substantial reshufflings have taken place with regard to the contribution of certain countries or groups of countries to the cause of civilization. It also seemed warranted to say ''All that is new in technical mass products that appeared on the market after World War II, has been taken up by the highly developed Pacific nations. The Asiatic threshold countries are able to produce anything that can be manufactured with ancient techniques without any special refinements.[37]

If one accepts the contribution to technical progress as a criterion for evaluating the viability of a system, the Eastern countries must be ranked in second place. Of course, the Soviet Union and some of the other Eastern countries have chalked up some substantial achievements in technological development. But on the whole, they still tend to import much more than they export of know-how and modern products. The causes of this situation are generally known. The most important is not so much due to historical continuity, e.g., the assertion that Russia has imported its advanced technology from the West since the days of Ivan the Terrible, as to the effects of the existing economic system. It rewards an orientation to short-term efficiency more abundantly than it does efforts with an eye toward the future. The Eastern economies have been spared the pressure of serious worldwide competition. The absence of ''creative destruction,'' to use a nice phrase of Josef Schumpeter's, makes life easier for the manager in the planned economy, but more difficult for the socialist citizen. Indeed, creative performance in the future is extremely limited without competition.

The Soviet Union spares no means for research and development; expenditures for this item make up 4 percent of the national product. This is as much or even somewhat more than in industrial countries of the West: 5,284,000 students[38] are studying in 891 colleges and universities for a highly qualified and responsible job. Some very relevant inventions have been devised. The elitist research center in Novosibirsk enjoys international recognition. The unresolved problem, however, is the considerable discrepancy between an invention and its practical implementation; while in the United States and in West Germany more than 50 percent of all innovative proposals find their way into production within a year, in the Soviet Union the time gap between the research result and its practical implementation is no less than three years; 8 percent of machinery is replaced because of physical wear, only one-seventh because of obsolescence.[39]

The managers in the planned economies are the most eager investors in the world. Nowhere is the share of capital investments in the national product as high as in the Eastern countries. As a rule capital investments are financed from the state budget. But nowhere does the completion of a capital investment project take so much time as in a planned economy. At the end of 1981, the volume of incompleted investment products in the Soviet Union was 86 percent of the annual value of investments.[40] The socialist system, which was supposed to help the Eastern countries out of centuries of backwardness, proved to be an almost unbridgeable barrier. This system, which had made possible an unprecedented progress in its building up phase, is hardly able to meet the challenge of the industrial countries of the West at a time when a new technical revolution is taking shape.

The planned economies had higher growth rates than the industrial countries of the West in the early stage of industrialization with its mass production and old technology. However, they became backward in the later stage, in which a flexible, adaptable steering system and progressive management methods became the indispensable conditions for the creative teamwork of highly qualified producers and for concentrating on solving problems and on technical innovation instead of on routines. The planned economies lacked these qualities, and for this reason they have neglected computer technology, semiconductor technology, communications technology, data processing. They have lagged behind the world level and have even been passed by others; they must import advanced knowledge from the West.

Japan proved to be the most able to meet the challenge of the new technical era; as the American sociologist Bruce Nussbaum put it, Japan has become "the center of the economical tornado." Japan's strength lies first and foremost in its comprehensive quality control and the high quality automation of the production process, as well as in its preferential, selective export strategy. But the Japanese know how to combine rationality and rigid discipline: the state and private industry work together like a cohesive enterprise.

Japan's enterprises have a control system which allows a visible and thorough analysis of the efficiency of every worker. The results are presented in a daily diagram. In these carefully sketched diagram curves, the worker finds the mistakes he has made in production while management obtains the overall picture of company productivity and information on the achievement of each individual participant in the production process. This perfect control system is linked to a perfect gap-stopping procedure. The rules of promotion are subordinate to quality. Quality must be achieved within the framework of the existing wage schedule. However, the Japanese can also thank their well-thought-out educational policy for their economic success: 94 percent of Japan's youth attend school until the age of 18; half finish an institute of higher learning. The fusion of physical and intellectual labor is the most advanced here.

The advanced market economies must acknowledge above all the close cooperation between research institutes and technology firms for the lead they have achieved in modern industrial production. "In the United States, universities and high-tech companies are often located next to one another and their communication ties are short and intensive."[41] Hewlett Packard, a leader in the development of modern technology, is close to Stanford University in Palo Alto, which is financed by several technology firms and oriented to the most modern technology projects. However, the Americans are eclipsed by the Japanese when it comes to having an educational structure which promotes productivity. While management is given priority in the United States, in Japan, stress is placed on the training of engineers. Between 1971 and 1981 the number of practicing lawyers in the United tates increased by 64 percent to 590,000; there is currently one lawyer for every 400 inhabitants. The number of engineers increased by only 15 percent during the same period and the number of workers increased by 25 percent. In Japan, on the other hand, one citizen out of every 10,000 is trained for a law career, while one out of every twenty-five Japanese is trained to be an engineer.

In Japan 65 percent of the seats of the management boards of industrial firms are occupied by engineers, but in the United States the same percentage is occupied by lawyers and financing and accounting experts.[42] The effect of this difference is described by Harvard professor Robert Reich as follows: "In Japan many problems that arise in business are viewed as problems of engineering or science for which technical solutions can be found. In present-day America the same problems are apt to be viewed as problems of law or finance, to be dodged through clever manipulation of rules or numbers."[43]

The Japanese are far ahead in automation of the production process: 13,000 robots have already been installed. The Americans and West Germany have only 4,000. The Japanese have also stepped up their exports of robots: in 1983 exports reached a volume of 40 billion yen or almost one-fifth of the total output. In 1983, the export volume almost tripled.[44]

The leadership in the industrialized world shifts from one country to the other. At one time Great Britain was in the lead, and later it was Germany; for decades the United States was in the lead, and today Japan is first in the production and marketing of key technologies. The above data also show unequivocally that the social system which has called itself socialistic, and which has been in existence since October 1917, has achieved superiority for that system neither in production relations nor in the results of production. Despite frequent setbacks and conflicts, the market economies maintain their world leadership position in the production and transfer of modern technology, followed by the threshold countries in second place rather than the planned economies. The market economies which best understood the changing conditions on the internal and world market and how to adapt to them, moved out ahead. They indeed have made the greatest contribution to the promotion of human civilization.

Of all the obstacles the planned economies have to face, their inadequate presence on the world market seems to be the single most crucial factor in maintaining their backwardness.

Monopoly over foreign trade and currency in the planned economies is inferior to the modern steering mechanisms of market economies

To be able to participate fully in the world market, one must have attractive and competitive goods to offer, and the prerequisite for producing competitive goods is an active participation in the international division of labor. The planned economies have neither a satisfactory range of exportable goods nor a viable means to bring them onto the world market.

The foreign trade system in existence today was designed in 1918, i.e., at a time when for various reasons the Soviet Union had no possibility of participating in world trade. But even later, after it had established diplomatic relations with almost all the countries of the world and had become a member of the League of Nations, almost nothing changed in this respect. Soviet foreign trade decreased from 10,090 million rubles in 1913 to 1,207 million rubles in 1939 (at 1950 prices).[45] However, in the period between the wars, the Soviet Union had unambiguously opted for an autarkic course. The monopoly over foreign trade and foreign currency, which was tailored to an autarkic economy, became a feature of all the countries of Eastern and southeastern Europe, which depended on intensive participation in world trade for their very existence. And this monopoly remains even today although no CMEA country, including the Soviet Union, any longer believes that it can compete with the industrial countries of the West in the development of modern technology without active participation in world trade.

Although some of the components of the foreign trade system have been modified and streamlined, the basic structure persists. The unit of currency in the planned economies is not tied to the world currency system through internationally accepted exchange rates. There is therefore no organic relationship between value relations on the world market and those on the domestic markets of the planned economies. Although the autarkic conception and the negative attitude toward the theory of comparative cost advantages have been put aside, there are still no functional mechanisms which could integrate the planned economies into the world market. The collective CMEA market is also unable to integrate its steering mechanisms into those of the world market. The collective currency, the transferable ruble, can be converted neither into the national currencies of the CMEA nor into the currencies of third countries. The basis for prices in intra-CMEA trade is not internal cost relationships, but costs on the world market. Of course, it is impossible to achieve any advantages with trade mechanisms tailored to an autarkic market. The planned economies, with their foreign trade monopoly, do not promote exports with credits or favorable interest rates, such as they demand from their suppliers and from the world banks. Usually they force their finished products upon their trading partner through compensation transactions in order to finance indispensable imports. The backward foreign exchange mechanisms are matched by a backward export structure.

Every industrial country of the world makes its own particular contribution to the rich range of products exported worldwide. Like the developing countries, the planned economies also export a good deal of raw materials and fuels. Out of a total volume for the world electronics industry of about 550 million dollars (1982), the Americans accounted for one-third, the Europeans 23 percent, the Japanese 19 percent, and the developing countries, threshold countries, and planned economies 25 percent; the latter accounted for about a third of that figure. Out of a total turnover of steam turbines with a capacity of 342,000 megawatts, the Europeans accounted for 40 percent, the Americans 23 percent, and the Japanese 20 percent, but the planned economies only 12 percent. The exports of the Federal Republic of Germany (535.6 billion DM or $185 billion in 1982) were almost twice as great as the total exports of the CMEA countries, more than four times as great as CMEA Western exports ($45.1 billion) and seven times as great as the Soviet Union's exports to the West ($26.1 billion). West German auto exports alone, amounting to 75 billion DM, equaled the total exports of the Soviet Union.

The expansion of Soviet foreign trade in the 1970s was regarded with amazement. Soviet exports in the period between 1971 and 1981 increased by 61 percent, somewhat less, however, than the national income (+ 68.5 percent).[46] The tremendous growth of its exports to the West, from 2,776 million dollars in 1971 to 23,800 million dollars in 1981 at current prices, was attributable to the extremely favorable terms of trade which had improved by 150 percent in trade with the Western industrial countries.[47] This explains why Soviet imports from the West increased by 321 percent in real terms, while exports increased in real terms by only 39.1 percent[48] without the Soviet Union having to raise any large credits. In real terms, Soviet exports to the West between 1971 and 1981 only increased from $2,589 million to $3,502 million. One commodity group made all the difference for the rapid growth in exports: crude oil and natural gas. At current prices, the value of petroleum exports increased from $608 million in 1971 to $12,287 million in 1981, while gas exports increased from $21 million to $3,965 million, but in real terms only from $490 million to $574 million and from $14 million to $322 million respectively.[49] Sixty percent of Soviet total exports to the CMEA countries and 85.6 percent of total exports to the Western industrial countries in 1982 were fuels, raw materials, and metals. The terms of trade, which showed a 45 percent improvement, also contributed to the expansion of Soviet exports to the CMEA countries.

The last two decades have seen a major reshuffling of the international division of labor, although three industrial countries of the West, the United States, West Germany, and Japan, still lead the exporting nations of the world. Despite the decline in their relative shares to the advantage of the Japanese, West Germany still remains the leading export nation, with 33 percent of its gross national product going for exports (1982). The Japanese figure amounted to 17 percent, and the American figure declined to 12 percent. Exports of the Soviet Union, the second greatest economic power of the world, are still 50 percent less than West German exports. The rapid rise in Soviet foreign trade in the 1970s was not due to an expansion of its competitive range of export products, but to the dramatic rise in prices for its most important export goods, i.e., crude oil and natural gas.

The systemic barriers in the planned economies do not favor the production of high-tech goods, nor do they promote exports. The economic system has reduced their foreign trade structure to one resembling that of the developing countries. A thorough reform of the economic system and its constituents, i.e., a modification of the foreign trade system, is an indispensable condition if these countries are to keep pace with the developed industrial nations of the world in both the production and export of technologically advanced goods.

Summary

A new technical revolution is paving the way for a modernized social system. But it is a revolution in the forces of production that is still in progress. Those aspects of the social system whose quantitative expansion may at some time in the future bring a better quality to society are very slow to change. In the short term, however, the new industrialization phase is bringing more disadvantages than advantages. Advanced technology is expelling much more of the labor force from the production process than it is creating new jobs. It has not yet been determined how, under the existing conditions, the redundant labor force should be employed: by reducing the number of hours worked per week or in a lifetime, by open unemployment as before or by unemployment behind the factory walls with all the negative consequences that this has for work morale and labor productivity, as is the case in the planned economies. But the employment problem is still not so acute in the planned economies as elsewhere, since the technical revolution is moving much more slowly there than in the industrial countries of the West.

The third industrial revolution is already assuming definable contours. Just as the agrarian society of the past gradually assumed more and more of the features of an industrial economy, the industrial economies are relying increasingly on more information technology, thereby effecting major transformations in the class structure and structure of production. But while the agrarian society paved the way for feudalism and absolute monarchy, and the industrial society paved the way to capitalism and bourgeois democracy, the physiognomy of the postindustrial society cannot yet be clearly perceived. Of course, the social and political forms of earlier economic formations were not one-dimensional: in the United States, the attributes of an agrarian society predominated down to the end of the nineteenth century. But there was no feudalism in the United States; in mid-nineteenth century, Germany began to develop the unmistakeable qualities of an industrial society, yet remained but an enlightened monarchy until 1918. Russia had been an absolute monarchy up to 1917, although the economy and the society grew increasingly riper for a bourgeois state system under the influence of progressive industrialization.

Of course, it cannot be ruled out that the real socialism into which the Russian "proletarian" revolution degenerated in the 1930s was the most logical outcome of the historical continuity of Russia and the psychology of its people, and that it more than any other state form accelerated the industrialization of this backward country. But the development of the two social systems also shows clearly that socialism is an inconceivable alternative to the bourgeois democracies of the industrial countries of the West.

The data presented in an earlier chapter show clearly that a traditional market economy, anchored in a pluralistic democracy, has met the challenge of the technical revolution more than real socialism has in the Eastern bloc; it can boast of greater prosperity, more coparticipation, more rights for the authentic representatives of the working man, more freedom of movement for management to develop its own initiative and creativity in the service of society, and better conditions for a transformation from physical work to intellectual work than has the real socialistic social system.

In meeting the challenge of the times, the planned economies are showing signs that they are more interested in introducing aspects of the market into their steering systems than they are in the ideological promises of utopian socialism. Both social systems are at a crossroads. The most recent experiences show clearly that a social market economy anchored in a pluralistic democracy has much greater chances for fostering the rudiments of a future, more humane social system than the other existing social systems.

Notes

1. Prof. Dr. Wolfram Engel, "Hat sich unsere Wirtschaftspolitik historische bewährt?" in *Ost-West-Journal*, 314/1983.
2. Yuri Andropov, "Von der sowjetischen Verstaatlichung in die gesellschaftliche Selbstverwaltung," in *Ost-West-Journal*, 3 April 1983.
3. V. I. Lenin, *Ausgewählte Werke* (Moscow: Progress Publishers, 1975), p. 456.
4. Ibid., p. 457.
5. Ibid., p. 493.
6. M. Simai, *Interdependence and Conflicts in the World Economy*, Budapest, 1981, p. 52.
7. O. Bogomolov, "Interdependence, Structural Change, and Conflict in the World Economy," in *Mirovaia ekonomika i mezhdunarodnye otnosheniia*, October 1983.
8. Robert B. Reich, "The Next American Frontier," *The Atlantic Monthly*, March 1983.
9. Ibid.
10. Simai, op. cit., p. 58.
11. Bogomolov, op. cit., p. 19; ibid., p. 19.
12. J. Stankovsky, "Ost-West-Handel 1982 und Aussichten für 1983," Bericht No. 86 des Wiener Institutes für Internationale Wirtschaftsvergleiche.
13. See *Deficits and Detente*, Report of an International Conference on the Balance of Trade in the Comecon Countries (New York, 1983), pp. 90 and 91.
14. Ibid., p. 92.
15. Ibid., p. 91.
16. Reich, op. cit., p. 44.
17. Ibid.
18. Ibid., p. 45.
19. Ibid.
20. "Statistical Trends: The USSR," *Financial Times*, 14 September 1983.
21. "Wir brauchen ein Apollo-Programm," *Der Spiegel*, 52/1983.

22. Ibid.

23. Ibid.

24. Yuri Andropov, "Von der sowjetischen Verstaatlichung in die gesellschaftliche Selbstverwaltung," in *Ost-West-Journal*, 3 April 1983.

25. Werner Bankhoff, "Studie über die Arbeitsmoral in ausgesuchten Industrieländern," in *Handelsblatt*, 6 December 1983.

26. By "superior work ethic" the authors mean an "inner drive toward optimum achievement without regard for compensation."

27. Reich, op. cit., p. 48.

28. G. Possaner, "Der starke Arm ist schwach geworden" (4 January 1984).

29. A. Zwass, *Planwirtschaft im Wandel der Zeit*, Europaverlag, 1982, p. 246.

30. *Pravda*, 26 July 1983.

31. B. Askanas and F. Levcik: "Die Europäischen RGW-Länder eine vergleichende Bilanz," Bericht No. 69 des Wiener Institutes für Internationale Wirtschaftsvergleiche.

32. *Narodnoe khoziaistvo SSSR* 1922 to 1982," p. 420.

33. "Sowjetunion," *Der Spiegel*, 16 January 1984, p. 112.

34. "Weniger von Orwell und Mehr von den Japanern reden," *Handelsblatt*, 13 January 1984.

35. Report of the International Labor Organization (Geneva), *Handelsblatt*, 14–15 January 1984.

36. Ibid.

37. Quoted in "Wir brauchen ein Apollo-Programm," *Der Spiegel*, 52/1983, p. 20.

38. *Narodnoe khoziaistvo SSSR*, 1922 to 1981, p. 506.

39. *The Economist*, 29 December 1979, p. 31.

40. *Narodnoe khoziaistvo SSSR*, 1922 to 1982, p. 377.

41. Quoted in "Wir brauchen ein Apollo-Programm."

42. Reich, op. cit., p. 58.

43. Ibid.

44. "Steigende Roboterexporte Japans," *Neue Zürcher Zeitung*, 18 January 1984.

45. *Vneshniaia Torgovlia SSSR 1918–1940*, Moscow, 1960, p. 14.

46. H. Machowski, "Tendenzen und aktuelle Probleme des sowjetischen Aussenhandels," *Neue Zürcher Zeitung*, 13 January 1983.

47. Ibid.

48. *Deficits and Detente*, pp. 86–87.

49. Ibid.

3. Conservative and liberal, state and market, in the West and in the East

It has become more and more apparent that the basic problem is the role of the state in the economy: the laissez-faire notion of an economy guided by Adam Smith's invisible hand in which a natural order reigns, in which the relations emerging spontaneously among men constitute the edifice upon which the system is built, and in which no state intervention is necessary, sounds just as utopian to us today as socialist notions of a society that administers itself without the authority of the state and in which, as Saint-Simon dreamed, man ruled over things and not over other men.

The countries which owe their victorious march to the promises of man's self-determination and self-fulfillment of human beings today have the most omnipotent states in the modern era. But, however thorough its grip on the economy may be, the state is continually compelled to yield to the laws and creative reason of human civilization. The dream of an economy *in natura,* without money, profits, and without differentiation of incomes, was abandoned long ago; market relations, not the ideals of utopian socialism, are making headway.

Radical turns in opposing directions are discernible in both world systems: in the planned economies, the market is suppressed by the omnipotence of the state bureaucracy. Market mechanisms are reactivated to protect human creativity from the stranglehold of the omnipotent administrative bureaucracy and, in general, to keep things functioning. It is not just any specific value categories adapted to the laws of a planned economy, e.g., viable money, sound prices, or functioning credits, which are being employed, but the distorted value categories of the traditional market; but these can change nothing due to the inherent functional limitations and the command character of the system. It is not the mottoes of equality of the great French Revolution and the October Revolution that are being implemented; quite the contrary, they are denounced as the most extreme of heresies. Income differentiation based on performance is being acknowledged as the driving force of civilizing progress. In real capitalism, on the other hand, the omnipotence of the market is being questioned. State planning is being tried to mitigate the proneness to recessions, to reduce unemployment to a tolerable level, and to help the weaker social layers whose very existence is being threatened. Planning under capitalism is not a broad all-embracing concept and a wide-ranging set of instruments, but rather *ad hoc* interventions that impair the ability of the traditional market mechanisms to function instead of reinforcing the instruments of economic control.

A hundred years after the triumphal march of Marxism, its protagonists seem to have discovered one of the most important teachings of the old master, namely, that the state of the productive forces is what determines the advance of human civilization. The progressive industrial revolution was able to revolutionize social relations far more than the most revolutionary ideologies of the modern era. The revolution which called itself socialist, was unable to even begin to implement the great socialist ideals in the politically and culturally backward Russia, with its industrialization still in its infancy and a proletariat that was still in embryo; the work and human conditions of the peasants were far from those of the industrial workers, nor had the latter acquired an equal footing with intellectual labor, and the path toward post-industrial society was not even begun. But the evolutionary restructuring of the industrial nations of the West was able to accomplish these things in some measure. These countries attained their economic and political maturity much earlier than the Eastern countries, and they embarked upon the path of the revolutionary restructuring of the social and economic system not by immaturely overthrowing the established social system, but by a parallel process of evolutionary development of the forces of production and of social relations adapting to them.

The retribution exacted for violating the law of development of human civilization is clear to all: despite victims by the legion, the Soviet Union is as laggard in carrying the third and the fourth economic revolutions to fulfillment as Russia was in the early twentieth century in the realization of the first and second phases of industrialization. And although both world systems (the West steeped in tradition going back hundreds of years, and the East still historically very young) are both showing unmistakeable signs of wear, the symptoms seem to indicate, more so in the East than in the West, that the crisis is a crisis of the system.

Despite numerous crises, the fourth industrial revolution is on the way

According to W. W. Rostow, we are in the midst of the fourth industrial revolution.[1] Each of the preceding revolutions was preceded by discoveries that revolutionized the mode of production. The first industrial revolution started with pioneering discoveries, namely Cort's method for producing steel using coke, Watt's steam engine, and the factory manufacture of textiles. These three advances all took place in the 1780s in Great Britain and secured for the British an economic head start in the world of that day.

The second industrial revolution started in 1830 with the railroad, especially in Great Britain, but also in the American northeast and in Germany. The third industrial revolution came with the discovery of electricity in the early twentieth century. The fourth started with new technological systems, in which synthetic fibers, plastics, and later, electronics, lasers, semiconductors and computers set the pace for dynamic economic growth and for the diversification of consumption.

Each great phase of development got its start in a particular country, and then spread to other countries of the civilized world. Each left its own unique stamp on the social system. The first industrial revolution, which started in Great Britain, struck the great historical note for a young and burgeoning capitalism. This was the capitalism of laissez faire, which Adam Smith and David Ricardo so thoroughly investigated, with all the horrible methods of exploitation of early capitalism and primitive accumulation, which Karl Marx, Georges Sorel and many others so graphically described. Great Britain experienced the first great economic crisis in 1825 and became the cradle of the labor movement, with Chartism as its most conspicuous expression.

The second phase of industrialization spread from Great Britain and Germany to the whole of Europe and then somewhat later to North America. The United States took the lead in the fourth great phase of industrialization, and it was there too that the fourth industrial revolution began. But American leadership in world technological progress seems continually to slip from its grasp. Only the first two industrialization phases took place in a homogeneous social system. The split into two fundamentally different social systems took place in the transitional phase from the second to the third industrial revolution, set into motion by the October Revolution in Russia, which interestingly was still immersed in the second phase of industrialization, with the third only barely beginning to emerge. The continuity of the traditional economic system was shattered in economically and culturally backward Russia and the partitioning of the world, with grave consequences for human civilization, became a reality.

Every phase of industrialization was accompanied by economic crisis, both domestically and worldwide. But despite heavy losses, devastating domestic conflicts, and catastrophic international developments, the prediction which Marx and Engels made in 1848 in the Communist Manifesto of the inevitable decline of capitalism has never been fulfilled. The economies of the world have not only rapidly recovered from every economic crisis, they have recently rebounded with a much greater boom than earlier. The first crisis of 1825, which struck only Great Britain, was followed at relatively short intervals by two other deeper and more extensive economic collapses: in 1836 and 1847.

The latter especially had a major influence on subsequent world history. It inspired not only the Communist Manifesto of 1848 but also ''The Spring of the Peoples'' which led to the fall of many established European institutions. The next economic crisis in 1857, the first to embrace not only Europe but also North America, seemed to corroborate Marxism, which at the time was enjoying an ever-growing popularity. The paralyzed economic capacities, the army of the unemployed, the hunger and need, all called into question the ability of the economic and political system to secure a tolerable existence for mankind.

The first Socialist International (International Working Men's Association), founded in London in 1864, aimed at the overthrow of capitalism and the establishment of a socialist society free of want, crises and unemployment.

But after the crisis of 1857 the economies recovered rapidly, just as they did in the next devastating crises of the nineteenth century: 1866 and 1873 (the longest and most difficult crisis of the century) as well as the crises of 1882, 1890 and 1900. Each of these caused considerable damage, yet, after each, economic potential was not only rapidly restored, but the economy experienced an unparalleled boom.

Revolutionary slogans may have been attractive for a growing number of the work force and intellectuals (the first Socialist International, which dissolved after eight years of activity because of the irreparable conflicts between Marxists and Proudhonists, was followed in 1889 by the second Socialist International). The traditional system itself opened the eyes of the world to the realization that it was unable to ensure unbroken development without crises and recessions; yet it also made clear that it was the cause of neither an absolute nor a relative immiseration of the working class and that it had advanced both the economy and the quality of life.

But faith in the ability of the West to secure a tolerable existence for its population was once again to be shaken. The world economic crisis of 1929–1933 put to shame all previous notions of the destructive elementary forces of an untamed market. It sentenced millions of human beings to hunger and need, destroyed moral values, and paved the way for antihuman ideologies to throw the world into a devastating war. Within two to three years, economic performance declined by 40 percent in the United States and Germany, 39 percent in Austria, and in the other countries of the world by one third. The number of unemployed was 15 million in the United States, 5 million in Germany, and 450,000 in Austria; at the height of the economic crisis, the ratio of the number of employed to the unemployed in Poland was 1,830,000 to 740,000. After the stock market crash on Wall Street on October 24, 1929, shares fell to but a fraction of their initial values: U.S. Steel fell from 375 dollars to 222 in July 1932. The situation in Germany and Austria, as well as in other countries of Europe, was even worse.

It was dismaying how the influential people of the world of that day looked on in perplexity and impotence as culture and society progressively decayed. The economic policy pursued before Roosevelt's National Recovery Act in June 1933 was designed more to deepen the worldwide economic misery: the Smoot-Hawley Tariff, which raised customs duties to the highest level in the history of the world, and the beggar-my-neighbor policy, which caused a rapid devaluation of the national currencies (between September and December 1931 the sterling exchange rate fell to 69.3 percent of its initial value) threatened to dry up world trade completely. U.S. exports decreased by 60 percent in only two years; between 1929 and 1932, Austria's foreign trade declined by 47 percent. And the situation in other countries of Europe was not better.

The social and political consequences of these terrible crises of the modern era were especially devastating: the radicalization of the popular masses; the bloody three-year-long Civil War in Spain; the continuous wave of strikes in France under the United Front government; the seizure of power by Hitler's bellicose party; and, finally, the attempted suicide of the West in fascism and war. Even though the American and European economies began to improve under the effects of Roosevelt's New Deal, Stalin's question and answer to the Seventeenth Party Congress of the CPSU on January 26, 1934, on the developments in the Western world still seemed thoroughly warranted: "Does this mean that we are here facing a transition from crisis to an ordinary depression, which will then give way to a new upswing and a new industrial boom?" "No," was his answer. And he continued: "Because this is a permanent and general crisis of capitalism." Indeed at that time the Soviet alternative still seemed quite attractive, especially as the cost of the successful Five Year Plans were not yet known. At a time when the West was careening from one economic crisis to another and a fascist dictatorship was spreading throughout Europe threatening to plunge the whole continent into an abyss, the Soviet economy was experiencing an unprecedented dynamic growth. The subsequent great victory in World War II and the establishment of the CMEA put the Soviet Union in a position of superiority not to be disparaged. The steering system of the planned economies seemed to be superior to the traditional market economy.

Who at that time could have suspected that the countries of Western Europe, devastated by long years of occupation, and the torso of a defeated Germany would be capable of mustering sufficient forces to restore economic capacities that lay in ruin, and bringing about a boom and prosperity almost beyond imagination for so many people? Forty years after the end of World War II, the market economies have clearly demonstrated that they have not overcome their tendency toward crisis, that they are incapable of securing full employment, and that economic capacities are not fully utilized. But they have also shown that they have not lost their lead in the development of modern technology, in the enhancement of the productivity of labor and capital and in the quality of life and that they offer the best conditions for a pluralistic democratic state system to flourish.

It is also an unmistakeable fact that the real socialist regime that has spread throughout the entire East and southeastern Europe has been able to free itself from the reign of terror of the Stalinist era, create a dynamic standardized mass production, and secure its population a minimum livelihood, but that it has also been incapable of competing with the industrial countries of the West in the production of modern technologies or in the creation of conditions for a democratic state system. The countries of the West have not been spared their periodic crises; deep-going social political upheavals have taken place in the East: in the GDR in 1953, in Poland and Hungary in 1956, in Czechoslovakia in 1968, and in

Poland in the late 1970s and early 1980s.

In the longest economic boom in history, during the 1950s and 1960s, the Western industrial countries were not only able to initiate a new phase in the development of modern technologies but were also able to break the undisputed superiority of the planned economies with regard to quantitative growth. This may be clearly seen in the data in the following table on economic growth, capital investments and productivity in several countries of East and West.

	GNP/labor productivity Annual average growth for 1950–1969 (in %)		Average share of capital investments in gross national products for the period 1950–1969 (in %)
West			
FRG	6.2	5.0	27.0
France	5.0	4.6	23.7
Italy	5.4	5.0	22.1
Austria	5.0	5.0	26.2
Great Britain	2.7	2.2	17.5
Japan (1955–1968)	10.1	8.6	30.0
USA (1950–1959)	3.7	2.3	18.9
Eastern Europe			
Bulgaria	5.9	—	—
GDR	5.2	4.0	—
Poland	3.1	2.6	32.0
Romania	5.0	5.0	—
Czechoslovakia	3.3	2.5	35.0
Hungary	4.0	3.2	35.0
Soviet Union			
1950 – 1958	7.1	5.3	25.0 (1950 – 1958)
1958 – 1965	5.3	3.5	30.0 (1958 – 1967)
1965 – 1972	5.1	3.3	—

Sources: Statistical books and Vaclav Holisovsky, *Economic Systems* (McGraw Hill: 1977), pp. 294 and 297

The leader in economic growth in the 1950s and 1960s was not the Soviet Union or any other CMEA country but Japan. Indeed the growth achieved by the CMEA countries was due first and foremost to the above average share of capital investments and the below average share of consumption in the Gross National Product, and much less to the growth rate of productivity than in the West. To achieve even a much more modest economic growth than previously, the CMEA countries found themselves forced to use a greater part of their GNP for capital investments than the Western industrial countries.

In the 1970s, economic growth slowed in both East and West. An economic recession spread throughout the West in 1973, bringing with it a higher unemployment rate than could be attributed to the effects of the recession alone. The experts are in dispute as to its causes. The former presidential advisor, Walter Rostow, claims that the Fifth Kondratiev cycle began as a consequence of the skyrocketing grain prices in 1972 and the fourfold rise in oil prices in 1973. The first cycle, which began in Great Britain in 1790, and brought about an explosive rise in prices of 66 percent between 1798 and 1801, was followed by a second cycle with an inflation of 71 percent between 1852 and 1854. The third cycle was between 1898 and 1900 with an inflation of 57 percent. The fifth price explosion occurred in the 1970s. According to Rostow, the leading symptom of the Kondratiev cycle is a restructuring of investment activity for the purpose of securing a viable rate of profit under the changed conditions.[2] The world economy has had to cope with this phenomenon since 1973.

The price explosion of the 1970s hit Western Europe, the United States, Japan, and the non-oil-producing countries of the Third World. The small countries of Southeastern and Eastern Europe also suffered its repercussions, although not so much through the direct impact of world developments, as because of the Soviet Union's successive adjustment of its oil prices to the world levels. The Soviet Union was, like the OPEC countries, one of the major winners. The Soviet Union is a gross exporter of oil and gas, not only to the industrial countries of the West (more than four-fifths of its foreign exchange proceeds in 1983 were from the export of oil and gas); it is also the main supplier of its partner countries in the CMEA. Consequently it was able to improve considerably its terms of trade during the 1970s and the early 1980s. But even the Soviet Union has not been immune to symptoms of crisis. Not only has economic growth in the CMEA slowed (although it is still higher than in some of the Western countries) and not only has unemployment reared its head (although officials would still like to keep it behind the factory walls), but there have also been unmistakeable symptoms of a deep-rooted dysfunction in the system, which is increasingly in contradiction with the level achieved in the forces of production. The symptoms of a dysfunctional defect have become evident: the productivity of labor and capital is low, and the specific expenditure of labor and materials in the production process is excessively high. Capital investment projects require a lot of time, much more than provided for in the plan. Technological progress is unsatisfactory compared with the amount spent for research and development. Social woes such as alcoholism, corruption, and theft of public property, have reached frightful proportions. The moral values essential to maintaining the social fabric are crumbling in this young social system much more rapidly than in the decadent West.

Reform is the key word in both world systems. But neither West nor East has any unified or consistent notion of a functional social system. Clearly, the role of the state in the economy must be redefined. But so far no country in either West or

East has as yet been able to integrate a viable market component into a state economy or a viable planning component into the traditional market economy.

In a state economy, the state by definition is omnipotent. There is no invisible hand of the market, i.e., no self-regulating mechanisms which basically create a functioning market, such as prices which are continuously adjusted to events on the domestic and world market as an allocation factor and orientations parameter at the same time, or a functioning currency, which is able to transmit signals from the world market on the basis of an economically realistic exchange rate integrated into the world system. The automatic mechanisms of a functioning market have been replaced in state economies by the command of a hypertrophied administrative bureaucracy. But this bureaucracy operates with counterfeit prices which it usually has set itself. It therefore has neither informative allocation parameters nor signals of an impending imbalance.

The more effective the hierarchic economic bureaucracy is, the less margin is allowed for personal initiative and creative activity. The crippling effect of the administrative apparatus is clear to all. Lenin himself, the founder of the state and the first head of government, warned about its devastating influence as early as 1920. Since then, however, the ruling bureaucracy has swollen beyond measure and the consequences are graver than ever. Every inauguration speech of a General Secretary of the ruling party contains such forebodings. But no Eastern country has found a substitute for its administrative apparatus.

The market economies of the Western industrial countries are also at a crossroads. It is generally accepted that the cybernetic age cannot be steered with the same methods and the same mechanisms as the mechanical age, that the invisible hand of the market is arthritic, and that only a rational, rigorously limited intervention through state planning can protect against excesses of the market and the devastating effects of economic breakdowns. The belief in the self-regulating force of market mechanisms as well as the belief in the healing effects of Keynesianism have been shaken. But no viable alternative has yet been found. The two superpowers, one leading the Western world, the second possessing hegemonic power in Eastern Europe, will continue to exercise a great influence on events in both world systems. The economic and social developments in these two countries will be discussed in more detail in the following section.

The United States and the Soviet Union have different social systems, but both are steered by equally conservative economic policies

No one who attempts to attribute the similarities in the basic features of these different systems and the considerable differences in their state systems, level of development, and quality of life exclusively to their social systems will ever find a suitable answer to the relevant questions. Real socialism, Soviet style, be just as inconceivable in the United States as American libertarian values in Russia. In his renowned book, *Présent Sovietique et Passé Russe*, Alain Besançon attempts to explain the Soviet present in the light of the great Russian past and lists the following properties of its style of government: Byzantine ritualism, Mongolian brutality, sixteenth-century Messianism, and Petrine voluntarism as a combination that recurs in every new phase of development of great Russia.

Russia's greatest philosopher in exile, Nikolai Berdyaev, was more consistent in his attempt to root Soviet communism in the Russian past: in his opinion, Soviet communism is not a mixture of Montaigne (1533–92) and Marx but a mixture of Marx and Ivan the Terrible. Alain Besançon rounds out Berdyaev's view with the following words: "The fathers of Soviet communism link up with the rich past of Russia in an the unbroken continuity with its concept of an everlasting authoritarian state" and for such a state, maintains Besançon, "there is no parallel model; no Western and even no Eastern state has ever had such an intention or such a function. . . ."

The October Revolution and its consummation later in Stalinism were marked by the omnipotence of the Russian state just as Sergei Witte, the most capable minister of the last Russian Tsar, had imagined it: "Russia is an empire, and to preserve it, the state must take every area of national life in its hands." The prominent theoretician and member of the Central Committee of the Communist Party of Italy for many years, Lucio Lombardo Radice, viewed this consummation of the Soviet state as follows: "In the Soviet model, the state not only does not wither away as a separate entity, but through its tendency to control everything it swells to enormous proportions and becomes omnipotent."[3] Under the conditions of real socialism, the state has swelled because the Party apparatus, both Communist church and state hierarchy at the same time, has reorganized the functions of the traditional great Russian bureaucratism into an all-embracing, almost theocratic state structure. To be able to have everything under its eye, it must be tyrannical and omnipresent. It has more powers than any other power apparatus of the modern era. Its most distinctive attribute is command and subordination; it lets the whip of state authority crack over the land, yet is itself not immune to the encroachments of the Party, which is one stage higher. But it is strong enough to bring down any Party leader who slights its claims to authority. This mighty apparatus brought down Khrushchev who fancied that he could transfer three-fourths of his apparatus from the metropolis to the lustreless provinces without having to fear its vengeance; this apparatus also prevented the late Yuri Andropov, backed by the omnipotent secret police, from being replaced by a dynamic top functionary of equal power.

Lenin, the founder of the Soviet state, knew that every state was "unfree, and not a state of the people," a special repressive force.[4] He wanted no such repressive state in the social system he founded and quoted the following from Frederick Engels: "The proletariat seizes state power and first transforms the means of production into state property. But in doing so it negates itself as proletariat, it negates all class differences and class contradictions, and thereby also negates the state as state,"[5] and further: "After this revolution, the proletarian state or semi-state withers away."[6]

After the October Revolution it was not the proletariat, still in its infancy, that seized power, but the Bolshevik Party, in numbers insignificant, but in quality the strongest, consisting mainly of intellectuals and the progeny of the bourgeoisie. Many years later, as well, when the Soviet proletariat had become numerically the largest social class in the world, it negated neither itself as proletariat nor the state. It became "more proletarian" and more politically dependent than the proletariat of any other country. The Soviet state is mightier than any other state and also mightier than ever before in the previous history of the country.

Lenin has realized this during his brief period as helmsman, when in December 1920 he wrote that the established regime was "a workers' state with bureaucratic excrescences." But it was already too late to turn back the tides of Russian history. Lenin wrote: "So long as the revolution in Germany tarries in being born, it is our task to learn from state capitalism of the Germans, to adopt it with all our forces, to shy from no dictatorial methods to accelerate this assimilation even more, just as Peter accelerated the adoption of Western culture by barbaric Russia without himself shying from barbarian methods in his struggle against barbarism."[7]

Lenin needed no examples from Germany or elsewhere to mold the Soviet state. His successors shied from no "barbarian methods" and established a social system which cannot function without an omnipotent state. Stalin's successors, from Khrushchev to Brezhnev, and Andropov, Chernenko, and Gorbachev, attempted half-hearted reforms without challenging the state and the omnipotence of the Party and the state apparatus. The Soviet state is more omnipotent in its style and more conservative in its functioning than any other state in history, either now or in the past, because it has extended its authoritative might not only throughout the whole of social and political life, but also into the economy and into foreign territories which had never belonged to great Russia. To be successful, any thoroughgoing reform would have to challenge the omnipotence of political power. But the ruling elite is not willing to reduce this power, i.e., its own sphere of influence.

Americanism is conservative in its moral values and its economic policies

The conservativism of Americans matches their fidelity to their social system which they regard as the embodiment of freedoms of universal and everlasting validity.

The fathers of the American state system, men such as Thomas Jefferson, Benjamin Franklin, James Madison, John Adams and George Washington, were not particularly influenced by ideas of the eighteenth-century Enlightenment and its idealistic successors in the nineteenth century such as the following: "the rule of the goddess of reason guarantees the unswerving progress of virtue, truth and happiness." They did not believe so much in human reason and high ideals; they placed their trust more in social institutions. Their Constitution does not stress so much the words "liberty, equality and fraternity," which the great French Revolution would be carrying on its banners a few years later, as political democracy and bourgeois liberties, as well as institutions that could guarantee acknowledged rights.

Herbert Simon, the Nobel Prize winner for economics in 1978, described America's founders as pragmatists with vast experience and knowledge of the human character, who desired to "achieve a high level of satisfaction and freedom for the individual citizen with the aid of the social institutions they designed."[8] For them, political democracy was not an end in itself but a means to an end, which was to be achieved through institutions that were optimally adapted to guarantee achievable human rights. They were quite aware of the attributes of the human material out of which they wished to build a functional state. The architects of the American state had no desire to build their state system using a fanciful new man as the great socialist dreamers of every era have done. Their material was men who knew how to behave "humanly" if not "heroically," and not with men who "sense a spontaneous need to act in a way useful to their fellow man" (Marx) or men "who will rise to the level of Aristotle, Goethe or Marx" (Trotsky). The fathers of the American Constitution did not dream, as did Frederick Engels, that the coveted social system would "bring about an optimal moral level which would make any external coercion superfluous," but rather attempted to build a state system on the realization that the regime would have to be based on the existing imperfect human material. "If men were angels," wrote one of the great architects of America, James Madison, "government would not be necessary"; "The actual government can only be a pale reflection of human nature," he said. For Madison, control over the government was just as important as the government's control over the governed. He was quite aware that "political democracy is the best means to prevent the concentration of power in a few hands," but he was also clear that "a political democracy can be abused to gain power in the name of a majority and to suppress the rights of those who are not a party to power."[9]

These views of the founders of the American state constitute the foundations of the American state system down to this very day. The discrepancy between ideal and reality was therefore never as great in the United States as elsewhere, where an ideology was developed to fit an imaginary, fanciful human ideal, while the state system was adapted to real human beings and conditions. The famous Russian writer, Ilya Erenburg, describes this dichotomy in his novel *Uskomchel* (The Perfect Communist Man), in which the hero of the novel drowns in vodka in his attempt to adapt his image to the visionary ideal.

The intellectual elite of the United States, liberal or conservative, is conservative with regard to the moral values proclaimed by the founding fathers. But even the most conservative of the conservatives no longer dream of a laissez-faire market and it is mistaken to say that state intervention in economic affairs began only with Roosevelt's New Deal.

Alexander Hamilton (1757–1804), Washington's adjutant in the War of Independence, a delegate to the Constitutional Convention in 1787, and founder of the U.S. Bank, distanced himself from Adam Smith's classical economic philosophy in his Report on Manufactures (1791). The influence of the mercantile school is unmistakeable. Hamilton advocated state protection for imperilled industries and subsidies for new ones. He maintained that protectionism was necessary to protect enterprises that were just getting started, to master the art of manufacture, and, last but not least, to secure deliveries for defense purposes.

The economic history of the United States reveals the quite considerable protectionist barriers set up in the second half of the nineteenth century to protect the domestic market. The tariff acts of the Republicans, e.g., the Morill Tariff Act of 1861 and the McKinley Tariff Act of 1890, justified their protectionist measures not only with economical but equally with ideological arguments, e.g., that the U.S. markets must be shielded for U.S. producers, or McKinley's comparison in 1888 of foreign competition with military interference from without. These are arguments more broadly conceived than merely as a spur to state intervention at that time.

But, more than in any other country, both conservatives and liberals have intoned the virtues of the free market. U.S. policymakers have been very hesitant to intervene in the affairs of the private economy and have shown an outright contempt for the establishment of planning functions. The rules of the free market have always had a preferential place in America's economic theory. The belief in fair play, i.e., that the interests of one economic group should not have preference over those of any other, was deeply rooted in economic practice. It was all but a universal belief that a policy of intervention in particular sectors could cause sectoral distortions, impair the market, and imperil the nation's prosperity. Champions of industry have never been singled out for preferential tax reductions, subsidies, or state supported research projects over other industrial sectors. Economic policy has never led to rampant nationalizations of basic industries such as steel, automobiles, coal or aviation. The United States has been very reluctant to nationalize traditional monopoly areas such as the telephone, railroad, energy, or gas facilities. There is a deep-rooted conviction that private enterprise does its job better than state enterprises.

The great depression of the 1930s for the first time raised the question of whether the free market economy was able to guarantee continuous economic growth. Nevertheless, when intensive intervention of the federal government in economic affairs was inevitable, limits had to be set to that intervention. The National Industrial Recovery Act of 1933 attempted to meet these requirements and worked out a code of conduct for every branch of industry. But from the very outset, the omniscience of the state planners was doubted, and no attempt was made even to socialize industrial enterprises. The Temporary National Economic Committees (TNEC), established to revive the economy, never even gave the impression that they would develop into a permanent instrument of government. Their temporary nature was explicitly emphasized, and the sphere of their activities clearly defined. They were to concentrate on encouraging capital investments through tax benefits, on expanding modern technology through easing the patent law, and on improving the quality of goods by setting clear product standards. It was stated that TNEC activity must take place within the market. The Reconstruction Finance Corporation (RFC), which released 40 billion U.S. dollars for the development of modern technology in the two and a half decades of its existence and the Tennessee Valley Authority (TVA), which concentrated mainly on improving conditions for farmers and on a few weapons sectors, were all designed so that they would never imperil the functioning of the market.

After World War II, ambitious government intervention into economic affairs came to an end. Macroeconomic measures, such as influencing aggregate demand by appropriate fiscal money and credit policies, were given precedence with the prime goal of creating a stable economic policy for free enterprise. This economic policy was backed by a theory whose defenders, whether liberal or conservative, attached even greater worth to the unadulterated rules of the game of a freely functioning market. The margin of maneuver for a far-reaching economic policy had narrowed: government decisions in 1962 and 1980 to accelerate the amortization of capital investment so as to promote the formation of capital and technical progress and the Trade Expansion Act of 1962 to promote the competitiveness of the U.S. economy were the only official acts of nationwide significance. The lingering depression has once again placed economic policy on the order of the day, more intensively in the United States than elsewhere. Economic policymakers have found themselves faced with problems that have a greater impact in the United States than elsewhere because of the momentum of the scientific and technical revolution.

No adequate software for a revolutionizing hardware

The new technology created in the United States, revolutionizing traditional economic and social structures, is threatening to boomerang on the American economy and society. The hardware is developing much more dynamically than the software, i.e., more rapidly than the institutional structures of the state and society. Before and directly after World War II, steel production, autos, coal and other principal sectors of heavy industry were the backbone of the U.S. economy just as in other industrial countries. Since the mid-1960s, however, industry, which in its day had driven agriculture from its leading position, has been receding into the background, replaced by a growing service sector.

In 1978 the share of the processing industries in the U.S. GNP was only 28 percent compared with 63 percent for the service sector broadly defined; similar are the disproportions in the total employment: 33 percent and 65 percent. Modern technology has brought about extensive shifts in the value-creating and employment structures of U.S. industry, as is evident from the following table:

Share in value creation and employment in the years 1960, 1973 and 1980 by factor intensity

	1960		1973		1980	
	Value creation	Employment	Value creation	Employment	Value creation	Employment
Technology-intensive goods	27	27	32	29	38	33
Capital-intensive goods	32	29	32	30	27	28
Labor-intensive goods	13	21	13	21	12	19
Resource-intensive goods	28	23	23	20	23	20

Source: Robert Z. Lawrence: "Is Trade De-industrializing the United States?" in *Economic Impact* 1, 1984, p. 15.

Between 1960 and 1980 the technology-intensive commodities have considerably increased their share in value creation in industry and in employment, while the share of resource-intensive commodities in other areas, but in particular in value creation and employment, has diminished considerably. The structural shifts taking place in the economy as a whole and in industry have caused grave problems with regard to employing the persons made redundant in the shrinking sectors of the economy. These problems have emerged in a relatively short period and in the context of an increasingly bitter war of competition with other Western industrial countries.

America's difficulties in the late 1960s and early 1970s were greater than those of other Western industrial countries because the true revolution of our time, the scientific and technical revolution, has entrenched itself much more quickly and much more dynamically in the United States than elsewhere. The restructuring of the economy and of employment has proceeded so rapidly that it is exceeding the capacities of existing economic policy-making institutions to deal with them. The unemployment rate, inflation, and interest rates were much higher in the second half of the 1970s than in other Western countries.

The greatest economic power of the world, in which the scientific and technical revolution has depressed the share of industrial production in the GNP to about 28 percent, and raised the share of technology-intensive goods in industrial value creation to 38 percent and that of the service sector in the gross national product to about 63 percent, is faced with problems of a completely different order than the second greatest economic power, the Soviet Union, where the share of traditional heavy industry in total industry is still 73.7 percent,[10] the share of industry in the GNP 51.2 percent, and that of trade and other services only 18.3 percent. The United States is facing problems that place the impending postindustrial revolution on the order of the day. The Soviet Union, on the other hand, must cope with problems of traditional, standardized mass production in industry and an extremely backward agriculture. The main and gravest problem of the Soviet Union is, as it always has been, that of supplying the population.

The Americans fear that the scientific and technical revolution, begun in America and expanding into the other industrial countries, might place its technology-intensive industrial branches at risk and that the dynamically growing mass production in the threshold countries might imperil its own basic industries. This fear is thoroughly justified if one considers that between 1950 and 1982 the U.S. share in the world GNP decreased from 40 percent to 20 percent, and its share in world exports decreased from 16 percent to 10 percent. In the period between 1980 and 1982 exports of the processing industries decreased by 17.5 percent while imports increased by 8.5 percent.[11]

It is feared that a macroeconomic policy based mainly on fiscal and monetary mechanisms may prove inadequate to prevent the erosion of traditional basic industries and to ensure the quality of brain-intensive, high-tech goods, which however has become an indispensable condition for improving competitiveness in commerce, especially with Japan. On the surface, the three main goals of social policies do seem to be at risk, namely: improving the quality of life, guaranteeing work for those willing and able to work, and stabilizing the buying power of the population.

But although the United States seems to be the clear loser in competition with Japan, it has maintained rather than lost its powers of leadership in the world economy. In the most difficult period of the postwar era, between 1973 and 1980, its GNP increased at an average rate of 2.3 percent yearly, which is only 0.3 percent slower than in the other OECD countries; moreover, its share in OECD exports decreased only from 17.6 percent to 17.2 percent. However, the United States has been more effective than Western Europe in creating new jobs: despite the oil shock, three recessions, and the severe collapse in the traditional key industries and despite a persistently high unemployment rate, 21 million new jobs have been created in the United States, and in 1983 another 4 million were added (on the other hand, in the Federal Republic of Germany the number of employed decreased by about 1 million in the same period compared with 1.3 million in Great Britain). Between 1965 and 1984 the number of jobs increased from 78 million to 103 million, i.e., by 45 percent. The U.S. economy showed an unexpected flexibility in the creation of jobs for women. Because of the growth of the service factor, which traditionally employs more women than men, the employment problem was more acute than in the other industrial countries of the West. But results were better than generally expected: by 1983, 53.2 percent of employable women had been brought into the labor process, compared to 43 percent in 1970. Among the industrial countries of the West, only Sweden has a higher employment rate, 60 percent of all employable women; in West Germany, the figure is 40 percent.[12] The United States was behind the countries of the European Community as regards increasing labor productivity: between 1973 and 1980 U.S. productivity increased by 1.1 percent, while in the EEC countries it increased by 2.7 percent. But the relationship between the productivity rate and the pay rate (1.1: 1.8) fit the market conditions better than in the European Community in which this ratio was 2.7 : 4.1.[13]

The Americans still lead the world in wage levels: in 1982 the cost of labor per hour in the United States was 28.48 DM, followed by Switzerland with 27.47 DM, West Germany with 24.35 DM, Sweden with 25.40 DM, the Netherlands with 25.38 DM, Belgium with 24.35 DM, Denmark with 22.20 DM, Italy with 20.87 DM, France with 20.8 DM, Austria with 19.04 DM, Great Britain with 17.3 DM, and Japan with 16.27 DM. The share of additional personnel costs in total costs was then 50 percent lower in the United States than in the FRG, in which the additional cost per working hour was 11.32 DM, which was only 3.44 DM lower than the actual gross hourly wage.[14]

In the United States, the state receives less taxes and social security payments than in the other Western industrial countries: in 1980 these two items made up 29.5 percent of the GNP as compared with 52.5 percent in Sweden, 48.9 percent in the Netherlands, 41.3 percent in France, 40.5 percent in Austria and 38.4 percent in West Germany. But in Japan this percentage was lower than in the United States (24.6 percent).[15] Despite a twentyfold increase in Federal expenditures in the past twenty years, the ratio of U.S. government spending to the GNP (34 percent in the budget year 1980/81) still ranks last among the seven industrially developed countries. In France, Italy and West Germany this figure was over 47 percent, while in Great Britain it was 44.7 percent and in Canada 40 percent.[16]

The United States is entering the fourth industrial revolution from a more advantageous position than the other industrial countries of the West, not only because of its traditionally lower level of state engagement in the economy, but also because of its lead in the development of science and technology. Of course, there are no undisputed indicators able to unequivocally demonstrate this superiority, but the Nobel Prizes awarded between 1950 and July 1981 may serve as some indication. The United States heads the list with 99 prizes, followed at a considerable distance by Great Britain (34), West Germany (12), France (6), and Japan (2). Expenditures for research and development are higher both absolutely and relatively than in the four other industrially developed Western countries: 35.2 billion U.S. dollars compared to 5.2 billion dollars in Great Britain, 5.0 billion dollars in France, and 10.6 billion dollars in West Germany.[17] The number of inventions relevant to economic growth was also above average: 315 in the period between 1953 and 1973 compared to 85 in Great Britain, 35 in West Germany and Japan,[18] and 20 in France. The only country approaching the United States in terms of expenditure for science and research is the Soviet Union: in 1981, total expenditures for this purpose in the Soviet Union amounted to 23.4 billion rubles or about 32 billion U.S. dollars at the official exchange rate. But expenditures for rationalization and innovations were rather modest—392 million rubles (550 million U.S. dollars)—as was the number of inventions: 58 between 1971 and 1975, and 94 between 1976 and 1980. The economic effect was also negligible: 2.6 billion rubles (3.5 billion dollars).[19] These figures, of course, do not include innovations that have gained worldwide recognition. The Soviet Union imports more modern knowhow than it exports.

Work morale seems to be higher in the United States than in Europe. An international team studying the problems of the labor market in the highly industrialized countries of the world revealed the following findings: to the question posed by the research team, "How proud are you of the work you are doing?" 84 percent of Americans and 79 percent of English responded "Very proud," but only 15 percent of the Germans said they were "very proud" of their work. The Americans also showed a much better attitude toward their jobs than the Germans: 100 percent of Americans and Englishmen were "very proud" or "somewhat proud" of their jobs, but only 53 percent of the Germans were so. The Americans also showed a higher work morale than the Germans in the next question, "I try always to do my best regardless of how much I earn": 52 percent of Americans, but only 25 percent of the Germans answered this question affirmatively. Further, 35 percent of Americans and 41 percent of Japanese, but only 23 percent of the Germans, said that having "a job in which they could put their abilities to use" was "especially important." Only 13 percent of Germans believed that "talent, ability, and skills helped to get ahead," but 31 percent of Americans and one-fourth of Japanese believed this. Forty-six percent of Americans, but only 18 percent of Germans, were satisfied with ther present jobs.[20] Americans (but not only Americans) believe that the United States has already lost its once undisputed first place in the world competitive struggle. The respected international foundation, the European Management Forum (EMF), which makes an annual evaluation of the competitiveness of twenty-two industrial countries, put the United States in third place in 1983 with 64.38 points, following Japan (70.31 points) and Switzerland (70.10 points), but ahead of West Germany (62.63 points), Sweden (58.77 points), Finland (58.77 points), Austria (57.18 points), and, winding up the list, Great Britain in fourteenth place (51.55 points), France in fifteenth place (49.77 points), and Italy (49.94 points) in seventeenth place.[21]

The long economic recession in the late 1970s and early 1980s posed the greatest of challenges to the American economic policy. Not only was the economy strained by high unemployment, rampant inflation, and high interest rates, but the leading role of the United States in the world economy was at stake. Western Europe was profoundly disappointed that the U.S. economy was unable to provide any impulses to revive the world economy, and, furthermore, saw its investment in economic activity jeopardized by soaring U.S. interest rates and the consequent capital drain. Faced with this recession, the Americans opted for a conservative economic policy. The Soviet Union, for its part, pursued its thoroughly conservative economic policy and the arms race, yet without venturing any thoroughgoing economic reform to meet the challenge of the new period and to eliminate the indifference and the waste of labor and capital.

Conservative economic policy:
Reaganomics and Thatcherism

Since the early 1930s, economic policymakers and theoreticians who advocate a policy of state intervention to combat economic recessions and gross social inequalities have been referred to as liberals. Keynesianism was their principal weapon and a strengthening of the role of the state was its consequence. Those who advocated a market economy shielded from any extensive state intervention, the conservatives, opposed economic and social liberalism, which in their opinion would weaken the national economy and undermine America's leading economic role in the world. William F. Buckley, Jr., in his book *Up from Liberalism* (1959) was one of the proponents of these views along with other prominent scholars such as Peter Viereck and Willmoore Kendall. They subjected the economic and social policies of liberal presidents to a severe criticism. But until the 1970s the conservatives remained a minority, scarcely meriting serious consideration. During Jimmy Carter's presidency, their criticism of economic and social policy found fertile soil for the first time and covered a broad range of issues: an inadequate economic strategy to combat the consequences of recession and America's diminishing competitiveness on the world market; rampant social evils such as drug addiction and crime; and a disillusionment with the state in general as a consequence of dissatisfaction with the way the government had responded to events in Iran, Nicaragua or Afghanistan. Then the champion of neoconservative ideas, Ronald Reagan, came to office, with an economic policy fashioned by neoconservative economists. Their hard core is the "technological right wing," represented by economists such as George Stigler (Nobel Prize laureate 1982), Milton Friedman and the Chicago school, the experts at the Hoover Institution, the Brookings Institute, and the Council for National Policy. The "new economics" school, which considers its theories to be the antithesis of Keynesianism, has a special influence on Reagan's economic policies. Arthur B. Laffer, originator of the supply-side theory, Jack Kemp, defender of this theory in Congress, and Martin Feldstein, former chairman of the president's Council of Economic Advisors, mapped out the principles of Reaganomics. *Commentary* and *The Public Interest* are the main organs of the neoconservatives. The following statement by the presidential adviser, Martin Feldstein, may be taken as programmatic for the neoconservative view: "We are witnessing a true revolution in economic theory: a turn away from Keynesianism, which has played the dominant role for thirty-five years. Fundamental changes in economic thought are to be expected in the upcoming years, changes which will have a thoroughgoing effect not only on the economy but also on quality of life.''[22] Feldstein criticizes the unqualified faith in the salvatory effect of state intervention, the consequence of which was state intervention in the economy at the least perturbation, which entailed considerable budget spending as a component of various government programs. Fortunately, observed Feldstein, many economists have, by reason of their experiences in the past decade, come to the conclusion that Keynes overestimated the effectiveness of state intervention and that ''we are witnessing a rethinking of the basic principles of economic growth.'' But his criticism is directed first and foremost against the inability to come to terms with the problems of the future: ''Shortsightedness is the archenemy of any reform,'' says the former presidential adviser.[23]

Arthur Laffer's supply-side theory and Martin Feldstein's rethinking of the basic principles of the traditional market constitute the backbone of Reaganomics. Its prime objectives—long-term economic growth with minimal unemployment, a low inflation rate and workable interest rates as well as a balanced budget—differ very little from programs of other governments. The difference is in the methods of implementation. Reagan's economic program is to be implemented with four packages of measures: a monetary policy, providing for a slow but steady growth in money supply; 30 percent tax reductions for wages and salaries; tax reductions for investors to stimulate investment and economic activity; and the dismantling of official controls and reduction in government expenditures from 22.4 percent to 19.0 percent of the gross national product.

The upswing may have come somewhat later than expected but when it did come, it set in more rapidly in the United States than elsewhere. In 1983 and early 1984 the growth rate was higher than expected. Inflation fell from 12 percent to 4 percent and the unemployment rate decreased from 10.8 percent to about 8 percent.

No one, however, has gone so far as to claim that it was Reaganomics alone and not the still healthy driving forces of the market or both together which effected the turn from recession to economic upswing and restored the regular functionings of the business cycle.

But one thing is sure: a balanced budget was not achieved. The massive tax reductions and the tremendous state arms expenditures resulted in an enormous deficit of 199 billion dollars for the budget year 1983/84. Deficits of 200 billion dollars per year will be unavoidable to the end of the decade unless massive tax rises and spending cutbacks come soon. No less a person than the former chairman of the Presidential Economic Council, Martin Feldstein, announced in an interview with *U.S. News and World Report* in February 1984 that a new recession was on the horizon and that the budget deficit could rise to 300 billion dollars by the end of the decade if the government and Congress did not come to an agreement on reducing it.

The tremendous balance of trade deficit produced by Reaganomics brings to light another no less important aspect of the supply-side strategy, namely, that its massive tax reductions have the same consequences as did the deficit spending of Keynesianism.

Reaganomics is more a sign of the times than a characteristically American phenomenon. Thatcherism in Great Britain is akin to it as is economic policy in the FRG under Helmut Kohl. Thatcherism has become a concept in itself, even though Great Britain's economic policy under Margaret Thatcher has no qualities that identify it as a coherent doctrine. Its catchwords are less state and less nationalization, scarce money and thriftiness, fewer rights for the trades unions and fewer conflicts between employers and employees. Nor has Thatcherism been spared the fate of Reaganomics. The state intervenes everywhere where the self-regulating mechanisms of the market break down because the laissez-faire market is simply no longer feasible. But, more than any other conservative tendency, Thatcherism has made inroads into traditionally liberal England (the two great reformers of Great Britain in the twentieth century, Keynes and Beveridge, belong to the liberal wing). The well-known British sociologist, Stuart Hall, says that the influence of the right wing under Margaret Thatcher has been more thorough than generally assumed. In his opinion, Thatcherism has shifted the parameters of consensus and brought about a clear turn toward authoritarian populism and reactionary ideas; it has penetrated deeply into the moods of the skilled workers, employed women, and youth.[24] Hall attributes the success of Thatcherism to the fact that the right wing, and not the left wing, takes its ideas seriously.[25]

Margaret Thatcher may have won a large majority over the opposition in the second election, but she has done nothing nearly as spectacular for the economy, which continues to stagnate. The main reason is low productivity: in 1980 output per worker in the British manufacturing industries was one-third lower than German output and 50 percent lower than Japanese output. Great Britain invests less than its main competitors. The share of capital investments in gross national product has been regularly below 20 percent since the early 1960s; in 1980 it was 17.8 percent, while in the FRG it has always been 23.6 percent. The strict fiscal and credit policies dampen the desire to invest. The rate of replenishment of the work force has been kept low by age limitations on education and a relatively high minimum wage. The ratio to the FRG is 5:9. Skilled workers have, however, become a rarity. At a labor cost per hour of 17.34 DM, Great Britain is last but one among the twelve largest industrial countries of the world, followed only by Japan. On the competitive list of the twenty-two industrial countries it occupies seventeenth place.

The oil-related rise in the exchange rate of the pound rounded out the country's economic woes. England's manufacturing industry lost about half of its international competitiveness on this account in 1980/81. Most affected were the traditional export branches: until just a few years ago, British Leyland had exported 10,000 trucks per year. In 1983 it was only 2,700. The effect of the depression on employment has been devastating. There are only 5 million people still employed in the manufacturing industries, about 1.5 million less than a few years ago. More than 13 percent of the employable population was unemployed in the first quarter of 1984. As in the United States, economic structures are undergoing a radical change. Great Britain is being transformed from a classical industrial nation into a "service society and petroleum economy"[26] as the British sociologist, Dorian Clayton, put it.

The explosion in oil prices spared Great Britain, like the Soviet Union, from even greater problems. The export surplus due to oil exports was 6.9 billion pounds in 1983, which meant that, despite the miserable performance in the manufacturing industries, current accounts still had a positive balance of 1.5 billion pounds, even if this was 1.5 billion less than the preceding year. North Sea oil brought in about £10 billion of tax revenues in 1983/84 and became the main source of financing for the sharply increased payments to the unemployed. In one area, however, British economic policy has been successful: the rate of inflation was reduced from 20 percent to 5 percent. The rise in the exchange rate of the pound, which reduced export competitiveness, had a positive influence on internal prices.

The economic and social woes of Great Britain are different from those of the United States. Their causes are also different. The problems in these two industrial nations differ in turn from the economic and political malaise in the East, and the methods for combating them also differ accordingly. But a conservative tendency is as noticeable in the economic policies of the United States and Great Britain as in those of the Soviet Union.

Notes

1. W. W. Rostow: "The Fifth Upswing and the Fourth Industrial Revolution," in *Economic Impact*, 1983/4.

2. Ibid., pp. 58 and 59.

3. Lucio Lombardo Radice, "Die DDR—Despotischer Sozialismus," in *Spiegel*, 42/1978, p. 126.

4. Lenin, op. cit., p. 300.

5. Ibid., p. 297.

6. Ibid., p. 298.

7. Ibid., p. 486.

8. Herbert A. Simon, "What is Industrial Democracy?" in *Economic Impact*, 1983/4.

9. Ibid., p. 79.

10. *Narodnoe khoziaistvo SSSR 1922–1982*, pp. 152 and 157.

11. Robert Z. Lawrence, "Is Trade De-industrializing the United States?" in *Economic Impact*, 1984/1, p. 16.

12. Carola Caps, "Das amerikanische Beschäftigungswunder" in *Frankfurter Allgemeine Zeitung*, 24 February 1984.

13. Martin Feldstein, "The United States in the World Economy," *Economic Impact*, 1983/3, p. 14.

14. *Salzburger Nachrichten*, 17 February 1983.

15. *Handelsblatt*, 4 November 1981.

16. *Time*, 19 July 1981.

17. United Nations Statistical Handbook, 1977.

18. *Economic Impact*, January 1984, p. 16.

19. *Narodnoe khoziaistvo SSSR 1922–1982*, p. 128.

20. Prof. Dr. Elisabeth Neumann, "Arbeit und Arbeitslosigkeit in den achtziger Jahren," in *Frankfurter Allgemeine Zeitung*, 14 May 1983.

21. *Die Presse,* 14 February 1984.

22. Martin Feldstein, "The Retreat from Keynesian Economics," *Public Interest*, 64/1981.

23. Ibid.

24. Quoted in Malcolm Rutherford, "The left adapt to Thatcherism," in *Financial Times*, 23 December 1982.

25. *National Economic Review* 3/1982.

26. *Die Presse,* 27 February 1984.

4. The planned economies are in need of reform

Leonid Brezhnev's successor Yuri Andropov lost no time in initiating a reform of the economic system. It had taken Nikita Khrushchev more than three years to smash the central economic bureaucracy, which had swollen to monstrous proportions under Stalin's rule, with a horizontal decentralization. Brezhnev and Kosygin took a year to dismantle the regional economic administrations created by Khrushchev, to restore the central economic machinery, and to concede some powers of decision-making, if very limited, to enterprise managers. But in his inauguration speech, Yuri Andropov proclaimed his intention to make up for "what had been neglected," and, as he later put it, to overcome the "accumulated inertia" as rapidly as possible and institute changes in planning, administration and the economic mechanism.

In his long career in the state and the Party, Andropov had been a diplomat, Central Committee official and secretary, as well as head of the secret police for fifteen years; but he had never held an active post in the economy. After he and his colleagues had sought for eight months for a suitable therapy to heal the ailing economy, he admitted candidly at the meeting of the Central Committee in June 1983: "If we are honest, we have to say that we have not yet completely discovered the laws of the society in which we live and work, and especially the economic laws." Presumably the General Secretary did not take too seriously the hundred-year-old revelation of Friedrich Engels that Marxism had discovered "the laws of development of man, industry and society with scientific precision," nor Stalin's economic legacy, "The Economic Problems of Socialism in the USSR." He also had good reason to doubt these and other economic laws that had been handed down as absolute truths. Their "scientific precision" had not helped the Soviet planned economy to bring about a crisis-free development for the good of the Soviet population. But the General Secretary was as well aware as Western specialists that the average monthly wage of 172.5 rubles, or about $220 at the official exchange rate,[27] was nearer to what a Western worker pays out for social security than to what he receives in salary.

The Party leadership was not so much concerned with the relatively low incomes of the Soviet population, as with the modest range of goods offered to meet the buying power created, with low productivity and poor quality, and above all with the significant decline in economic growth. The days when the Soviet planned economy had astonished the world with its extremely high growth rates and could overlook the exorbitant costs of growth were gone. Between 1966 and 1970 average growth was 7.5 percent; in the next five-year period it was still a respectable 5.8 percent. But between 1976 and 1980 it declined to 3.8 percent and in the first two years of the current five-year plan it has fallen to as low as 2.5 percent. Although in 1983 a growth of 3.1 percent was achieved, there was a clear awareness that this level was not sufficient to meet the needs of the population and that not enough food was produced to feed the Soviet people. Although six times more people out of the total number of employed (20 percent) were employed in agriculture than in the United States, the Soviet Union bought grain from America, and not vice versa.

Of course, the economic system established in the early 1930s did contribute to the country's accelerated industrialization. But it was heavy industry and the armaments industry that benefited most. An economy of steel and iron was created. The share of the capital goods industry in the total product was about 70 percent, at least one-third higher than in the Western industrial countries. But the price paid for this by the Soviet population was high. Nowhere in the West was the accumulation rate as great and the consumption rate as low as in the Soviet Union. But in the flush of this all-embracing euphoria of growth it was forgotten that the reserves of raw materials and fuels were not unlimited. The territory of the Soviet Union, covering 22 percent of the world's surface, is the largest national territory in the world, and the most abundantly endowed with raw materials and fuels. But for years more has been consumed than replenished. The plunder of raw material deposits was most severe in the European part of the country, in the closest proximity to the industrial regions.

The centrally administrated economy is and always had been oriented more to quantity and less to quality. No great worth has been attached to a frugal use of materials and labor. The more material manufactured products contained, the higher was gross output, which has always been the principal criterion of performance. The Soviets were very proud that their output of coal, ore and steel per capita was higher than elsewhere. But the fact that the specific expenditure was 30 percent to 40 percent higher than in Western industrial countries first began to cause concern when the rich deposits in the Caspian Sea, the Don Basin, and later in Bashkyria and even later in the Tatar Autonomous Republic began to show signs of depletion. The Soviets had tarried a bit too long in opening up Siberia and the Far East, and when they finally did begin, the costs of exploration and exploitation had become unmanageably high and without Western technology nothing could be done.

A planned economy not only consumes more capital, raw materials and labor than a market economy, the quality of the goods produced is lower. The Soviet Union is a great power that uses its advanced technology not only to meet the needs of the people. The days are gone when qualitatively better products could be obtained in the GDR or Czechoslovakia than those produced domestically. The uniform economic and political system is also uniform in the sense that it reduces performance to a common denominator: the once highly productive countries of Eastern Europe have slipped to the lower level of performance characteristic of Eastern Europe instead of keeping pace with their peer countries of Western Europe such as France or Austria. The Soviet Union and its Eastern European allies have found themselves forced to import modern technology from the West. But while the Soviet Union has attempted to fill up its technological gaps through the export of raw materials and fuels, which accounted for 68 percent of its total exports to the West, the Eastern countries have had to finance these efforts by building up a mammoth mountain of debt. With available raw materials and energy resources diminishing perceptibly, meeting the growing need of the CMEA partners for additional imports is all the more a cause for concern to the Party leadership. While the other CMEA countries are increasingly less able to meet Soviet needs for modern technology, they have allowed their own energy needs to increase in direct proportion to the slowdown of the steering system imposed upon them.

It has been costly to maintain the inefficient economic system and has sometimes even required the use of force—not only domestically, but also throughout the Soviet Union's huge sphere of influence. No longer can the Soviet Union simply force its allies to help bear the burden of hegemony. The security buffer zone around the Soviet Union is changing from an asset to a costly liability. The Soviet Union not only raised the oil quota for CMEA partners from 138 million tons in the five-year period from 1966 to 1970 to 364 million tons in the five-year period from 1976 to 1980, it also had to yield to pressure to accept a price lower than world prices. According to some experts, the subsidy required by this measure was 20 billion dollars yearly. But the costs of expanding the Soviet sphere of influence beyond Europe are even heavier: Cuba and Vietnam absorb 61 percent of the total economic help to the Third World. The Soviet Union pays 0.34 dollars for a pound of Cuban sugar compared with a world price of 0.09 dollars, but even this impressive aid package was insufficient to obviate Cuba's need to reschedule its debt to Western banks of 3.2 billion dollars.

The Soviet Union has been able to draw on the labor and construction materials of the CMEA partners to tap its energy resources, but it has had to import modern technology from the developed industrial countries. Japan is involved with a credit of 450 million dollars and equipment for getting the Neryungri project in Yakutia under way. But instead of the agreed-upon import quota of 5 million tons of coal per year from 1985 onward, Japan received no more than 50,000 tons in 1983. The conditions for opening up the Eastern territories proved to be more difficult than expected. The Soviet economy is not able to meet internal needs and, even less, its worldwide engagement and the gap between what is desired and what is possible is growing wider. Yuri Andropov was aware of this, and his hurry to improve the economy was thoroughly justified.

The economic crisis is a crisis of the system

There is no problem of cyclical crises in the planned economies. There are hardly any difficulties in disposing of products produced in excess supply, since both the population and industrial enterprises suffer from chronic supply problems. What characterizes daily economic life in a planned economy is queueing up for the most ordinary products, clandestine exchange of products from one firm for materials supplied by another, forced stoppage because of supply gaps in the first twenty days of the month and frenzied work in the last ten days. When raw materials and fuels, as well as labor, were available in plentiful supply, the work conditions, which were not particularly favorable, nevertheless did not prevent a remarkable growth of the Soviet economy. But nowadays the situation is different. Material resources and manpower have become scarcer. The tremendous costs of economic growth and, above all, the boundless endemic waste of labor and capital have grown beyond bearable measure. There may be no outward signs that the inner forces of the Soviet economy, which accomplished a tremendous growth despite all the flaws in the system, are dwindling. But a spontaneous, rather passive rebellion on the part of the pillars of social activity is becoming ever more apparent, reflected in declining productivity of labor despite labor discipline, and declining product quality. The problem is not merely one of passing difficulties, bad weather that dashes the expectations of agriculture, or a transitory cooling down of industrial activity, but an unambiguous failure of the steering system which can no longer keep pace with the level of productive forces or cope with the problem of scarcer and more expensive resources. A study by the Novosibirsk section of the Academy of Sciences of the USSR,[2] which fell into the hands of Western journalists, arrived at this conclusion.

The statement is made unopposed that the steering system for centralized economic management is more appropriate to the level of the productive forces in the 1930s than their level today. Since then, it is pointed out, political and economic conditions have changed radically. Workers are now better trained and better educated, and more competent and aware than in the 1930s. They are therefore able to evaluate critically the actions of the political and economic leadership of the country and, moreover, are capable of defending their own interests if necessary.

The Novosibirsk research team sees the main cause of the malaise to lie in the declining ability of the economic bureaucracy to function. The efficiency of economic management based on the administrative control of subordinate units is being steadily eroded; further, the existing system is incapable of making appropriate use of the intellectual potential in the Soviet society because any competition for a job, for money, for sale markets, as well as competition between the state and private sectors of the socialist economy, has become impossible. In this system, so say the experts, the authority of enterprises and their responsibility for the results of their activity, as well as every form of uncontrolled economic activity on the part of the population, are limited.

The Novosibirsk team makes mistaken theory responsible for declining efficiency. Theory has denied any contradiction between the forces of production and the organizational structure and the existence of deep and antagonistic contradictions between social groups and public interests. There is, in fact, no essential difference between this pessimistic evaluation of the efficacy of Soviet theory and the views of the late General Secretary. Andropov observed, "We would be poor disciples of our teachers if we contented ourselves merely with repeating the truths which they discovered and relied on the magical powers of quotations memorized at some time in the past." Andropov knew clearly enough that one cannot merely rely on the ideas of the classics of Marxism about the functioning of real socialist economy, nor for that matter on the views of the founder of the Soviet state. Lenin said that if all citizens "had become remunerated employees of an all-embracing state, extremely simple operations of supervision and keeping records, within the powers of any illiterate, would be sufficient, and simple arithmetic and writing receipts would suffice." The steering of a modern socialist economy proved to be much more complicated, however, than the ingenious dreamers could have expected, if for no other reason than the traditional market mechanisms such as money, prices, profits, and competition were abolished. Economic control could not be reduced to the administration of relating material processes, nor could supervision be placed in the hands of semiliterates as Lenin had imagined. A gigantic hierarchically structured economic bureaucracy evolved, which placed working people and their performance under an all-embracing control. This bureaucracy, as the researchers from Novosibirsk say, reduces workers' initiative and creativity to nil, compels management to indulge in poor economics, accustoms workers to practices harmful to the system, and drives the most active part of society into the shadow economy.

Official theory, aimed at justifying the existing regime, was unable to come up with any suitable options for development. But the KGB, headed by Andropov for fifteen years, had permitted no opposition opinion, branding all of it alien and hostile. "That there are dissidents," said Andropov on the occasion on the one hundredth birthday of his predecessor and founder of the Soviet secret police, Feliks Dzerzhinskii, in 1977, "is due solely to the fact that the opponents of socialism make use of the Western press, diplomatic secret and special services." Thus Andropov regarded dissidents not only as imperialist agents but also as simple criminals. "There are among our population a few persons of this type, just as there are thieves, speculators, bribe-takers and other criminals, and we deal with them appropriately." How those opposed to the regime in the Soviet Union are "appropriately" dealt with we all know. But we also know what value an economic theory can have that must operate within a system at a time when that system no longer fits the relations of production.

The malaise of the Soviet economy is inherent to the system. The official theory and economic management are, however, not inclined to take realities too seriously and show no intention of seeking a solution outside the given system. The top layers of the society are not affected by the inefficiency of the economy, and the lack of a legal opposition makes their task easier. The Novosibirsk team, who are certainly not unused to thinking in the categories of class struggle, admit quite openly: "The existing system could only be changed by social groups who have high positions and consequently are tied to this system by personal interest." The ruling "real socialist" elite is just as little interested in revamping the Soviet regime as the ruling elite in the industrial nations of the West are interested in revamping the market economy.

Measures to improve the existing steering system have been introduced from time to time, but the term "reform" tends to be avoided so as not to arouse the suspicion that the measures undertaken were meant as a challenge to the fundamental principles of the system. In the whole of Soviet history only one General Secretary has dared to break up the central planning and administrative bureaucracy. But the entrenched Party and economic apparatus proved to be stronger than the Party leader. Khrushchev was also the only General Secretary who was forced to step down because he had jeopardized the vital interests of the ruling elite.

Andropov was a man of the state apparatus which he had had a direct hand in shaping over the years. He also made clear that he would be faithful to the desires of those who put him where he was, namely, the KGB hierarchy and the military and economic leadership. He was not made head of the state to contest the principles so dear to them, and to him, but rather to stimulate the productive forces that had fallen dormant in the last years of the Brezhnev era. He had demonstrated his ability to discipline Soviet society and to alleviate its uncurable ills, and he endeavored in a similar fashion to bring some order into the economy. But he did not call into question the existing economic system; for him it was a monolithic structure. But if liberalization of economic command is to have any meaning, political power must be trimmed of some of its authority, and this Andropov was not willing to do.

An economic mechanism that functions in a well-organized and trouble-free fashion is a prime objective

Rigid discipline was to guarantee work free of disruptions and new penalties were introduced to keep people on the job. Some of the measures included in the Brezhnev-Kosygin reform of 1969 were to be carefully reconsidered with an eye toward a wide-ranging restructuring of the steering factors. Baibakov, the former head of planning, set definite limits to the proclaimed structural changes when he said: "There can be no thought of abandoning the principle of centralism of the economy." The same claim was made by Prime Minister Nikolai Ryzhkov during the Twenty-seventh Party Congress, on March 3, 1986.

The most important document of the new era of leadership was the law on "work collectives and enhancing their role in the management of enterprises and organizations." The work collective was declared the basic unit of socialist society. It is granted broad powers and duties. A member of a collective may exercise his rights through the collective. The work collective may influence enterprise activity, housing construction, etc., and may evaluate the results of enterprise activity. Of course, neither this consultancy function nor the evaluations ensuing from it, are binding. But the duty imposed upon the collective to promote labor productivity, ensure the fulfillment of the plan, and combat violations of labor discipline, is significant. The work collective is given the right to grant or deny permission to a worker to leave an enterprise and to sponsor or not to sponsor his continuing education. The collective is also obliged to ensure the political and ideological education of the work force. Of course, the right of self-determination was also considered. However, as Politburo member Geydar Aliev explained, this was not an "anarchist syndicalist concept" but "actual socialist self-administration" which could be based on the "limited principle of democratic centralism." Aliev illustrated how this tried and true principle would be applied as exemplified by the procedure followed in preparing the recently ratified law on the work collective: 130,000 amendments were approved in 230 meetings with a participation of 110 million Soviet citizens. But the fact that only seventy unimportant amendments were accepted is illustrious proof of the wisdom and clairvoyancy of Soviet legislators.

The Party leadership places little reliance on the powers of worker participation councils supervised by the Party or on the effects of political ideology; rather disciplinary measures are preferred. The law on work collectives, therefore, was followed up by harsh penalties for violations of labor discipline; for each day of absenteeism, vacation time (usually fifteen days) is cut by one day; three hours absent from one's job is counted as a whole day, and shirkers and drinkers can be remanded to a lower-paying job for three months.

Narrow limits imposed on the decentralization of economic powers

Andropov was aware that punishment alone is not enough to reactivate the slumbering potential of the Soviet economy. He explained to Party veterans, "We should reflect on whether workers have been given the necessary conditions for productive work." Evidently the Party leadership had come to the conclusion that existing conditions were not conducive to labor productivity. Indeed, on July 26, 1983, the Party and government decision "on supplementary measures to expand the rights of production associations (enterprises) of industry in planning and in economic activity and to enhance their responsibility for the results of work''[3] was announced. Interestingly, this was initially to be an experiment to be carried out in two union ministries, i.e., the Ministry of Heavy Industry and Transport and the Ministry of the Electronics Industry, and in three republic ministries, the Ukrainian Ministry of the Food Industry, the Belorussian Ministry for Light Industry, and the Lithuanian Ministry for Locally Administered Industry.

Many important decision-making powers were transferred to the production units: the number of binding plan indicators was reduced to a minimum so that the production enterprise could plan the details on its own responsibility. In the experimental production units, centrally set indicators would be limited to the quality, the range, and the terms of delivery of contracted output, and would contain recommendations for the development of science and technology, for improving productivity and quality, and for reducing costs.

In addition, the experimental factories would be able to decide on the use of their own investment funds; they would also pay taxes on their profits to the state budget, but retain the rest for their own needs; "quality products on a world standard or above" would mean higher wages and rewards; more incentives would be provided for the fulfillment of production and delivery plans: bonuses would increase from a present 10 percent to 15 percent, but a 1 percent shortfall would be penalized by a 3 percent cut in bonus. The experimental factories would have more control over their own funds for science and technology, for social and cultural purposes, and for housing construction.

A number of other perhaps no less important enterprise powers were to be tested for two years, after which it would be decided whether they should be generalized. However, the objective observer of Eastern Europe and the Soviet Union was not at all surprised to see that most of the enterprise prerogatives proposed for testing had already been included in the Brezhnev-Kosygin reform of October 1965 and July 1979. In a few branches, they had been functioning for some time; for example, they had been tested since 1966 in the nitrogen factory in Shchekino. One of the more important ingredients of the present experiment, namely the "economic norms" which determine the size of the wage and bonus fund, were already part of managerial practice in Czechoslovakia in the pre-Dubcek era. One gets the strong impression that steering experiments have the aim more of postponing long due reforms than fulfilling them.

The results of the Shchekino experiment, which has been going on since 1966, are excellent. In fourteen years the factory was able to triple its output, increase its average wage by two-thirds, and reduce its work force by one-fourth. But instead of applying this practice throughout the country, the experiment was reduced to additional bonuses for the exercising of several jobs, after which the established bonuses were abolished, later reintroduced, and somewhat later still reduced to one half.

Limited options

No one doubts that the Party leadership had the best of intentions to improve the existing economic system to make it more efficient. But what alternatives to the existing planning and administrative methods exist? An economy can either be steered with economic mechanisms as in market economies, or planned and administered as in the state-controlled economies. Steering mechanisms heteronomic to the system, such as planning in a market economy or market mechanisms in a planned economy, have so far found only limited use.

The steadily growing planning and administrative bureaucracy has purged the traditional economic mechanisms from the state economies and considerably weakened their effectiveness. Lenin was well aware of the danger of a bloated bureaucracy, and his "New Economic Policy" vastly curtailed its powers. Stalin abolished Lenin's successful experiment and set a gigantic economic and political bureaucracy into operation. Khrushchev attempted once again to remold the system, but was overthrown, and Brezhnev and Kosygin made several experiments but returned to the old steering system with an even more self-conscious administrative bureaucracy.

Yuri Andropov was a few illusions poorer and a few experiences richer. He was therefore more cautious because he understood better than his predecessors the limits of a reform to restructure the economy. As long as the military industrial complex absorbs 15 percent of the national product and the best forces of the country, it will assuredly insist on deciding economic priorities itself and not abandon decentralized production units to the blind forces of the market. Andropov was, and Gorbachev is, no less conservative in his system than Ronald Reagan is in his. But there can be no doubt that the escalating East-West conflict is one of the most important reasons of the new conservatism that is spreading in both world systems.

Decentralization as an integral part
of an untouched central steering system

The pilot proposals broaden decision-making powers at the micro level over wages and bonus funds and over profits and their use for innovative measures. But the system is left untouched. The preamble to the government decision of July 26, 1983, states that the goal of the measures is to "strengthen the central administration of the economy, giving due regard for democratic principles." On the occasion of the one hundredth anniversary of Karl Marx's death, Yuri Andropov wrote: "Our system functions, it simply needs repair in many places; problems, poor harvests, a shortage of food, and poor consumer goods exist because Lenin's norms have not been observed with utmost exactitude." Oleg Bogomolov, one of the most influential Soviet economists and member of the

Academy of Sciences, calls the reforms a measure to "perfect central state planning, the task of which is to determine economic proportionalities and fulfill the plan not only by means of state directives, but also by means of economic mechanisms such as credit, prices, taxes, and other financial normative parameters."[4]

For Soviet ideologues, central planning and administration are the state mechanisms whose function is to safeguard the primacy of politics from the chaos of the invisible hand of the market. P. Ignatovskii, the editor-in-chief of the respected economic journal *Planovoe khoziaistvo* (Planned Economy), stated more or less the same thing in the theoretical Party organ *Kommunist* (12/1983). "Politics and the politicization of the economy are indispensable conditions for economic success," he says, with one qualification: politics must give due regard to the economic laws of socialism. He invokes Lenin, who always stressed the primacy of politics and would never have permitted the "political" to be supplanted by the "economic." In his opinion, a purely economic conception which places politics in the background would result in the building of socialism on the basis of mere economic performance and would favor group interests. Politics must maintain primacy, continues Ignatovskii, not only to eliminate negative phenomena in the economy, but because "it is an objective necessity, which alone is able to ensure that social interests have priority."

Ignatovskii also offers an answer to the recurring question of why the policy traditionally pursued has not been able to cope satisfactorily with the needs of the economy and the population: it is not politics, but the fact that politics was not given sufficient priority, which is to blame. Money, writes Ignatovskii, was "transformed from a means for the exchange of goods into a goal of economic activity, factories concentrated on profits, and not on meeting the needs of the population, and profit became the principal measure for competent economic management." Ignatovskii regards the desire of some reformers to expand the domain of commodity and money relations as a "romantic hope" for infallible economic indicators which do not exist and cannot exist. His criticism is aimed above all at the powerful economic elite which regards state property as group property and forgets that the state has placed only a part of the means of production under their administration for the purpose of meeting the needs of the population.

We have reported Ignatovskii's view in detail because it reflects the opinion of official economic policy-makers. It was also the basis for the government decision of July 26, 1983, the purport of which was essentially as follows: primacy of politics and central planning as far as possible, decentralization and economic mechanisms as far as necessary. But it was just this formula which doomed previous economic reforms to failure. The Soviet experiment, to be carried out over a period of two years which began with January 1, 1984, has no better chances.

Konstantin Chernenko continued
the reforms of his predecessor

The new Kremlin chief was not inclined to deny the flaws in the Soviet economy. Quite the contrary. In his programmatic speech to the Electoral Assembly on March 2, 1984, he spelled them out directly: "There are many economic sectors that are strikingly backward; existing economic potential is far from being fully utilized; the spirit of innovation in the mechanical engineering industry is not satisfactory; the proportion, still relatively considerable, of manual and unskilled labor in industry and construction is declining only very slowly, etc." The Party leader proposed decisive and far-ranging measures to improve administration of the economy and to give new dimensions to economic mechanisms. The first steps, said Chernenko, are included in the action package agreed upon by the Plenary Session of the Central Committee of November 1982, which took place after Andropov had been appointed General Secretary of the Party. The measures agreed upon, said the Party leader, were able to arrest the negative tendency apparent in the first two years of the five-year plan, i.e., the slowdown in economic growth. An especially encouraging sign for Chernenko was the fact that labor productivity efficiency indicators had risen risen in many sectors of the economy. There were, in his opinion, areas which were still lagging. In the five-year period from 1986 to 1990 new organizational structures will be introduced whose content will depend on the reform experiments initiated in early 1984. Thus, said the Party leader, enterprises will be given more powers of decision-making and also more responsibility for meeting production targets, while the excessive control of central authorities will be diminished. At the Plenary Session of the Central Committee of April 10, 1984, Chernenko reproached management for "being a swollen bureaucratic masterdom that was out of all proportion to the actual productive labor force at every level of the economy."

Chernenko was even clearer in a speech held in late April 1984 before the Central Committee commission for the preparation of the new Party program. He warned his prominent listeners against any thought of neglecting short-term tasks in favor of the "relatively distant, beautiful and rosy future." For Chernenko, too, winning the race against capitalism was a top priority task. In his opinion, success would depend on "the internal development" of the Soviet Union. However, he expressed his confidence that socialism would win the race although, as he stressed, capitalism has considerable growth potential still to be tapped. The Party leader warned against "idealization and overhastiness" in portraying Soviet reality and "an over-sanguine notion of how long the transition from socialism to communism would take." It is interesting that the Soviet leadership had no desire to conceal the flaws in the economy and, moreover, demanded that managers and economists present a realistic picture of the situation minus embellishments. But it is also interesting that the new leadership has opted mainly for organizational measures and not radical economic reform to cope with the growing problems.

The 27th Party Congress, which took place under the Gorbachev leadership, produced a new version of the Khrushchevian Third Party Program (adopted by the 22nd Congress in October 1961) by considerably revising its aims. The target of the original version of the Program—to overtake the United States in per capita income by 1981—was, understandably, not mentioned in the new document. Per capita income in the USSR is now not much higher than 50 percent of that in the United States. We also no longer find in the Program the promise that the present generation will live in a communist society. These statements are replaced by the following: "The way from socialism to communism is determined by objective development laws; any attempt to introduce principles of the communist society regardless of the material and mental maturity will be doomed to failure." The new edition of the Program defines the next stage of Soviet society not as communism but as "developed socialism," where everyone should be rewarded "in accordance to the quantity and quality of his performance and not in accordance to his need." This contraction of goals to match the existing possibilities characterizes the new leader as a realist who does not promise more than can be delivered.

The specification of the targets, policies, and measures in the new Program makes all speculations about the *modus operandi* of the new leadership useless. It will neither go the way of little Hungary, nor adopt the direction of the disciplined GDR. The world's second economic power in the world, which strives for first place, for absolute dominance, will take the Russian way.

The target envisaged by the Party Program is very ambitious: production capacities are to be doubled by the end of the century. In order to realize such a goal after many years of very modest growth rates, "deep shifts in all decisive fields of human activity and a shift from extensive to intensive factors of industrial performance" will be required. Most impressive is the envisaged growth in labor productivity, to be increased 2.3–2.5 times in the next 15 years. Lenin is quoted in this connection: "Without a perceptible growth of productivity, a shift to a communist society will be impossible." The present level of labor productivity is 50 percent lower than in the developed countries of the West.

Notes

1. *Narodnoe khoziaistvo SSSR 1922–1982*, p. 405.
2. An abridged version was published in the *Frankfurter Allgemeine Zeitung*, 10 August 1983.
3. Yuri Andropov in a speech at the Plenary Session of the Central Committee of the CPSU, 22 November 1982.
4. O. Bogomolov: "RGW-Ökonomische Strategie der achtziger Jahre" (*Kommunist*, July 1983).

5. Liberalism in the West, revisionism in the East

Every movement likes to proclaim its liberalism. But, as Daniel Bell trenchantly put it, "Apart from the ideology no one actually desires economic liberalism."[1] Liberal ideologies are as old as capitalism itself—which, however, has changed over the course of centuries. The capitalism which the thinkers of the eighteenth century observed and analyzed was fundamentally different from the capitalism of the nineteenth century, and the liberals of the nineteenth, as well as the neoliberals of the twentieth century would have had considerable difficulty identifying the ideas and arguments of their predecessors with their own. Nevertheless, one line of continuity is discernible between the liberal theories of the past and those of today. Each is concerned with the relationship between the state and the economy, although, to be sure, in the specific context of the particular time and the particular country.

The founders of classical economics, Adam Smith (1723–1790) and David Ricardo (1772–1823), developed their theories in the second half of the eighteenth and beginning of the nineteenth century, roughly at the same time as the Physiocrats in France. Liberal ideas marked both classical economics of Great Britain and the teachings of the physiocrats in France. Both were against the mercantilism of the governments of Europe and advocated a free competition and free trade undisturbed by the state. But in the late eighteenth century Great Britain already had a relatively developed industry, while in France, industry was only being born. Agriculture and the interests of the peasants were the prime concern of French thinkers of that time.

The "natural order," spontaneously evolving relations among men, fair play in politics, and the unrestricted right to property were the fundamental principles of a liberal social system for Smith and Ricardo as well as for the founders of the Physiocratic school in France, Pierre Boisguilbert (1646–1714) and François Quesnay (1694–1774), author of the reproduction process in the famous *tableau économique* (1758). For the liberal British and the French of that era labor was the principal source of value and social wealth. But while the classical economists were primarily concerned with the interests of industry, and Ricardo directed his criticism against landowners and advocated a free trade with comparative cost advantage as its driving principle, Boisguillebert and Quesnay and the Physiocratic school of France generally regarded agrarian labor alone as productive. Labor in all other sectors of the economy was ''sterile.'' Only the peasants were a productive class; craftsmen and merchants were a ''sterile'' class.

The nineteenth century was dominated by economic liberalism: in the first half by the Manchester school and in the second half by the Cambridge school. These two schools shared a common liberal current of thought. They were against state intervention, which in their opinion adulterated the objective laws of economic growth with subjective decisions, and disturbed economic equilibrium. But the second half of the nineteenth century was qualitatively different from the first. The Cambridge school stressed different aspects of economic and political relations than the Manchester school.

A cofounder of the Manchester school and the creator of Great Britain's Liberal Party, John Bright (1811–1889), fought for the right to vote for workers and, as representative of the Anti-Corn Law League, for the abolition of the tariff on grain imported by Great Britain. Richard Cobden (1804–1865) advocated Great Britain's expansion as a colonial power and Nassau William Senior (1790–1864) fought vehemently against reducing working hours—which at that time were still twelve hours per day—in the belief that profit was created in the last hour. The contradictions of monopoly capitalism in the last years of the nineteenth century were discernible in the ideas of the Cambridge School; the founders of the neoclassical school, e.g., William Stanley Jeromes (1835–1882) and Alfred Marshall (1842–1924), described these contradictions in their monumental studies. The neoclassical school introduced the concept of marginal value, enriching the research methods of price formation which were then further expanded in the Austrian School, particularly in the studies of Karl Menger (1840–1921). But it also opposed the growing monopolization of the economy and advocated a juster distribution of the national product.

The neoclassical school, like the classical school earlier, demonstrated its liberal credentials in economics. But the times were at odds with both these currents; it was no longer on the side of either classical or neoclassical liberalism. Economic theories had become more complicated and more multifaceted but were increasingly less able to deal with the realities of the times. As Jürgen Habermas justly remarked, ''In each new stage the economic system creates new and more complicated problems as it attempts to resolve the problems of yesterday.''[2] National and multinational concerns have created a new market which differs fundamentally from the market of early capitalism. Liberal theoreticians spoke then, and still speak today, of free competition. But there can be no free competition between concerns, which sometimes embrace entire industrial sectors, and individual enterprises. The expansion of the oligopolist power structures has placed narrow limits on the competitive market of yesterday. Today's market is no longer homogeneous. John Kenneth Galbraith sees the market split into two basic areas: a planning sector, which affects large concerns, and the authentic market, which embraces unorganized individual enterprises and small enterprises. As Galbraith sees it, "Uneven development of economic sectors, unequal distribution of incomes, unequal and chaotic distribution of state expenditures, environmental pollution, and inefficient methods of stabilization policy,"[3] is a picture that hardly compares with the traditional market described by classical and neoclassical liberalism.

Today's state is absorbing an ever greater share of the national product for defense and social purposes, is increasingly assuming the role of investor to mitigate the crisis-proneness of the traditional market, and, to quote Habermas, "is intervening more and more frequently to fill in the ever-deeper gaps in the functioning of the market,"[4] and, in the process, is broadening the margin of action of the state bureaucracy, but narrowing that of the free market and of free competition. The path from classical and neoclassical liberalism to organized liberalism is straight and direct.

Are the liberals still liberal?

In the home of the neoclassical school, Cambridge, John Maynard Keynes asked the question in 1925: "Am I a liberal?" and answered it affirmatively, not so much by accepting liberalism as by rejecting conservatism and socialism. "They (the conservatives) offer me neither food nor drink, neither intellectual nor spiritual consolation. I am neither encouraged, stimulated, nor edified," said Keynes. But he rejected the Labour Party just as curtly: "In the first place it's a class party, and this class is not my class."[5] Keynes rejected not only Marx but Say's law, according to which supply and demand were equal by definition, and consumption equalled production; this was a law that considered neither "overproduction" nor "underconsumption" as possibilities, and regarded unemployment only as a temporary phenomenon. But, unlike Marx, who rejected classical economics (along with the capitalist system), and who in his own words attempted to predict the destiny of mankind "from the bowels of the economy" and had developed scientific socialism, Keynes rejected Say's law of the market as "an opinion that contradicts correct theory and experience" in the belief that the solution for a society shaken by crises should not be sought in a visionary social system, but was, on the contrary, to be achieved by perfecting the mechanisms of the existing system. Keynes had the advantage of being able to look back over the fifty years of capitalism since Marx and the two decades of real socialism built in Marx's name.

Of course, the state intervention which Keynes proposed as the salvation of the existing economic system was a negligible quantity compared with the suffocating grip of the state colossus and its monstrous bureaucracy which a planned economy had to bear as a replacement for the self-regulatory mechanisms of the traditional market. For him, the conceptions of the utopian socialists of his time, such as Oskar Lange and J. P. Lerner, who thought that a pure market economy was possible only under socialism, were "pure utopias." In real socialism, such conceptions are dismissed as rank revisionism. That, in fact, was the term used in real socialistic Poland to describe and disparage Oskar Lange's own theories and activities. Keynes created no new social systems. He rejected classical economics and "the natural order" and attempted to institute order with the help of the state. For him, classical economics was dead. He therefore sought a solution in a politicization of the economy. Social goals and, above all, full employment, no longer achievable as the resultant of individual decisions, were henceforth to be "organized" by the collective will, embodied in the state. The proneness of the market economy to crisis was to be eliminated, or at least alleviated, through the state's economic policy. Socialization of a portion of capital investments and "euthanasia" for the rentier were his measures to combat crisis. According to Keynes, state investments could be planned over the long term and were less unstable than private investments. They would therefore have a stabilizing influence on economic development. A long-term reduction in interest rates would make for productive utilization of capital. Over-saving, which according to Keynes was the principal cause of depressions, would thus be eliminated.

Keynesian liberalism invokes limited state intervention to prevent the total state

Keynes's yes to the question "Am I a liberal?" was correct. Although the state intervention he proposed conflicted with the views of classical and neoclassical liberalism, compared with the existing alternatives of total nationalization of the economy and of the whole of social life, it was the much lesser and, hence, acceptable evil. When he wrote his book *The End of Laissez Faire* in 1926, he had already realized that the days of free competition were gone for ever. Late in 1936 when he wrote his principal opus, *The General Theory of Employment, Interest and Money*, he had digested the lesson of the deepest economic crisis of modern times, namely, that today's economy could no longer be steered by the invisible hand of the market. Roosevelt's New Deal, for which Keynes served as an adviser, convinced the world that the state had to intervene where the free market no longer functioned. Keynes's limited state intervention in economic affairs was a middle way between the utopian vision of a self-administered economy and the omnipotent and almighty state in real socialism, which indeed had come into being because a self-administered economy had proven to be a pure utopia.

Keynes was a liberal because he wished to deal with economic and social conflicts within the existing social system of a democratic state and not with the aid of a totalitarian state at a time in which the traditional mechanisms of the market had ceased being effective. At that time he was less orthodox than the SPD, which in the early 1930s had come out in favor of the gold standard, and less orthodox even than Ramsay MacDonald, who fell under the impact of the economic crisis of 1931 because, following the advice of the Bank of England, he elected to overhaul the state budget rather than reduce unemployment.[6]

The renaissance of economic liberalism

If economic liberalism remained a possibility after the chaos of the world economic crisis and World War II, credit must go to the Freiburg school, persons such as Friedrich August von Hayek, Ludwig Erhard, Franz Boehm, Alfred Miller-Armak and Franz Eucken, who had steadfastly maintained their belief in the effectiveness of an unadulterated market. Friedrich von Hayek's notions— that the state was not the executive committee of the ruling class, but a bureaucratic power which tended to the use of force by reason of its leviathan nature; that any economic policy which strengthened the state, weakened liberalism; and that the laissez-faire market tended toward equilibrium, but that the state hindered it from doing so because it caused inflation and other symptoms of crisis—became the leitmotif of the Freiburg school and the guidelines of economic policy of West Germany's post-war governments. After the command economy of the first post-war years, which had become dysfunctional and chaotic, attention turned again to the advantages of the market and private enterprise as growth-promoting institutions. The Federal Republic of Germany was the only major country of Western Europe that undertook no serious nationalizations after World War II. Later developments—the economic miracle, expected by hardly anyone, and the integration of ten million German refugees—were its fruits and seemed to ratify the neoliberalism of the Freiburg school. As long as the economy of the Federal Republic and of the West flourished, the correctness of this economic policy and the liberal ideology of the Freiburg school that served as its justification brooked no doubt. However, when growth ground to a halt in 1967 after a period of annual growth rates of 4 to 8 percent, all talk of a "pure economy" abruptly ceased. The stability and growth law of 1967 was, to use the words of its author, Karl Schiller, "a synthesis between the Freiburg imperative (the competitive system) and the Keynesian message (global control)."[7] It was Karl Schiller who coined the programmatic slogan of the West German social democracy: "self-regulation in micro-relations and global control in macro-relations" and "competition where possible—planning where necessary," which was incorporated into the Bad-Godesberg program.[8]

The lingering recession of the 1970s marked the end of neoliberalism and of Keynesian global control. But even the "alternative economic policies, such as monetarism and supply-side economics, appear not to be as successful as they had augured to be."[9]

As usual, failure was an orphan. Yet all economists and economic schools were eager to take the credit for the revival in economic activity in 1983 and 1984. Success, even moderate success, has a hundred fathers. But the clearest claim to paternity doubtlessly lies with "tried and true" Keynesian deficit spending, although it seemed to be generally realized that the much-disdained market economy still had some meat on its bones and that even a perfect economic policy was only one of the instruments of a self-sustaining private enterprise economy.

Revisionism in the East

In the centuries of its existence, the traditional competitive market has undergone radical changes in the way it functions and in its relationship to the state. But even the traditional planned economy has been through some thoroughgoing reforms, and perhaps even more failed reform attempts, in the few decades of its existence. If the reformers incline more to the advantages of the mechanisms of a market economy than to the fine-sounding but utopian promises of the revolutionary *Sturm und Drang* period, it is because, perhaps, of the undisputable fact that, although the market economy is the worst economic system in the world, the alternatives are even worse.

There is no legal opposition to the ruling party and the ruling state ideology in the Eastern bloc. Reformers who strive for more than the ruling Party is ready to accept are dismissed as revisionists. Of course, this revisionism has nothing to do with the classical revisionism of Eduard Bernstein (1850–1932) and his famous slogan, "the goal is nothing, the movement is everything." It has become a term used by state ideologues to designate a kind of heresy, a deviation from the officially preached, but never realized, utopian ideology. Of course, the revisionists are closer to the pledges of the past than those who mouth the official ideology yet have shaped a reality that totally contradicts it. The ruling technocracy has, however, little to do with ideology, and the ideologues have no more than a very negligible influence on the economic and social life fashioned by the technocrats. The ideologues of today are worlds apart from the proclaimers of the exalted theories of salvation of yesteryear.

Revisionism is an Eastern European phenomenon. The communist leaders of Eastern Europe, who were appointed rulers of their own countries after World War II, without ever having been elected to those posts, and who were still convinced when they began their troubled days in office that the *force majeur* would bring them communism and not Stalinism unadulterated, were revisionists relative to Stalinist socialism, caretakers of the state rather than its leaders. Leafing back through history, it is evident that none of these persons had ever imagined that a one-party regime and a state economy enveloping all areas of social life would be built under the leadership of their party, just the opposite to what they had been proclaiming for years under the harshest conditions of illegal activity. Georgi Dimitrov, leader of the Comintern (dissolved in 1943) and Bulgaria's prime minister since November 1946, desired least of all such a coercive regime. In September 1946, Dimitrov declared "Bulgaria is not a Soviet republic and not a form of dictatorship of the proletariat, but a people's republic, in which government functions are exercised by the overwhelming majority of the people, by the workers, peasants, artisans, and the national intelligentsia.''[10] Indeed on January 23, 1948, Dimitrov was still speaking of a Balkan Federation which was to have embraced not only the Balkan countries, but also Poland, Czechoslovakia, and, in the event the Communists emerged victorious, Greece as well.

The Czech coalition government in the first three postwar years was far from the idea of a total nationalization of the economy. The nationalization program of October 1945, based on the thoroughly democratic Kosice declaration, bore a closer resemblance to Mitterand's nationalization project of 1981 than to the total deprivatization, of even the smallest industrial and service enterprises, that followed upon the coup d'état of February 1948. The far-sighted prognosis of the then foreign minister, Hubert Ripke, who said that total nationalization must necessarily lead to the dictatorship of a single party, unfortunately turned out to be correct.

The goals of the Communist Party of Germany (KPD) of June 11, 1945, contained no signs of an intention to establish a one-party regime. Instead, they aimed at the fulfillment of radical democratic ''minimal demands,'' and the ''socialization of certain firms and assets,'' but otherwise maintained that ''the initiative of private entrepreneurs on the basis of private property should be given full freedom to develop.'' The Socialist Unity Party of Germany (SED), founded at the Party Unification Meeting of the KPD and the SPD on April 22, 1946, expressly declared that ''Germany's special situation at present includes the possibility of a democratic path to socialism, and that the SED would only resort to revolutionary means if the capitalist class departed from democracy.''[11]

In contrast to what later occurred in Eastern Europe and in comparison with the current official state ideology and practice, these declarations of the earlier communist leaders sound ''rather revisionist.'' But they fully accord with what Lenin proclaimed a few weeks before the Revolution in October 1917: ''By taking over full power—and this is probably the last chance—the Soviets could ensure the peaceful unfolding of the Revolution, the peaceful choice of deputies by the people, the peaceful struggle of the Party within the Soviets, the testing of the program of various parties in practice, and the peaceful passage of power from the hands of one party into another.''[12]

However, the ideas shared by all the communist leaders of Eastern and Central Europe, of a people's democracy in the countries governed by them, suffered the same destiny as that of the Western architects of the Yalta Agreement of an independent geopolitical constellation in this area. But it bears mentioning that the Eastern architect of this agreement made no secret of his sympathy for the principle ''*Cuius regio eius religio.*''

The communist leaders of Eastern and Southeastern Europe have found their place in the real socialist system. They are quick to label as revisionism the same declarations they or their colleagues made in the early days when they hear them repeated by their critics today, while the policies of the totalitarian state which they helped to create are put out as socialism in pure form. But every liberal movement in Eastern Europe consciously or unconsciously goes back to the original program in demanding less nationalization and less state, less central planning and administration, and more decentralized economic powers, more competition, and more freedom for the traditional mechanisms of the market.

It has not been so much the pressure from the critics of the regime as the pressure of actual events that has forced the institution of reforms to combat the waste of labor and material resources and to encourage creative effort. Often, a major fraction of the Party and state apparatus has entered the reform movement. So it was in Poland and Hungary in 1956 and in Czechoslovakia in 1968. Its protagonists saw in the Prague Spring the realization of the liberal Kosice program. But it is becoming increasingly clear that a thoroughgoing reform in a state-owned and state-administered economy will only be successful if the entire state system is recast in a more liberal and democratic mold. The realities of the situation in Eastern Europe, ever more complicated, and the nascent fourth industrial revolution, create different, but by no means less difficult, problems in the East than in the West. Governments find themselves compelled to take measures to eliminate the now evident symptoms of crisis. The history of the Eastern bloc has been a history of reforms tried and failed since the mid-1950s. The most radical and most liberal reform took place in Hungary after 1968. Limits were set to central planning and administration, and certain decision-making powers were devolved to economic units. In the West the problem has been to keep state intervention in economic matters within limits, and to maintain those forces which have made a competitive market economy undisputedly superior in developing the productive forces and in promoting technical progress. But the nationalization of key economic sectors has also reached considerable dimensions in the West. The data presented in the following section will show that this has more to do with national traditions than with the economic program of a conservative or liberal party.

Nationalization is neither a conservative nor a liberal project

Nationalizations are not a monopoly of the East. They were an important ingredient in the election program of the socialist, Mitterand, in 1981, and they were no less important in the economic program of Charles de Gaulle after World War II. The ultimate goal of the Communist program was nationalization and socialization and not total state control of the means of production. Nationalized enterprises were to become the property of the people, i.e., of factory collectives. A democratically elected Factory Council, and not the state bureaucracy, was supposed to administer nationalized enterprises. This indeed was also the gist of the nationalization program of the October Revolution: "Industrial enterprises belong to the workers and the land belongs to the peasants," proclaimed the revolutionary slogan, and that is what actually happened immediately after the Revolution. If after a very short time the nationalized enterprises were placed under state control, i.e., taken from the workers and transferred to the state bureaucracy, this second expropriation was due to a catastrophic fall in labor productivity to one-fourth of the prewar level. The utopian goals of the Revolution proved unachievable and had to be reduced to realizable proportions. There were, in fact, only two forms of property: private and state. *Tertium* (ownership of the means of production by the industrial workers) *non datur*.

The social implications of state control of production units, whether partial or total, are the same everywhere regardless of the social system. Although corporate property need not necessarily be regarded as the most humane form of property, state administration of the means of production is certainly no more democratic than self-regulating mechanisms of a competitive market. The Bad Godesberg program of the SPD of November 15, 1959, therefore states: "Any concentration of economic power, even in the hands of the state, entails dangers. Therefore, public property must be steered in accordance with the principles of self-administration and decentralization.[13] But the rights of self-determination are no greater in the state enterprises of either East or West than they are in private firms. When state control over production is an ingredient of certain social democratic programs, including the Bad-Godesberg program, it is seen as a means to "safeguard freedom against the excessive power of large economic complexes." But in actual nationalization procedures, power taken from the large corporations was still given directly to the state bureaucracy and not to the workers. The establishment of state control over large concerns and the curtailment of the misuse of power by anonymous forces was an undeniable social victory, although its value was diminished considerably by the state's assumption of ultimate responsibility for the nationalized industries. The recent recession and its grave effects on state-owned firms have made this point painfully clear. In Charles de Gaulle's nationalization program, the power of large corporations played no decisive role. De Gaulle simply had no confidence in the ability of the market to restore within a short period the economic capacities destroyed by the war or the competitiveness of French industry. De Gaulle's nationalization program was not only aimed at restoring economic capacity; it also had the ambitious goals of the second and third industrial revolutions in France in view. Similarly, the socialization of the means of production in the Soviet Union, later adulterated to direct state control, was to have served the ends of industrialization and the elimination of centuries of Russian backwardness.

Two conservative post-war governments
—one turning to the free market,
the other to state control

The post-war policies of the West German and French governments show clearly that state control of heavy industry is neither a liberal nor a conservative measure. Both were thoroughly conservative. The Ahlen program of the CDU of 1947 did not totally rule out the socialization of enterprises and economic sectors in certain cases, but when the CDU emerged the victor in the first Bundestag election and went on to mold economic policy in the Federal Republic, it did its utmost to free itself from the command economy of the post-war period and fundamentally to reconsider the advantages of the market and private enterprise.[14] Nationalizations were hardly even considered. A currency reform to bring wage and price policies into line with the market, make possible a straightforward cost-benefit analysis of investment and production activities, and tie the domestic monetary and price system to the world market, was the basic pillar of this thoroughly liberal economic policy and the fundamental condition for the West German economic miracle. The totalitarian practices of the Hitler era and the command economy of the early post-war years were all too fresh in people's memories to permit any coercive measures whatsoever to be made part of the economic policy of the new democratic Germany. In 1958, the nationalization of the Volkswagen works was annulled and it was returned to private shareholders. The brilliant achievements of the West Germany market under the conditions of the free market also left their mark on the SPD Bad-Godesberg program, which dissociated itself both from the unrealizable slogans of utopian socialism and of the practice of ''really existing'' state socialism in the East. In the recession years, both the social liberal government under Helmut Schmidt and the CDU-FPD government under Helmut Kohl have allowed state intervention into economic affairs, but have never even considered nationalization.

De Gaulle's nationalization program had nothing in common with any utopianism. His intent was simply to make the French economy more functional and competitive, but within a pluralistic political system and market economy. For him, the nationalization of some economic sectors dominated by large corporations did not mean not a departure from the traditional system, but rather a strengthening of that system by improving its overall efficiency. He also wished to penalize collaborators by nationalizing their assets. De Gaulle's intention of strengthening the market economy through the hand of the state may not have concorded with his philosophical views, but it fit in well with the political traditions of the state in France. The state sector has always been larger in France than in any other country. Indeed, as early as the sixteenth century, royal printing houses were founded, succeeded by the Imprimerie Nationale in 1829, and the Chamber of Commerce was founded in the seventeenth century and made a state institution in the nineteenth century. Unlike in other countries, these institutions not only represent industrial and commercial business, but also administer the waterways and airports, transportation and communications, and even state museums. Another interesting institution is the Caisse de Depots et Consignation, established by the state in 1816 to accept private deposits as well as to attract the deposits in savings banks to finance investments in social services (housing construction loans, loans for building hospitals, schools, etc.). The first attempt to nationalize the French railroads dates back to the early nineteenth century, but this was not actually achieved until 1878 when 2,500 railroad routes, operating at a loss, were purchased by the state from private firms.

The first nationalization of an entire sector was projected by the Socialist-Communist united front government in 1936. The railroads, the Banque de France, and the armaments industry were to have been purchased from private capital and put under state administration. In 1937 the Societé Nationale de Chemin de Fer was founded, although private firms were to hold 49 percent of the stock, and the interest rate was to be kept at 6 percent until 1982. Private banks were also to hold shares in the capital stock of the Banque de France and be represented on its board. In the armaments industry, however, only the aircraft sector was nationalized.

De Gaulle's nationalization program went far beyond the program of the united front government of 1936: he proposed to nationalize the fuel industry, the production and distribution of gas, the coal mines, the Banque de France, a number of other banks, and a major portion of the insurance sector. In April 1946, the fuel and gas sector was taken from private hands, and two state enterprises, Electricité de France and Gaz de France, were established; on May 17, 1947, a law was passed nationalizing coal mining and distribution. Nine coal trusts, called Hoillers de Bassin, assumed control of the nationalized private firms; Charbonage de France was to coordinate their activities and the Caisse Nationale de l'Energie, founded in 1948, was to participate in the financing of their investment ventures. The law of December 2, 1945, nationalized the following major banks: Societé Générale, Credit Lyonnaise, Banque Nationale pour la Commerce et l'Industrie (BNCI), Comptoire Nationale d'Escompte de Paris (CNEP). The BNCI and the CNEP merged on July 1, 1966, to form the Banque Nationale de Paris. The same law of December 2, 1945, completed the nationalization of the Banque de France, begun in 1937. At the same time, thirty-four insurance firms were nationalized and amalgamated into four major insurance companies following a 1968 reorganization: L'Union des Assurances de Paris, Les Assurances Générales de France, Les Assurances and the Mutuels et Générales Françaises. On January 16, 1945, the Renault automobile works was nationalized because of the owner's collaboration with the Nazi authorities.

The extent of the nationalizations undertaken in France after World War II was considerable; in 1963 there were 1,372,000 persons, i.e., 11.2 percent of the total number of workers, in the state sector. The state sector was largest in transport, accounting for 52 percent of the total state sector, and 65 percent of the total number of employees in the transportation sector, followed by the energy sector, accounting for 26.2 percent of those employed in the state sector, and 90 percent of those employed in the energy sector.[15]

De Gaulle's nationalizations had not a trace of socialist thinking in them, although they did bear a resemblance in some respects to the practice under real socialism: in the East, nationalization served the purposes of industrialization, then in its beginning stages, while in France it was undertaken to restore the economic potential destroyed during the war and to boost French industry up to the highly advanced technological level of the other Western industrial nations. French industry was much more decentralized and far less extensively equipped with modern technology than in other countries. The nationalized sector was therefore intended to be a progressive cog in the economy as a whole, the purpose of which was to promote the modernization of other branches of industry. Defeated West Germany showed a deep aversion to any kind of state *dirigisme* and the Freiburg school prepared the theoretical groundwork for a liberal economy. In France, however, nothing of the kind was discernible in the post-war period. The country's intellectual elite, rallying around de Gaulle, worked on sweeping nationalization programs. The wave of nationalizations also fit in well with the French predilection for state planning. As John Sheahan, an American expert on France, put it, "France's planning practice proved to be a substitute for the dynamic stimulus of competition in a country in which the competitive spirit had traditionally been weak, but state interventionism strong and readily accepted."[16] Indicative planning and an extensive state sector were supposed to intermesh organically with the rest of industry still governed by market principles and to create conditions which, in the opinion of France's post-war government, were indispensable for entering into the mainstream of worldwide technological progress. Further, it is no coincidence that such great stress was laid on the control of credit activities in the general blueprint for expanding state intervention in the economy. Nationalization of the Banque de France and the four other major banks was accompanied by other measures to strengthen state control of monetary and credit transactions. The National Credit Council (Conseil Nationale de Credit) and the Insurance Council (Conseil Nationale des Assurances) were established, and their activities were to be coordinated by the Ministry of Finances. The state-controlled credit system was to finance top-priority state investment projects on favorable terms. Nationalizations have deep roots in the economic structure of France. From de Gaulle's resignation in 1946 to his comeback in 1958 a number of governments of various complexions had been in power and he himself ruled in an authoritarian way for ten years. But neither he, his predecessors, nor his successors have attempted to curtail the state sector, which did not undergo any major expansion until the Socialist-Communist coalition government in 1981–1982.

Great Britain's Labour Party supports nationalization, while the Conservative Party supports reprivatization

Before World War II Great Britain had little experience in nationalizations on a large scale. Although the Labour Party had been in government twice before

World War II, in 1924 and 1929, and was a coalition partner in 1940, it was not until the postwar government under Clement Attlee that it undertook an extensive nationalization program. Unlike in France, this program was part of an ambitious reform program that brought the Labour Party to power in the first postwar elections in 1945. Roughly the same economic sectors were to be nationalized as in France: coal-mining, fuel, gas, railroads, the Bank of England, a few municipal transit systems, and the steel industry. Nationalizations were carried out in stages: first the coal mines and the Bank of England in 1946, then fuel and the railroads in 1947, and finally the gas sector in 1948. Nationalization of the steel industry did not begin until 1949 and ended just before the end of the government's term in office, i.e., in 1951. However, after the Conservative Party gained the majority in Parliament in 1951, it denationalized the steel industry and part of the nationalized transport system. But once again, in 1967, the Labour Party renationalized the steel industry.

Although the Labour Party's nationalization program was an integral part of its socialist economic program, it is interesting that the factor motivating it was the same as in de Gaulle's France; indeed the sectors nationalized were the same, and in both countries efficiency was dropping, while the degree of concentration and profitability was low. The decapitalization of the nationalized sectors continued. The coal mining industry was in a chronic crisis: it had reached its peak output in 1913 with 287 million tons but by 1938 had fallen to 230 million tons. The railroads and the power industry showed no inclination to innovate, and, in fact, two-thirds of their capacity had been in public charge even before World War II. It bears mentioning that the economic reasons given above were also decisive for the Conservative Party, which until Margaret Thatcher had contented itself merely with the denationalization of the steel industry. But even the Labour Party under the leadership of Hugh Gaitskell and Harold Wilson showed no especial predilection for continuing nationalization in Great Britain. The share of the state sector in the gross national product increased from 10 percent in 1953 to 12.9 percent, while the share of the state sector in the market of capital goods increased from 20.5 percent to 21 percent.[17]

The Austrian nationalization program was neither conservative nor liberal but neutral

In Austria, a nationalization program had the support of a mass movement following World War I. On March 14, 1919, a law was passed creating a Nationalization Committee; on August 14 the nationalization law came into force. But only a fraction of this program was realized. Fifteen unimportant joint stock companies in the textile industry, twenty-five in the banking system, and seven in the leather and shoe industry became state property.[18]

The nationalizations carried out in 1946 and 1947 were not part of an economic program. The reasons for nationalization were also different from those in France and Great Britain. German property and property of persons who had collaborated with the Nazis were nationalized. The owners had left the country and only the state had the means to get the abandoned factories going again. The nationalization took on greater proportions than elsewhere because the German share in Austria's industry and banking was so large. After the 1938 annexation Hermann Göring's firm took over 76 percent of the capital shares of the Steyer-Daimler Puch, Chronag AG, and the Simmeriger Waggonenfabrik. The Austrian National Bank and the Creditanstalt were incorporated into the German banking system. In 1944, Germany owned 82 percent of the Austrian banking system, 96 percent of its mining, and 81 percent of its engineering industry.[19]

All three coalition partners, the ÖVP, the SPÖ, and the KPÖ, voted for nationalization, but only the KPÖ advocated total nationalization of all industrial plants.

After the nationalizations of 1946 and 1947, the state share in the capital stock of the 276 largest corporations of Austria was 49.5 percent in industry, 59.5 percent in the finance and credit system, 46.6 percent in tourism, making a total of 47.1 percent.[20]

Austria's state sector has undergone major organizational changes over the course of time, but its share in the overall economy has remained stable and is the second largest in the world after Finland; the proportion of nationalized industries is also much greater than elsewhere.

Nationalization—An international comparison

The state sector plays some role in every Western country, especially in areas involving the public good. It has also acquired a place in industry in Austria, Finland, Great Britain, and France, as is evident from the table on p. 116.

The degree of nationalization varies from country to country, but it is the smallest in the Federal Republic of Germany (9 percent), Japan (19 percent), and Switzerland (11 percent). It is largest in Finland (34 percent), Austria (31 percent), and Great Britain (25 percent). Unfortunately, precise data are as yet unavailable on the size of the state sector in France after the nationalizations of 1981 and 1982. The state sector has reached considerable proportions in public utilities (electricity, gas, water), but in this area too there are major differences: 20 percent and 28 percent in Japan and the United States, 43 percent and 53 percent in the Federal Republic of Germany and Finland, and 100 percent in Austria and Israel. Nationalization has reached major proportions only in Austria, Finland, France, and Great Britain.

Regardless of the reasons, it has been first and foremost those sectors providing public services, e.g., water, gas, and energy, that have been nationalized. Basically, the state monopoly, which earlier had also included such sectors as tobacco or salt, is expanded. In addition, in France and Great Britain nationaliza-

Share of the state sector in the various branches of the economy

	FRG	Japan	Switzerland	USA	France*	Sweden	Israel	Great Britain	Austria	Finland
Total	9	10	11	15	17	20	24	25	31	34
Public utilities	43	20	60	28	83	71	100	70	100	53
Transport	74	42	63	18	69	53	32	—	78	59
Construction	0	14	6	12	1	12	6	8	4	31
Processing industry and mining	1	0	1	1	8	4	2	9	25	14

*The statistics do not include the nationalizations effected by the Mitterand government in 1981–1982

Sources: Frederic L. Pryor, *Property and Industrial Organization in Communist and Capitalist Nations*, (Bloomington: Indiana University Press, 1973), pp. 46 and 47; and Vaclav Holesovsky, *Economic Systems*, p. 335.

tion was undertaken in economic sectors that had been operating at a loss for some time and were on the verge of decapitalization, such as the coal and steel industries. The measure was not a matter of "socialization of losses," as was generally assumed, but an attempt to make the particular sector profitable by concentrating small firms out of existence. However, subsequent practice has shown that painful adaptive measures, such as personnel cutbacks, and even reductions in wages and social services have been unavoidable in state enterprises. Moreover, the state has had to assume the burden of larger subsidies to make these nationalized enterprises competitive on the world markets. However, areas instrumental to state control over the overall economy have also been nationalized: e.g., parts of the banking system and, above all, the issuing banks.

In those Western countries where nationalizations have reached considerable proportions, the influence of the state on economic matters has been strengthened considerably. But the above data indicate that even where ideological factors were operative nationalization was still subject to the constraints of the system. If any conclusion at all could be drawn from a comparison with the total state control of economic and social life in the East, it would be that, if socialism is an ideology for restructuring the society, "real socialism" is a concept for establishing a state.

France's socialists opt for more state intervention while the West German socialists affirm the "free market wherever competition truly prevails"[21]

France is pursuing a different course than Germany in the present phase of the technical-industrial revolution, just as it did in the immediate post-war period. The socialist parties of France and Germany have economic programs that diverge on fundamental points. France's socialists gained absolute majority in the elections in May 1981 with their program, replete with promises, of socialism à la Francaise, which proclaimed a radical onslaught on traditional property relations; nevertheless it chose to form a coalition government with the great losers in this election, i.e., the French Communist Party, which was more orthodox than liberal. The SPD, ever true to its Bad-Godesberg slogan of "Competition as far as possible, planning as far as necessary"[22] in thirteen years at the head of coalition governments, lost power in October 1982 to a coalition of Germany's middle-class parties.

The left in France has evolved differently from its German counterpart over a historical period of many years of great change. After World War II the French Socialist Party was a negligible quantity; the CPF was one of the country's strongest parties and by far the strongest on the left. In the 1970s, however, it lost almost half of its voters and the cream of its intellectuals. The socialists doubled their number of voters. The Communist Party of Germany, whch had been a powerful political force until the Hitler era, never recuperated in West Germany after World War II. While the SED, a motley union of socialists and communists, exercised power in the GDR by the grace of Big Brother, the Communist Party of Germany (KPD) remained a marginal group on the political landscape of the Federal Republic. Not only was SPD only able to recover the ground it had held before World War II and even expanded at the expense of the communists, but it also led a coalition government for thirteen years. Neither before nor after World War II had it ever sought a united front with the communists or contemplated any major nationalizations. Its Bad-Godesburg program contains the portentous and unambiguous statement: ''Any concentration of economic power—and that includes in the hands of the state—entails dangers.''[23]

The socialist-communist coalition government of France in the 1980s was not a novelty of the post-war period. In 1936, a popular front government led by the SFIO leader, Leon Blum, gained a majority and governed the country for two years. But the nationalizations undertaken by the pre-war government of Leon Blum and by de Gaulle's post-war government were not of comparable scale to those undertaken by the coalition government of Mitterand in 1981 and 1982. In the aftermath of the nationalizations following World War II, the share of the state sector in the total economy was only 2 percent higher than the comparable figure in the United States, with main emphasis on public utilities (83 percent of this sector) and transport (69 percent). The Mitterand government, on the other hand, has placed key sectors of industry and the banking system in public hands. The state sector in industry rose from 8 percent to 30 percent, and 50 percent of industrial enterprises with more than 2,000 employees were nationalized. In addition, 75 percent of the country's industrial research and development and thirty-six major banks were nationalized.[24]

This radical onslaught on property relations has established a precedent among the world's market economies. Nowhere is the state sector as large as in France. No other social democratic party has dared to undertake such a sweeping nationalization program and, moreover, in a united front with the communists as well. Only in the planned economies of the East is the state sector larger.

The nationalization program was one of the main economic points in the election platform of the French Socialist Party, which was an unambiguously democratic platform, rich in ideas. The majority of the French approved. But the question may be legitimately asked whether nationalization is indeed a problem of ideology or just a purely organizational problem within an overall economic program. Neither the socialist movement before its split into socialist and communist parties nor either of these parties separately, it should be recalled, had made the nationalization of the means of production the ultimate goal of struggle. Nationalization and socialization have always been the revolutionary watchwords of the socialist movement. In the Soviet Union the total nationalization of the means of production was not an act of the October Revolution, but a framework prefatory to the forced industrialization initiated by Stalin in the 1930s, in which heavy industry and the armaments industry were given absolute priority. However Mitterand's nationalization program comes to be labelled by future French historians, i.e., whether ideologically or organizationally inspired, the forces prompting it arise more from France's economic history than from the history of its political parties, that is, French confidence in the capacity of the state to establish and maintain order and in French mistrust of the self-regulating forces of the competitive market. This attitude has been a constant factor in French economic policy from the eighteenth and nineteenth centuries to the Popular Front politics in 1936, de Gaulle's postwar economic policy, and the new edition of the Popular Front under Mitterand. Indeed, Laurent Fabius, the second Minister of Industry and Prime Minister under Mitterand, described the greatest wave of nationalizations in France's history as follows: Change must take place more rapidly in France than in the other "old countries" because France, in Fabius's view, had not modernized its production apparatus between 1975 and 1980 as had the United States, Germany and Japan. "In the upcoming years, France will not only have to catch up with this development, it will also have to keep pace with breakneck technological change."[25] The key words "to catch up" (if not even "surpass"), first echoed in the East, are equally conspicuous in Mitterand's program of goals. The goal of nationalization is unequivocally stated. It is seen as a means to improve France's competitiveness with regard to the major industrial nations, which have attained their superiority on the strength of their market economies, and are resolved to preserve that system to maintain their superiority in the future. Which of the two, i.e., the traditional market economies with limited state intervention or France with its already considerable state sector, will gain the upper hand in the even more bitter competitive race, cannot be foreseen; but one thing is clear, namely, that the state sector, vast as it is, has hardly changed the ideological image of the country and the network of social services, now quite extensive, is necessarily limited by the financial resources made available to it, and these the state sector has not augmented.

The state sector is omnipresent in the planned economies of the East, but since, however, they are not fully integrated into the world economy, maintaining competitiveness is not a primary issue for them. Exporting and importing industrial enterprises are shielded from the foreign market by the state monopoly on foreign trade and currency. While Hungary and Poland have given their large enterprises a margin of free play in foreign trade, industrial enterprises in the Soviet Union and the other Eastern countries still have no knowledge of the prices for which their products are sold on the world market, or of how much is paid to their foreign trading partner for the goods they import from abroad. The instrument of the state monopoly, namely, the foreign trade organization, is the link between them and their foreign partners. It pays the production enterprise and is paid by the purchaser of imported goods at domestic prices. The difference between the domestic price and the foreign price is paid into or covered by the state budget. Today every reform proposal for improving competitiveness looks to the mechanisms of the market for salvation. But the state and administrative bureaucracy have banished forever the self-regulating mechanisms from the economy.

In France, people are well aware of the dangers of nationalization, i.e., the bureaucratic stifling of the creative initiative of a state-controlled firm. Mitterand granted full freedom of decision-making and autonomy to the presidents of industrial groups at the time they were appointed. However, reality tells a different tale. Complaints abound about the continual interference of ministerial officials of almost every sort. "Every minister thinks that the state enterprises are his own personal affair," write France's newspapers. The president of Rhone Poulenc, Jean Gandois, resigned in protest against the continual interference of state officials. This official "interventionitis" became too much even for the President. He reminded his ministers that coherent industrial policy must be safeguarded against the encroachments of a creeping bureaucracy. He made this comment two years after the state's assumption of control over what are now state firms. Whether the presidential admonition will be heeded is uncertain. But France's economy stands and falls with its foreign trade, since 21.7 percent of its manufactured goods are sold abroad. If the state, instead of industry, assumed control of foreign trade, France too would sooner or later be forced to export raw materials, of which it is in short supply, or semifinished products which have never been profitable, just as do the planned economies of the East.

But growing conflicts with labor are even more serious than this problem. The people expected more from the Socialist-Communist government it helped to power in May 1981 than it could give. But workers in a state enterprise cannot be given more rights or higher wages and more social services than workers in the private sector. If they are allotted more than would be warranted by calculations of cost, based on using the profit rate as a source for financing expanded reproduction, the state must make up the difference, and do so at the expense of the private sector. Even in the planned economies, state enterprises must sustain themselves, balance their accounts, and make a profit. But their productivity is 50 percent lower than the productivity of the industrial states of the West, and lower productivity is also paid at a lower rate. The planned economies have always produced more iron, steel and machinery and relatively fewer consumer goods, fewer than the volume required to meet the buying power created. This has been possible because the employees in those economies have no authentic representatives to defend their interests. The trade unions are state organizations like every other organization, and identify the interest of the workers with the interest of the state, i.e., with the interests of the state bureaucracy. But the French have a glorious democratic history behind them and will know how to defend their authentic interests in the future. The Socialists also will not want to wish this dismal fate on the French people. The French Communist Party wanted to nationalize much more than the Socialists were able. But the Communist Party has always been deft at destroying what exists, but never at replacing what has been destroyed.

The problems of the French coalition government had roots that go beyond nationalization; they were a consequence of an overestimation of the role of the state in a democratic society. The wave of nationalizations was accompanied by a massive "demand-side" policy. The intention was to prompt an explosion in demand by broad increases in wages and social services, which was supposed to stimulate economic activity. Naturally, the consequences were different from what had been expected. Wage increases drove up the costs of manufacture, dampened expectations of profit, and reduced state revenues; stimulation of consumption did not increase domestic demand as much as it promoted the import of expensive goods. This demand-side policy drove the budget and foreign trade deficits beyond bearable limits. The fifth holiday week, reduction in the working hours, and many other social services are among the major conquests of French workers. However late in joining the modernization wave, France will not have it any easier in world competition, now that a worker's time on the job in 1983 has been reduced to 1,780 hours, which put France in second place after the Federal Republic of Germany (1,746 hours) but far ahead of its greatest competitors, the United States with 1,904 hours and Japan with 2,096 hours.[26]

The euphoria of the first months after the establishment of the left coalition was abruptly deflated when the *patronat* (Association of Employers) presented its first big bill. From 1973 to 1983 total tax and social welfare outgoings increased by 9 percent to 44.7 percent of the GNP compared with 26.9 percent in Japan, 31 percent in the United States and 37 percent in West Germany. During the same period, the gross profit rate decreased from 27.8 percent to 21.7 percent, while the rate of wages and social outgoings increased from 64.2 percent to 70 percent. This discouraging balance sheet was a consequence of the drastic wage increases of the three previous years which saw wages rising by 51 percent, but prices by only 32 percent. The explosion of the wages bill has caused 20,000 bankruptcies annually, with small and medium-sized enterprises the worst hit. Even after the great wave of nationalizations, there are still 150,000 firms in France employing between 10 and 500 workers. And only these enterprises are able to create jobs to replace those eliminated by automation in the large enterprises. Firms with less than 100 employees created more than 700,000 jobs between 1974 and 1980, while those with more than 200 employees created only 560,000.

Measures to prevent a further increase in unemployment and to alleviate the conditions of the unemployed (the *traitment social*) have been instituted, but still the number of unemployed is increasing steadily: at the end of March 1984 it was 11.4 percent higher than a year previously and 10.3 percent higher than in October 1983. Within five months, the unemployment rate rose from 8.7 percent to 9.6 percent and the total number of unemployed reached 2,247 million in March.[27]

The state sector is unable to eliminate
the flaws of the market economy

The measures undertaken in 1982 and 1983 to relieve the budget and foreign trade deficits, which had grown rapidly in the interim, as well as the measures taken to restructure basic industries, demonstrate that Mitterand and his followers had intended to use nationalization of the large enterprises and the major banks more as a means for modernizing a halting industry than as an ideological ingredient to socialism French style. The generous wage and social policy, the *traitement social-politique* of the first months, was followed by an austerity policy. In state sector and private sector alike, there is only one way to modernize: i.e., by introducing new technology and automation of the production process. "The robot's gain in man's loss," said the competent ministers of the left coalition. The pragmatist, Laurent Fabius, used an example from the Renault works to demonstrate the consequences of modernization: "Today twenty-five hours are still needed to manufacture a model R5, but its successor, which will be ready for the market in about a year, will require only sixteen hours."

Modernization means job redundancy, especially where the modernization process has been delayed. New jobs will be created in the industries of the future only later, and only when these obsolescent basic branches can be replaced. Furthermore, it is questionable whether workers made redundant in these branches can be employed in the newly created industrial branches or in the service sector.

The painful restructuring in the Peugot-Talbot auto works in early 1984 was followed by an even more painful elimination of jobs in Lorraine. Although the *traitement social* remains the basic premise of economic policy, the available resources to effect this policy are all but exhausted. The retirement age has already been drastically reduced, job time is the second shortest in the world after the Federal Republic, while a considerable number of persons, especially youth, are already in retraining programs. The elimination of jobs has increased from 1.3 percent to 2.5 percent annually since 1981, and the process of restructuring is still far from complete even as technological development continues unrestrained.

The austerity policy did not begin with the press conference of the president on April 4, 1984. In March 1983 the finance minister, Jacques Delors, had already proclaimed drastic economizing measures and devalued the franc for the third time since the elections of May 1981. Deference to the *peuple de gauche* who had helped the left coalition to victory is still maintained. But François Mitterand sees himself as the president of all the French and his credo is now "He who creates wealth, must not be punished." He made this even clearer at a visit to the north of the country in early 1983. "Funds used to subsidize unprofitable business," said the president, "will be lacking to support new industries more viable for the future." The *mutation industrielle,* conceived as a component of French-style socialism, is showing itself more and more clearly to be one instrument of modernization among the abundant arsenal of other measures which his predecessors, de Gaulle, Pompidou, and Giscard, had already employed. Laurent Fabius, in fact, saw this to be the mission of his government: "De Gaulle completed the institutional transformation; the task of the left is to undertake the economic and social transformations."

The government is pursuing a traditional austerity policy and the employees are responding with traditional methods of class struggle. The wave of protest reached its high point with the unrest in Lorraine and the March on Paris. Good Friday ended with a strike of Citroen workers and a demonstration, organized by the Communist Party trade union, to protest almost 6,000 redundancies. In late April, hospital service personnel and some aircraft dispatchers struck. Arnold Toynbee's proverbial statement, "The worker remains a wage recipient regardless of who his employer is," retains its validity even in the nationalized enterprises of France. In October 1982, the head of the Communist-led CGT said, "We are at the beginning of a very difficult learning process," but in April 1984, at the high point of the wave of protests led by the CGT, he called Mitterand's new economic course "modernization with axe in hand." Even the trade union, CFDT, which is close to the socialists, finds "sociopolitical ambition" to be lacking in the government's goals. The Communist leader, Georges Marchais, participated on April 18 in the March on Paris of the Lorraine steelworkers. On April 20, the leader of the CP faction in Parliament declared his confidence in the government under Pierre Mauroy in a statement that suggested a purely formal membership in the government majority: "Its declarations are a long way from eliminating our worries and fears concerning the problems of buying power, unemployment, and industrial policy." And he continued even more clearly: "We are in the left alliance and the government majority just as much as we are on the side of the workers." The socialist faction acknowledged this remarkable vote of confidence of its "ally" only after an interruption and further internal discussions. The further path of the CPF was not difficult to guess: the coalition government ceased to exist.

"Privatization is not a question of ideology"[28]
—the same applies to nationalization

An honest social democrat and an honest communist can pursue a common goal only very briefly before they reach a parting of the ways. For the socialist Mitterand, nationalization of the large corporations was only a means to accelerate technical progress and strengthen the competitiveness of his country; for the Communist leader Marchais, partial nationalization was a step toward total nationalization, i.e., a step toward the destruction of the existing system, which since the Russian Thermidor has been synonymous with state ownership of the means of production in neo-Marxist terminology. The process of adaptation initiated by Mitterand cannot be carried through without sacrifice, i.e., without the reduction in jobs and unemployment. If underemployment could be kept behind the factory walls, France too would fall prey to the fate of the planned economies—low productivity and low wages. It would be unable to strengthen its competitiveness and would gradually be reduced to the status of an underdeveloped country. The Mitterand way to economic grandeur is painful, but it is surely the lesser evil. His coalition partner Marchais, however, did not wish to strengthen the existing economic system in France but to destroy it. He misused the indignation of workers threatened with dismissal and organized proclamations and protest actions against the economic course of a government in which the CPSU was a coalition partner. The "common way" was of short duration.

In this context, the statement of a former presidential candidate and current Minister of Agriculture in the coalition, Michel Rocard, at the fifteenth International Congress of the Common Market in Florence in April 1984 is interesting. He pleaded for the state to show broad restraint in intervening in the economy. The state should limit itself to defining the general conditions and leave the task of shaping the production process in the hands of the social partners.[29] But this statement no longer describes the practice of his government.

The resolutions of the Florence Congress are interesting as well because the view was accepted that privatization of publicly owned enterprises should be seen not as a question of ideology, but as a pragmatic question. Nationalizations undertaken in a market economy need not necessarily be seen as a purely ideological issue. But in France, nationalization as well as the overall process of adaptation and its painful effects have become key points of contention among the political parties. And even as the Mayor of Paris, Jacques Chirac, is saying that the government should not be spared its lashes in this difficult phase of adaptation, the political battle between the former allies, the social democrats and the Party-line communists, is becoming more embittered.

The SPD decides for a competitive market economy

This was a pioneer decision, inspired by the painful experiences of the Nazi era and total nationalization in the name of socialism. The Bad-Godesberg program is without a doubt a return to the principles of socialism "which in Europe is rooted in Christian ethics, humanism and classical philosophy." The program refrains from proclaiming any ultimate truths "Out of respect for the convictions of men, over which neither a political party nor the state must have control." After all the failed attempts, it was high time to stress man's inability to create an ideal and eternally just social system, just as it was the right time to stress that the SPD "opposed every dictatorship, every type of totalitarian and authoritarian rule, as they abuse the dignity of man, reduce his freedom to nothing and destroy the law." In light of events of recent memory, the criticism of the communists is also fully warranted: "Indeed, they have falsified socialist thought. Socialists aspire to achieve freedom and justice, while the communists take advantage of the conflicts in society to establish the dictatorship of their party.''

The principles the Bad-Godesberg program, laid down to describe its economic and social system, are of special importance in our present concerns. The goal of economic policy was unequivocally defined: "Steadily growing prosperity and a just participation of all in the fruits of the economy, life in freedom without unworthy dependence and without exploitation." The authors of the Bad-Godesberg program were aware that the question of the present could not be: "whether allocation and planning are expedient in the economy, but rather who this allocation affects and who receives its benefits." Further, the program does not relieve the state of its responsibility for the economy: "It is responsible for a forward-looking cyclic policy." But it should also "restrict its method essentially to that of direct intervention in the economy." Important elements of Social Democratic economic policy are: "free choice in consumption, free choice of jobs, free competition and free business initiative." Further, "the autonomy of the employer and employee associations in the conclusion of wage contracts" is stressed as an essential ingredient of a free society. Since "a totalitarian command economy destroys freedom, "the Social Democratic Party affirms the free market, wherever competition truly reigns," but not without reservations since where " . . . markets come under the dominion of individuals or groups, manifold measures are necessary to preserve freedom in the economy."

The importance of the state sector is also stressed: "Public property is a legitimate form of public control which no modern state can forgo. It serves to defend freedom from the encroachment of the power of huge economic structures." It continues further, "public property is useful and necessary wherever a healthy order in economic power relations cannot be achieved by other means," but with the following qualification: "Every concentration of economic power, even in the hands of the state, entails dangers."

A few years after the Bad-Godesberg program was adopted, the SPD assumed responsibility for the government in a coalition with the FDP. In the thirteen years of its tenure in government, no program of nationalizations was carried out. Just before the social-liberal coalition fell on September 17, 1982, the SPD Party Congress in Munich (April 19–23, 1982) sought a way out of the crisis in the German economy not in nationalization, but in a further democratization: "Only an unrestricted parity between workers and capital in large concerns is a sufficient guarantee that technological innovations and structural change will not take place solely at the expense of the workers. . . ."[30]

The German economy in the post-war era has always been stronger than the French economy. Various factors have played a role here. Even the expectations for 1984—a forecast growth of 3 percent—are better than the expectations in France (+ 0.8 percent). Nowhere has nationalization proved to be the best means to eliminate economic backwardness, nor has it proved effective as a means to promote social justice. François Mitterand was right when he said that "he who creates wealth, should not be punished." France's difficulties after this painful intervention should not be necessarily seen as an argument against nationalization, but they are a warning signal that should not be disregarded.

In Austria the state sector is being neither expanded nor reduced

Before May 1981 the state sector in Austria was greater than anywhere else in the Western world. But this was not the result of a conscious economic program of an influential political party. Neither the government of the People's Party nor the government of the Socialist Party of Austria expanded or reduced the state sector. The Socialist Party's economic program of May 24, 1981, ventured to praise private small and middle-sized enterprises: "Two-thirds of all employed work in this sector. It is necessary for local commerce and hence makes an important contribution to our quality of life. Small and middle-sized firms have shown themselves to be inured to crisis in difficult times in their ability to adapt and their closeness to the market."[31] The state sector has not shown itself to be inured to crisis in difficult times. State subsidies amounting to billions were created to cover the considerable losses. It should be borne in mind that the steel industry, which dominates the Austrian state sector, is in chronic crisis throughout the world and also receives state subsidies. In times of crisis, Austria's state sector has shown more concern for maintaining underemployment than the private sector could permit. But this only delayed adaptation, it did not render it unnecessary.

The SPÖ has defined its position on the nationalization problem more precisely in light of recent experiences. It has become more skeptical. One of the most prominent authors of the party program of 1978 and of the economic program of 1981, Professor Egon Matzner, observed the following: "The elimination of private and decentralized capital by the nationalization of private capital can no longer be regarded as satisfactory; nationalization as such changes only ownership relations. The requirements inherent to certain situations, which are critical for decision making at the enterprise level, are not essentially affected." Matzner goes on to argue that, even though the presence of the state in a major portion of industry and the banking system makes the bourgeoisie's control over capital in Austria weaker than in most capitalist countries, nonetheless "on the other hand, and according to the requirements inherent in certain situations, nationalized industries have also been found to be acting against the interests of society. . ."[32] After the heavy losses of more than 11 billion shillings in 1985, some influential political groups in Austria postulated the reprivatization of a huge part of the nationalized economy. The predilection for nationalization is also conspicuously absent in other influential social democratic parties: in Sweden, where the Socialists have governed the country for fifty years with an interruption of only six years, and Spain, where they assumed the government in 1983.

Sweden's Social Democracy, in power for fifty years, nationalizes only declining industrial sectors

Sweden's socialists have been in power longer than any other social democratic party in Europe. In October 1982, they assumed control of the government once again after an interruption of only eight years. In Sweden, the share of the state sector in industrial production is no more than 4 percent, although its share in public utilities and the transportation and communication system is extraordinarily high (71 percent and 53 percent respectively). But this does not mean that the Socialist-governed state has little influence on economic life or on the shaping of income; quite the contrary, state expenditure is 68 percent of the Gross National Product, the highest in the entire OECD. Public expenditure for health, education, and welfare increased by 6 percent in the last decade at a time when the economy was growing only by 1 percent annually. [33]

The state attaches great value to the modernization and rationalization of the economy since Sweden, perhaps more than any other OECD country, is firmly anchored in the international division of labor. However, adaptation to the needs of the technical and industrial revolution was effected not by restructuring property relations, but through an all-embracing fiscal policy and through organizational measures to restructure the economy. The steel industry was thoroughly revamped, perhaps more so than in any other country, but there was no question of nationalization. Redundant plants were closed down and reorganized for the production of high quality goods without appreciably reducing output. The largest private steel company in Sweden, Johnson and Co., purchased the stainless steel manufacture of the Udderholm and Fagersta companies for about 56 million dollars and became the leading producer of stainless steel piping and sheet metal with an annual output of about 600 million dollars. The restructuring meant a loss of jobs for about 1,500 persons, i.e., 15 percent of the total personnel; two foundries and two rolling mills were closed down. Diversification and quality improvement maintained exports at a high level, and 200,000 to 250,000 tons of stainless steel as well as 1.3 million tons of top quality steel products, i.e., about 33 percent of the country's steel output, were exported to Europe. Compared with other European countries such as Great Britain, which exports 14 percent of its production, the Federal Republic of Germany (20 percent), or the EEC average (16 percent), [34] Sweden's performance in steel export is unsurpassed.

Sweden attaches great value to automation of production, stimulated by a state-supported development program. The principal focus is on the mechanical engineering industry, which accounts for 45 percent of the country's industrial production; 50 percent of the manufactured machinery is marketed abroad. Two-thirds of total expenditures for research and development is therefore concentrated on mechanical engineering. Sweden's mechanical engineering industry has become a world leader in computer-formed machine models, and the industry has the highest number of robots. Foreign trade is supported by the state, and all economic sectors are actively involved in it. The first important act of the Swedish socialist government after their election victory was to devalue the Swedish crown by 16 percent in October 1982.

Sweden's socialist government exercises a major influence on the economy and on the shaping of incomes through its extremely high taxation rate, its restructuring program, and its extensive redistribution of incomes. This economic policy has encountered severe criticism from business circles, which Lars-Erik Thunholm, President of the Scandinaviska Enskilda Banken, summed up as follows: "Job security ordained by the state and codetermination, regulated by law, replaced growth oriented mobility. In addition, public interventions in the use of resources, in price setting, incomes policy, and all the other relations in the labor contract, put the mechanisms of the market out of commission."[35] Still, Thunholm concedes that Sweden's economic policy has not pursued a socialist model, but rather has developed along the lines of a mixed economy, or rather a special version of it, which he has dubbed a "negotiation economy."

One of the most important objectives of economic policy is to combat unemployment. Sweden's unemployment rate of 3.4 percent is the lowest in Europe after Switzerland, but the highest in Sweden's post-war history. In addition to the official number of unemployed of 147,000, 4 percent, or 180,000 persons, are in the various labor market programs.[36] This is a costly policy if one considers that the budget expenditures earmarked for this purpose, 7.2 billion Swedish crowns, has had to be supplemented by additional programs costing 16.2 billion Skr., altogether making up 11 percent of the total budget expenditures. More than one-fourth of a work force, totaling 4.3 million persons, work less than 35 hours per week.[37] But Sweden's government feels that the cost of supporting open unemployment and the harm done to society by unemployment, are far greater than these budgetary expenditures to combat unemployment. Wages in Sweden are perhaps the highest in the world, and the redistribution and transfer rates are also extremely high. A typical, "fully employed" industrial worker or a commercial employee with an average income had a marginal tax rate of 57–63 percent in 1979. Ten years earlier it was 45–50 percent. Many transfers are income-dependent. Only households with low factor incomes receive large state subsidies for rent and child assistance. Thirty percent of households with the lowest incomes receive by far the largest portion of their purchasing power from state transfers.[38] The total marginal burden of the household is highest in the middle income groups because of income tax and the loss of state transfers. There are also groups which are marginally taxed at more than 100 percent. The existing system of overproportioned redistribution has been called into question since it has led to a growing shadow economy and is undermining incentives to improve performance.

An important component of the Social Democratic program for "economic democracy" is the "employee funds" which are built up out of profits and wages, and are to be used mainly for the purchase of shares. The dividends due in 1983 were subject to a special one-time tax of 20 percent. The Swedish Employers' Association began an extensive campaign against these initiatives, but neither the government nor the Confederation of Trade Unions are at all prepared to renege on this election promise.

The Swedish Socialist Party, which has been in government longer than any other social democratic party, is no more inclined to intervene directly into property relations than the Socialist Workers Party of Spain, which gained an absolute majority on October 28, 1982 for the first time in history. "In its present economic situation, Spain can not afford nationalizations," proclaimed the young socialist head of government and leader of Spain's Socialist Workers Party, Felipe Gonzalez. The new government intends to begin its program of reforms with the legal system, the state administration, public health and culture. The state administration is to become more flexible; in the future, civil servants may be moved from one ministry to another, something which had never previously been possible, and Madrid will cease being the sole host to the country's great swollen bureaucracy. The left wing of the party reproached the Minister of Economics, Miguel Boyer, for planning a right-wing economic policy with the votes of the left, but the Minister replied: "If we carry out this policy of earlier governments, who were much further to the right, better than they did, i.e., if we succeed in it, we will have achieved quite a bit."[39]

But it is not only the Social Democrats who harbor doubts that nationalization is a panacea for the steadily growing number of conflicts. The planned economies as well, for which nationalization of the economy and of the whole of social life amounts to the fulfillment of the revolutionary goal, and for which socialization is a means to the self-administration and emancipation of the workers, are seeking the solution to their grave economic problems not in the inefficient instruments of a planned economy, but among the perennial mechanisms of the traditional competitive market. Hungary took the giant step in this direction, and in the next chapter we shall examine the achievements and the problems of that country.

Notes

1. Daniel Bell, *The End of Ideology* (Glencoe, Illinois: Free Press, 1960), p. 73.

2. Jürgen Habermas, "Problems of Legitimation in Late Capitalism," in *Critical Sociology: Selected Readings*, ed. Paul Connerton, 1976, p. 364.

3. J. K. Galbraith, *Economics and the Public Purpose* (Boston, 1973), p. 221.

4. Habermas, op. cit., p. 365.

5. Quoted in Karl Schiller, "Bin ich ein Liberaler," *Der Spiegel*, 14 February 1983.

6. Bell, op. cit., p. 71.

7. Schiller, op. cit.

8. *Grundsatzprogramm der Sozialdemokratischen Partei Deutschlands*, Bad-Godesberg, 15 October 1959, p. 14.

9. Clement August Andreae, "Vorbild Osterreich?" in *Wiener Journal*, April 1984.

10. Vulko Chervenkov, "The Activities of the Bulgarian Workers Party," in *For a*

Lasting Peace, for a People's Democracy, 3/1947, p. 2.

11. D. K. Flechtheim, "Kommunismus in Deutschland 1918–1975," in *Die Sowjetunion, Solschenizyn und die westliche Linke* (Rowohlt, 1975), pp. 98, 99.

12. V. I. Lenin, *Works*, Vol. 26, p. 50f.

13. *Grundsatzprogramm*, op. cit., p. 15.

14. Heinz Dietrich Ortlieb, *Die verantwortungslose Gesellschaft oder wie man die Demokratie verspielt* (Munich, 1971), p. 38.

15. *Les Enterprises publique dans la CEE*, Paris, 1967.

16. John Sheahan, *An Introduction to the French Economy* (Merrill, 1969), p. 75.

17. Central Statistical Office, *National Expenditure 1958 and 1968*.

18. *Handbuch der Österreichischen Wirtschaft* (Vienna, 1939), p. 70.

19. Kurt W. Rothschild, *Austria's Economic Development between the Two Wars* (London, 1947), p. 80.

20. *Berichte und Informationen*, 13 August 1956.

21. *Grundsatzprogramm*, op. cit., p. 14.

22. Op. cit., p. 10.

24. *Handelsblatt*, 15 February 1983.

25. Quoted in "Talbot als Modellfall" in *Neue Züricher Zeitung*, 11 January 1984.

26. *Salzburger Nachrichten*, 7 April 1984.

27. "Anhaltender Anstieg der Arbeitslosigkeit in Frankreich," *Neue Zürcher Zeitung*, 18 April, 1984.

28. From the Fifteenth International Congress of the Community, held in Florence, April 1984.

29. *Die Presse*, 20 April 1984, "Privatisierung ist keine Ideologiefrage."

30. Quoted from "Sozialdemodraten/Wirtschafts-und Steuerpolitik," *Handelsblatt*, 20 November 1982.

31. *Das Wirtschaftsprogramm der SPO*, ratified at the Twenty-sixth Federal Party Congress of the Socialist Party of Austria, held in Graz, 24 May 1981, p. 9.

32. Egon Matzner, "Strategy for the Transformation of the Crisis" (Paper presented to the International Conference on Socialist Alternatives in Economic Policy, organized by the Socialist International, Vienna, 20–22 November 1982).

33. Kevin Dunn, "Sweden," *Financial Times*, 25 January 1984.

34. "Rationalising for Europe," *Financial Times*, 25 January 1984.

35. Lars-Erik Thunholm, speech at the University of Zurich (*Neue Zürcher Zeitung*, 4 February 1983).

36. D. Brown, "Crisis package aims to cut unemployment," *Financial Times*, 25 January 1984.

37. Ibid.

38. Prof. Dr. Bruno S. Frey, "Einkommensverteilung in Schweden," *Neue Zürcher Zeitung*, 4 February 1983.

39. Quoted from Walter Haubrich, "Ganz auf Zukunft eingestellt," *Frankfurter Allgemeine Zeitung*, 4 December 1983.

6. The search for a "third way" and the Hungarian experiment

The search for a "third way" did not begin in 1968 in Hungary. Two years before the end of World War II, in the summer of 1943, the cream of the intellectual elite of the country met to discuss Hungary's fate. The Szarszo Conference on Balaton Lake set itself the goal of outlining an economic program for the postwar era, then about to dawn. The organizers of this conference defined themselves as a non-Marxist socialist movement, the goal of which was to carve out a place for Hungary in a democratic league of nations of the countries of central and eastern Europe. Under the aegis of the Magyar Elet Publishing House, headed by Sandor Püski, the conference assembled 600 people: journalists, artists, writers, agrarian experts, workers, and students representing every political nuance in the country. There was even a small communist group present. Although the participants did not wholly reflect the political landscape of the country at the time, they could be regarded fairly as representative of Hungary's political and social structure. Also among the participants were politicians who would have a major influence on the history of Hungary in the post-war era, such as Ferenc Nagy, later Prime Minister, Istvan Dobi, Prime Minister between 1948 and 1952 and head of state between 1952 and 1967, as well as Bela Kovacs, leader of the small peasants party until 1947 when he was arrested and transported to Siberia.

For six days, from August 23 to August 29, discussions went on on the role of the state in social life, future relations with neighboring countries, religion, culture, and even popular music. Two talks were especially exciting: one by Ferenz Erdei, member of the government from 1948 through 1956, and one by Laszlo Nemeth, awarded the Kossuth and Herder Prize in the post-war years. It was Erdei's view that a bourgeois government was no longer possible after Hitler's defeat and that socialism was the only possible option; however, only the Transylvanian writer, Istvan Nagy, and a member of the People's College, as it was called, shared his opinion. The vast majority rejected this view, not because they were unwilling to cooperate with the communists but because they were afraid of being dominated by them. It was claimed, with justification, that the Soviet army would bring Stalinism, not the socialism so ardently desired.

On the other hand, Laszlo Nemeth's notion of a "third way" found broad support. Nemeth rejected both national socialism and communism; neither Hitler nor communism would bring the good life to the Hungarian people, he said. Communism would force the peasants into collective farms and the skilled craftsmen into communal shops; the intellectuals would be forced to submit to strict state control, continued Nemeth. "This socialism would be barely distinguishable from slavery, since Hungary would be governed by alien outsiders," he said to conclude his talk on a socialist alternative. The only solution, in his opinion, was a "third way." Just as British or Dutch rule would be no viable solution for New Guinea, which required an independent government of Papuas, so for Hungary, only an authentic Hungarian government was worth striving for, argued Nemeth as he defined what this "third way" would entail. The political philosopher and author, Istvan Bibo, member of Imre Nagy's government during the 1956 uprising and political prisoner from 1957 to 1963, interpreted Nemeth's "third way" as an alternative to both fascism and bolshevism.

The dispute over Hungary's post-war regime grew more acute after the publication of the outcome of the Szarszo Conference in 1944. It was becoming steadily more obvious that the vast majority of the Hungarian people and its intellectual elite rejected the Horthy regime and the country's feudal capitalist structures. They desired a pluralist system in its stead and not a one-party regime, regardless of its form.

A number of the suggestions of the Szarszo Conference were later reflected in the program of the coalition government established immediately after World War II. However, this government was of short duration. What happened was precisely what the far-sighted at the Szarszo Conference had predicted: the Soviet army brought brutal Stalinism, not a pure and humane utopian socialism, and it befell Matyas Rakosi, Hungary's head of state, to "Hungarianize" it.

The Szarszo Conference, its organizers, and the notion of the "third way" passed into oblivion. The attempt to embark upon a third way, a Hungarian way, foundered, as did similar attempts in Poland and Czechoslovakia. The Hungarian people swept away the Stalinist regime in the bloody October uprising of 1956, and barred the way to its restoration forever more.

Halfway to the third way

Janos Kadar, the communist martyr of the Rakosi regime, realized that a new edition of the reign of terror of his predecessor and a *dirigiste* economy would have no possibilities of success. For years he searched for a steering system that could give Hungary more freedom, and industrial firms more decision-making powers, without a reign of terror, without *dirigisme*, while maintaining intact the basic principles of a one-party regime and a state economy. That would thereby revive dormant creative potential and improve upon the extremely low economic performance. Calm gradually returned to agitated minds. The people resigned themselves to the thought that in the given geopolitical realities not much could be changed, while the workers endeavored to get as big a slice of the pie as they could within the existing system—not always in accord with the interests of the state.

The country's best economists worked zealously on a steering model that could raise the performance of the economy and secure a higher standard of living in accord with the geopolitical situation and with centrally determined priorities. Of course, the margin of action, which could not call into question the basic principles of the political regime, was much too narrow. Nevertheless, when on January 1, 1968, the Gomulka regime with all its promises approached its bitter end after having reverted to traditional methods of government, and the "Prague Spring" had warmed the icy climate of the Novotny era for a brief period, Hungary's new economic mechanism came into force. Eighteen years have passed since then, time enough to assess the results.

The reform has powerful opponents

Hungary's economic reform is undoubtedly the boldest, most far-sighted, and most multifaceted attempt to bring new life blood into the hardened arteries of an economic system that had been invested with the attribute of infallibility. Of course, existing practice and accumulated inertia could not be overcome at the snap of a finger. The reform was a resuscitation process that attempted to overcome the loss of initiative plaguing the system. Success was not always forthcoming, and setbacks were inevitable. After five years of growth, it seemed that the ability and the will of the reformers to carry the country's economy further had finally run out.

The oil crisis and its devastating consequences for the economy, as it plodded along to recovery, dealt a fatal blow to the reform. It was not officially declared dead, but all talk of reform ceased. It could plausibly have been argued that the orthodox wing of the Party, which had always followed the reform with suspicion and had branded the reformers as unregenerate revisionists, had assumed control of the Party leadership. The reform movement slumbered for five years between 1973 and 1978. But when the traditional centrally administered economy was restored, its typical parasitical symptoms reemerged. For Hungary, whose economy was more dependent on the international division of labor in the Eastern bloc than that of any other country, the sluggish, innovation-shy *dirigiste* steering system was more intolerable and more irreconcilable with the desire of an enlightened management to embark upon a rationalization. The reform current once again came into its own in 1978. It had powerful advocates, but no less powerful opponents.

New accents after the 1973–1978 pause in the reform

The efforts of the reformers to expand the competitive market intensified after

1978, no mean task considering that a centrally administered economy bars competition and thwarts any response to salubrious impulses coming from the world market through the state monopoly over foreign trade and currency. Everywhere, "the mediocre was preferred, . . . everywhere the weaker was supported," to quote Bela Czikos-Nagy, one of the architects of the economic reform. Translated into economic terms, this meant that even normative rules were based on average conditions.[1] Rezsö Nyers, politician and economist, spelled out the intrinsic weaknesses of a reform-resistant planned economy even more clearly: "For years we promoted average performance and failed to respect the performance of highly skilled people and to remunerate them accordingly. The number of capital investment projects delighted the planners; they would have liked to have undertaken even more, but almost no one was concerned about their efficiency.[2]

After 1978, the reformers placed even greater stress on the decentralization of economic powers. The production unit, which had been demoted to the status of a unit in a monolithic state syndicate, was to be endowed with the attributes of a responsible enterprise.

Henceforth, profit was to resume its traditional economic role, i.e, a production unit would have a free hand to use its profits as it deemed best. But this would only be possible if a firm could also decide on resource allocation. A firm would also bear full responsibility for losses, however, i.e., the state would no longer make up any discrepancies between costs and prices. Hence prices would have to cover costs if they were to be able to serve a parametric function. A comprehensive price reform was implemented. But the reformers wished first and foremost to make firms sensitive to international competition. These goals were in fact not exceptional in the Eastern bloc, although in no case had they ever been achieved. Hungary had undertaken effective measures to transform the traditional value categories from technical instruments of accounting into economic steering and allocation factors.

To avoid the failures of the other Eastern countries, Hungary's reformers had to proceed more resolutely; i.e., they had to prepare systematically, step by step, the way for the introduction of economic mechanisms. The greater the margin given to economic steering mechanisms, the narrower becomes the range of action of the state planners and the state executive. But political power does not so easily relinquish a sphere of influence once it has been acquired. The allocation of decision-making powers between the central authorities and the production unit, which will also define the areas where central directives applied and where economic mechanisms would be allowed to operate, is still going on in Hungary.

The reform spreads

Over the eighteen years of reform many bureaucratic barriers have been eliminated, and many sometimes very original organizational innovations and administrative methods have been introduced. For the orthodox party wing these had always been much too radical, while for the reform-inclined managers and intellectuals they were too half-hearted to achieve the desired improvement in economic performance. As the Eastern specialist of the *Financial Times*, David Buchan, wrote, "Hungary's bankers and innumerable economists would like to see more pressure on the accelerator. Others cry wolf while some trade unionists and local Party leaders look anxiously for the brake."[3]

But Buchan observes correctly that the forces of those for and of those against the reform seem to be about equally matched. However, the arguments of the reformers are becoming less and less convincing in view of the stagnation of the economy and the real incomes of the population even though some important measures have been implemented. The traditional steering methods, which promote growth at the cost of quality, have already been abandoned, but a solid efficiency-promoting system is as far away as ever. The production units have been largely unshackled from the central plan and the administrative hierarchy. The state plan, more indicative than binding, determines their place in the overall economy, their resources, their customers, cost expenditures, and their share in the state budget, but within these limits they can operate more independently than formerly. The entrepreneurial qualities of the industrial firm have acquired some weight. It no longer works to fulfill the plan with consumer needs taking a back seat but instead is attuned to the domestic or the foreign market. The needs of the population, and not the preferences of the central planners, have become paramount. Despite tremendous economic problems, Hungary's population is better supplied with food and industrial consumer goods than the other CMEA countries.

Decentralization of decision-making meant cutting the umbilical cord to the central planners and the central administrative executive, but it also meant a turning away from the centralization of economic powers in mammoth firms, i.e., a turning away from the gigantomania that has been the typical feature of every administered economy. The breaking up of the huge factories and trusts built up over the past several decades in fidelity to an alien model has been a central task of Hungary's economic policy since 1982. The iron and metal works, Csepel, which, though nationalized, retained the same structure of a multileveled production conglomerate as conceived by its earlier owner, Manfred Weisz, has been broken up into fifteen technically homogeneous production units. A trust which had centralized all the country's repair shops was also dismantled.

Developments, not only in Hungary but also in the West, have clearly demonstrated that middle-sized firms are more flexible and more adaptable than unwieldy large factories. The same view was expressed by the Hungarian Vice Prime Minister, Jozsef Marjai, in a talk with the *Financial Times* editor: "I should also like to see Hungarian companies stick less rigidly to their established profiles and show more courage and flexibility in branching out into other activities."[4]

The breaking up of the trusts and large firms placed 170 production units under central economic authorities and 122 under local executive authorities.

The decentralization of decision-making by shifting it to the micro-level also meant a major reduction in the administrative apparatus. Three economic ministries were merged after the reform; many medium-sized factories under central administration were dissolved, and the production units were freed from the stifling grip of the state bureaucracy, which throttled any free initiative coming from below. As one of the principal architects of the economic reform, Professor Rezsö Nyers, put it, "The interests of the state were submerged in a swollen apparatus of economic ministries and associations."

Direct links were established between production enterprises and the foreign market. The state monopoly over foreign trade and currency, regarded as an organic component of the steering system of a large autarky-oriented economy, was least of all suited for a small open country like Hungary, which procured 40 percent of its national income through foreign trade. Modernization of the antiquated foreign trade system was a central issue of the economic reform of 1968; 150 industrial and agricultural enterprises were authorized to establish direct links with foreign markets. But even where traditional foreign trade enterprises were responsible for foreign trade transactions, they would usually accept export goods on commission from a production unit and the profits acquired would then be divided between the production unit and the foreign trade enterprise. Thus enterprise earnings depended on the prices at which goods were sold, i.e., on the quality and competitiveness of the goods offered for exports. In the early 1970s, about 70 percent of hard currency exports and half of ruble exports were based on a common interest.[5] Foreign trade transactions handled directly by production enterprises amounted to no more than one-fifth of the total volume.[6]

To make it possible to incorporate foreign trade earnings into the accounts of production enterprises, the traditional practice of autonomous price formation was gradually abandoned: in 1980 the second price reform since 1968 was instituted with a view toward adapting the Hungarian price system to world prices. Henceforth, fuels and raw materials would be valued on the basis of import prices while finished goods would be valued on the basis of export prices on the world markets. With a price system adapted to the international price system, an economically based exchange rate became possible. In the 1970s, a conversion factor was still in use, but on October 1, 1981, a unified exchange course (for commercial and noncommercial payments) of 35 forints per U.S. dollar came into force. After several devaluations (11 percent in 1982), one dollar was equal to 44.66 forints in early October 1983. On May 30, 1986, $1 was equal to 46.35 forints and 1 transferable ruble was equal to 28 forints. Hungary has been a member of the Bretton Woods Institute since 1982.

The decree of the Ministry of Finance and the Minister of Foreign Trade (Law Bulletin 69, 1982) establishing "free trade areas" marked an important step forward in the shaping of the reformed steering system. Joint ventures with foreign firms are authorized to keep their books in freely convertible currencies; amounts in excess of that paid in basic capital can now be deposited in any domestic or foreign bank and deposits in convertible currency are freely disposable; Hungary's regulations on wages, prices and investments do not apply to free trade areas, nor do the regulations on state controls; and the profit tax (40 percent) is relatively small compared to tax rates in force elsewhere. The number of joint ventures has increased to 65, mainly with West German (30) and Austrian firms (13), although so far only twelve have had earnings. Hungary has one hundred joint ventures with Western firms abroad as well.

One of the most profitable joint ventures is the "Central European International Bank" (CEIB) established in November 1979. It is the only joint venture so far with over 49 percent foreign shares. The Hungarian National Bank owns 34 percent of the share capital, and is thus the largest and also the most influential shareholder; with the other 66 percent of the share capital is distributed among six shareholders (Banca Comercial Italiana, Bayerische Vereinsbank, Kreditanstalt-Bankverein, Long-Term Credit Bank of Japan Ltd., Société Générale, and Tayio Kobe Bank Ltd. of Japan), each of which has the same share, 11 percent, of the total capital. The CEIB was founded by Hungarian legislation; but bank transactions are not subject to Hungarian law. The bank is not part of the Hungarian banking system and is not subject to Hungarian regulations on foreign currency. The president, currently Leopold Henri Jeorger, Vice General Manager of Société Générale, is elected by the Western shareholders. The CEIB, which began its activities in January 1980 with a capital of 20 million dollars and a credit line of 15 million dollars, was the brainchild of the promoters of joint ventures with Western investors, but it also finances Hungary's foreign trade with the West.

The bank has already proved its adaptability with notable successes in the first two years: its profits were 2.6 million dollars in 1980 and 2.7 million dollars in 1981, but in 1982 it began to experience the same problems which had beset the CMEA and the developing countries, especially as it had no central bank to fall back upon. It began to restrict its activities to low risk regions, modified its development plans, stressed stability, profitability and liquidity, and developed a new concept of export financing: its assets increased by another 4.5 percent to 232 million dollars compared with the preceding year, while profits rose to 2.8 million dollars after taxes. Three million dollars had to be spent to finance uncollectable credits. Net proceeds, 1.3 percent of the total assets and 10 percent of the bank's own resources, were modest but still quite acceptable compared with other banks.

The reform of the unwieldy foreign trade system had a favorable influence on the development of Hungary's economic relations with the West. Steady contacts with other countries created a favorable climate for resuscitating the idea of reform. But the oil crisis caused greater damage to import-dependent Hungary than to the other countries of central and Eastern Europe. Faced with the alternatives of covering losses suffered as a result of the deterioration in the terms of trade by raising production prices or by financing them with state subsidies, the Party leadership chose the latter path, thereby assuming direct responsibility for the economy. The reform was interrupted in 1973 and not resumed again until 1978. In the meantime, however, an immense mountain of credit built up, placing a great strain on Hungary's economy and making the reform movement more difficult to sustain further.

The reform promotes agriculture

Although it is not easy to estimate the ultimate influence of the reform movement on Hungarian industry, it may be definitely said that it has left lasting traces in agriculture. Hungary's agriculture has unequivocally found a middle way between the large, innovation-shy, inefficient Soviet collectivized or nationalized units and the fragmented small units of Poland and Yugoslavia, which are just as inefficient. Collectivization did not eliminate the peasants as an independent social stratum, but it also did not place them under the state economy. The liberal agricultural policy enabled the co-op member to resume his peasant existence, and as a result Hungary's agriculture has been experiencing an uninterrupted boom.

Agricultural output increased by 42 percent between 1970 and 1980, compared with only 9 percent in the Soviet Union, 14 percent in Poland, 24 percent in the GDR, 19 percent in Czechoslovakia, 28 percent in Bulgaria, and 63 percent in Romania;[7] Hungary's agriculture produces 30 percent more than is consumed, and the excess, amounting to 80 billion forints, is exported, 59 billion forints (about 1.7 billion dollars) against convertible currencies.[8] Several large units have been authorized to establish direct ties with foreign clients.

Hungary ranks among the five most efficient world producers of corn and wheat; the corn yield, about 6 tons per hectare, is equal to the U.S. yield. The expansion of fodder grains has enabled Hungary's economy to develop a productive stock-raising sector.

Peasant incomes are on a par with the incomes of industrial workers; there is therefore no migration of the rural population into the cities. 46 percent of the total population live on the land, and 19 percent are directly employed in agriculture.

The reform freed the farm units from the tutelage of the central state authorities. What is produced is what the country needs or what can be exported. The peasant has a vested interest in proceeds because he has a share in profits, but he also bears responsibility for failure.

One of the most important achievements of the reform movement is the ''production systems'' established during the 1970s, which have become crucial sources of innovation in agriculture. This institution is an authentic Hungarian invention, although it draws on the experience of the Netherlands, Denmark and the United States. The aim is to optimize the proceeds from the production of every member unit. The 21 production systems which are currently operative in

Hungary's agriculture account for half of the cultivated area and 49 percent of livestock, 74 percent of the grain crop, and 81 percent of the maize crop. The members of the production systems achieve the highest grain yields (45 double centners per hectare of tilled land), 12 percent more milk, and 20 percent more meat than the national average.[9] Each production system specializes in specific crops. Usually they use the same technology and the best organizational methods for production.

The largest and most successful production system in Hungarian agriculture is the "Taurina" system, which specializes in cattle-raising. It unites 134 farm units, which possess one-fifth of Hungary's entire livestock holdings. Taurina employs 300 highly skilled agrarian experts, thirty of whom are scientists. Each unit, reports the system director, Dr. Tibor Merenyi, very quickly brings its yield level up to the Taurina average. The system covers its own costs and receives no state subsidies. Its sources of financing consist of member dues paid each year (75,000 forints entry fee) and payments for services. Taurina has its own laboratories, carries out its own research and experiments, organizes a machinery service, cooperates with the manufacturers of farm machinery, prescribes an appropriate fodder composition and the best methods for stock-raising, and conveys the latest scientific and technical information to its member units.

But Hungary's agriculture also owes its success to the activation of small plots of cooperative members and the mobilization of hundreds of thousands of leisure-time gardeners. Hungary's agriculture has 1,500 cooperatives with a useful cultivation area of 70.2 percent and 130 state farms with a share of 15.4 percent of the total area; 4.5 percent of the farm land area is in the possession of cooperative members as small private plots, and 6.4 percent in the possession of private farms. The rest is in the hands of leisure-time gardeners, who account for no small share considering that only 25 percent of the approximately 1.6 million private farms belong to the peasants.[10] The small units produce almost half of the total amount of pork, 40 percent of poultry, and a large portion of vegetables and fruits. The private small units owe their extremely high yields to cooperation with cooperatives which supply the necessary fodder and rent out farm machinery. The owners of small private plots have been given the choice of selling their farm products either to the cooperatives or on the free market.

The reform in Hungary's agriculture is also responsible for its multifaceted profile: the farm units were not transformed into agrarian industrial complexes, as Khrushchev had considered in the early 1960s. Like the Chinese communes, they manufacture a wide range of industrial goods which have also been marketed abroad.

The work methods of Hungarian agriculture are being carefully observed by the other Eastern countries but certainly not emulated. There is also good reason to doubt whether they could in fact be successful under the socioeconomic conditions of other countries. Exceptions are the Naduvar and Babolna methods for the cultivation of maize, which has been planted in 379 production units over an area of 870,000 hectares. This extremely productive cultivation method was introduced in the early 1970s. Poultry and hogs are also fed with maize. The technology comes mainly from the United States. Hungary's method for cultivating maize is being watched especially attentively by the Soviet Union, which suffers from a chronic shortage of fodder. While the Babolna factories harvested 6 tons per hectare, the most productive units in the Ukraine have never achieved more than 2.8 to 3.4 tons per hectare. Since 1978, the Babolna method has been tested in various parts of the Soviet Union. In July 1983 an agreement was signed with Hungary in accordance with which the Babolna farm combinate is to build a poultry farm in Soviet Azerbaidzhan; the experiences of this pilot project will be monitored between 1984 and 1987 by Hungarian experts. The Soviet Union will pay 27.4 million rubles (700 million forints) for the buildings, equipment, technology and laboratories.[11]

The Hungarian agricultural model also seems to have inspired Bulgarian agriculture. One million inhabitants of 8.9 million of the total population have private plots; they cultivate about 12 percent of the total area of the country and also provide 30 percent of the country's meat supply and 40 percent of its eggs.[12]

The rise of private initiative

Hungary's private entrepreneurs could refer to the reform years as a golden age. In no other planned economy has the small private enterprise received such a broad margin of maneuver for doing business than in Hungary. Only about 30 percent of housing, as great a proportion as in Great Britain, is still in state possession: in 1982 almost twice as many privately owned dwelling units were built than cooperative or state-financed dwellings. Five thousand private restaurants, which do all they can to emulate the Parisian or New York style, offer the growing circles of the newly rich, the ruling bureaucracy, and foreigners exquisite dishes and drinks which are not to be found in state restaurants. The world-famous French fashion firm Pierre Cardin has opened some boutiques in Budapest. Magyar Hirlap writes that the production and the material come from Hungary, but the style and the price from Paris. With an average salary of about 5,000 forints, a Hungarian state employee will certainly not be able to afford a coat costing 7,800 forints, a woman's dress costing 11,500 forints, or even a "cheap" tie costing 1,000 forints. Cardin did not open his boutiques for small earners. Not far from the super-elegant Cardin boutique are the domestic shops where the average wage-earner can obtain less elegant mass consumption goods at one-fourth of Cardin's price. Neckermann, which established a mail order house on Western lines in Budapest and dispatches exquisite gifts to the furthest parts of the capital city within two hours, cannot offer its services to the average Hungarian; they are too dear.

The reform, in fact, introduced an income differentiation and Hungary's reformers understand all too well that prosperity cannot be built either on the basis of equality or the basis of state initiative. Hungary's supply policy follows the principle that the effective demand of the "high-level wage earner" and the small wage earner should both be satisfied. Queues are unknown in Hungary. Private small firms are springing up like mushrooms: in 1975 there were 84,000 small craftsmen, but in 1983 there are already 115,000; in the last two years, more than 3,000 small merchants have begun businesses, including 170 fashion shops, and 6,000 manual workers are offering their services in haircutting salons, and tailoring and shoemaking shops. Since the liberalized decrees of 1982 came into force, 3,500 car owners have acquired a taxi license and have considerably alleviated the bottleneck in state transportation. In Budapest alone there are presently twelve marriage arrangement offices. Five hundred somewhat dilapidated castles are being renovated by private persons as in Austria and placed at the service of tourism, which has been flourishing for several years. Every week auctions take place where nationalized small firms and restaurants are leased to the highest bidder of small entrepreneurs. The private firms achieve a much greater turnover and a greater profit with far fewer employees, and this is also of benefit to the state. In the meantime, the state has permitted private firms to raise the number of employees from three to six and, if the family is large, even twelve.

There are also small enterprises in the GDR and Poland, but straightforward promotion of private initiative is found only in Hungary, where there is no intention of treating it as a foreign body in the state economy or of nipping it in the bud by burdensome taxes. Quite to the contrary, the state encourages private individuals to perform creatively and to strive for higher earnings. New incentives are constantly being tried. Translation teams have been founded, private persons direct sports stadiums and many other institutions which formerly had suffered considerable losses as state property.

One of the most recent are the "worker communities." Volunteer teams of workers are formed in state-owned factories who then undertake private activity after working hours or on Saturdays and Sundays. After finishing the work for their firm, the team remains to carry out special activities of various kinds. They have been successful because they use no capital and entail no risks, yet they always have sure customers for their products and services. There are already 28,000 workers who make use of this opportunity. In Budapest alone, there are 1,000 worker teams that have concluded such partnership agreements with their companies. They take on jobs in light industry and small activities in the machine industry which large plants cannot undertake because of their cumbersome organizational structure. They make use of industrial wastes and other materials which are of no use to their parent firm and fill gaps in needs which the central planning authorities would be unable to discover. The goods produced are usually sold to the parent firm or other customers.

These worker communities owe their success mainly to the close cooperation with their parent firms which allow them to use machinery, waste and other means of production and provide them with outlets for their products and services. Cooperation of the worker teams with state-owned factories has proven to be useful to both sides as has the close cooperation between private farms and their agrarian cooperatives.

Small firms and workers' collectives not only cover the gaps in supply that often arise domestically but have also been able to export a growing portion of their products. They export horseshoe nails to Irish horse-breeders, electronic cutting tools to Japan, and road maps and hiking maps to Austrian hikers. Hungary's planners report that the craft collectives not only have achieved a productivity twice that of large concerns but already account for 8 percent of total industrial exports.

The reform movement has been a major factor in the increased respect shown by the socialist state, which is fundamentally collectivist oriented, for the interests of the individual. Since mid-1983, Hungarians have been permitted to earn money abroad on the condition that the applicant show proof of a job offer from a foreign firm. Of course, it is not only the individual who benefits; the collective also gains from respecting the interests of the individual. A citizen returning from abroad will have been able to improve his professional skills and perform more valuably.

The average wage is relatively low in Hungary, and there has been no rise in real income for several years. But Hungarians are able to earn money in private enterprise and save money on favorable terms. Hungary has adapted Western methods of saving to its domestic needs more than the other Eastern countries and uses this money in these savings deposits to finance useful undertakings: state and municipal savings certificates are no longer an alien concept and within a short period these new forms of saving have grown even further.

The beginning took place in the state sector with the gas loan, issued in March 1983, by the State Development Bank together with the State Trust for Petroleum and Natural Gas for fifteen years at 11.5 percent interest. The intention was to transfer unused capital to enterprises urgently in need of it. This type of capital transfer is a novelty in the planned economies; hitherto a redistribution of capital was possible only via the state budget, through redistribution of profits or appropriation of surplus capital stock by the competent ministry. By decentralizing decision-making, Hungary's reformers have turned capital transfer into a matter between firms, requiring no intervention from the state or the competent economic ministry.

The reformers clearly did not expect that their proposed method for capital transfer would elicit such a lively response, and, accordingly, the first loan was issued in the modest sum of 200 million forints. But against all expectations, within a very short time it was oversubscribed and doubled in value. Bonds became the fashion in Hungary. When this bond, the first in the history of the Eastern countries, was issued, no one had thought that these securities, which had been intended merely for capital transfer between enterprises, might be acquired by the population. The interest it bore (11.5 percent) was set much too high in comparison with the interest rate (a maximum of 5 percent) on private savings accounts. The authorities were unwilling to offer such a high interest rate to private persons as well, but Hungary's bankers quickly realized that private money could be used more efficiently than hitherto for public purposes.

In mid-1983 the National Savings Bank (OTP) issued a municipal bond subscription to finance infrastructural projects, but only for the population, this too was very quickly oversubscribed. A few months later, a step forward was made toward unifying the capital market, which was still rather modest: the petroleum and natural gas bond issued in November 1983 was released for purchase by private persons as well. The interest rate was set as the average between the somewhat higher rate for enterprises and the somewhat lower rate for private persons, i.e., 7.5 percent for five-year bonds, and 9 percent for eight-year bonds. The average rate was however still much higher than the interest rate on private savings accounts. Bankers therefore looked for a means of promotion which would make earmarked loans attractive while maintaining the interest rate for private persons. The most recent municipal bond, therefore, entailed the commitment to ensure the subscriber the installation of a telephone within three years. The promise is certainly attractive, considering that the waiting period for a telephone can normally be as long as twenty years. Though such an incentive may seem somewhat extraordinary, it will not only promote savings, but will also help to eliminate a chronic bottleneck. Proof that Hungary's government is serious about expanding the telephone network is provided by the agreement concluded with Austria in November 1983, providing for a major expansion in the next three years.

The reform strengthened the people's confidence in the state considerably. Compared with 1982, savings increased by 18 billion forints to 194 billion forints (about 4.5 billion dollars). At a population of only 10.5 million, this is a very high per capita savings rate. Hungary is also the only country in Eastern Europe that permits foreigners to have foreign currency accounts. For short-term deposits the interest rate usually offered is one percent higher than in Central Europe.

The rise of private enterprise is an essential component of the economic reform, although by no means the most important. Its share in total production is not that large if one considers that 98 percent of the industrial plants are state-owned, and that this accounts for 96 percent of total output. Nevertheless, even this aspect of the reform has been harshly criticized by the counter-reformists. The incomes of the "private" entrepreneurs are the envy of many. The opponents to the reform see the private sector as a source of unjust enrichment and a temptation for skilled engineers and workers to leave state-owned enterprises to earn more money. One hundred fifty thousand people who left the large enterprises in the last few years now work in the service sector in small businesses. The critics of the reform see in this social layer, which is still quite small, the embryo of a class that will be alien to socialism. The workers' communities have been attacked especially harshly; it is feared that the utilization of machinery after work could lead to a fall in labor productivity in state-owned industry. But what is not taken into consideration is that the private entrepreneurs not only fill up gaps in the supply to the population but also are accepted by the large concerns as reliable suppliers and, moreover, also bring in hard currency.

A moratorium on the criticism of private enterprise has been called for one year at the behest of Janos Kadar. Its ultimate fate will undoubtedly depend on the development of other more important aspects of the economic reform.

The contradictions in Hungary's economic system have not diminished after eighteen years of reform

The economic reform introduced in Hungary in 1968 was not the consequence of a mass movement as in Poland in 1956 and 1980 or Czechoslovakia in 1968. Hungary's reform in 1968 was a pragmatic reform of the economic mechanism within an overall economic system left largely unchanged, and remains that fifteen years later. Most of the measures projected in 1968, and many others as well, have been implemented over the past eighteen years of reform. The effects of the reformed steering mechanisms are discernible in every sector of the economy, although Hungary's economic managers and economists are today more skeptical than they were initially. An essay by Marton Tardos, published in late 1982 in the weekly, *Heti Világgazdaság*, and the debate it set off cast new light on the progress of the reform and on the country's economic growth. Opinions vary, but the overall picture seems grim. Marton Tardos calls for proposals from many quarters since the "economic situation is serious and the tasks which must be resolved are extremely complicated." One of the most active participants in the discussion, Laszlo Antal, thinks that the situation is more serious than generally assumed and that any solution will demand sacrifices.[13]

Some of the participants in the discussion, such as Robert Hoch, adjudge the reform results on the basis of the country's economic development; hence, they attribute the economic successes of 1968–1973 to the salubrious effect of the new economic mechanism, and the economic recession, which set in subsequently, to the retreat from the original principles of reform. However, the connection is by no means beyond dispute: from 1968 to 1973, the economic boom was not confined to Hungary, while developments after 1973 were influenced by the effects of the oil crisis, just as elsewhere. Hungary, poor in energy and raw materials, suffered perhaps more than the other countries of East and southern Europe from the effects of inflation.

It is true that Hungary discarded the principles of economic reform after 1973: industrial enterprises were protected from the effects of the deteriorated terms of trade by state subsidies financed with Western credits. The industrial enterprises, shielded from the effects of developments worldwide, continued to function as if nothing had changed until, that is, the burden of debt became insupportable.

Nineteen seventy-eight saw a return to the basic principles of the 1968 reform in the hope that the shift of responsibility and of a number of decision-making powers to the micro-level would restore the lost equilibrium. Measures were undertaken, with some procrastination, which under the circumstances had become unavoidable: prices for fuels, raw materials, and mass consumption goods were raised drastically. Imports, especially from the West, were reduced and investment activity was damped. In 1980, the volume of investments was 25 percent lower than five years previously. But just as a recentralization of decision-making and a retreat from the reform in 1973 were able to postpone, but not avert, the deflationary economic policy that later became imperative, the revival of economic mechanisms could not shield against the effects of the deflationary policy introduced in 1978. Neither market nor planning mechanisms, and even less so a mixture of the two, were suited for this.

In the period between 1978 and 1983 the growth rate was no more than 1.5 percent annually compared with a 5.1 percent annual average for the thirty years between 1950 and 1980; the annual average growth of wages was no more than 0.7 percent between 1976 and 1980 compared with 3.3 percent in the period between 1971 and 1975.[14] In 1985 the distributed material product diminished in comparison with 1984 by 0.5 percent and the real income per capita rose by 1 percent. No one had expected miracles from the reform, but the reformers were bitterly disappointed over the plodding pace of adaptation of the nation's economy to changed conditions worldwide. It was claimed that productivity of Hungarian industries was 50 percent lower than in the industrial countries of the West. The erratic investment policy of earlier years, when the attempt was made to transform Hungary, an agricultural country, into a country of iron and steel, took its revenge in a period when worn-out capacities could no longer be replaced owing to lack of capital. Six of nine foundry furnaces in Hungary have a capacity between 300 and 600 cubic meters, but furnaces with a capacity of 1200 to 2000 square meters are considered optimal. The specific expenditure of coke per ton of iron is 38 percent higher in Hungary's foundries than elsewhere, and, moreover, the price of coke increased from 35 dollars in 1970 to 170 dollars in 1980.[15] The consumption of iron ore is also extraordinarily high and costly. Ores imported from the Soviet Union contain no more than 46 percent iron; usually, however, ores with an iron content of 50 percent to 60 percent are processed.

Current trends on the world markets are also extremely unfavorable to Hungary: although its volume of exports was higher than in the preceding year, in 1982 its foreign exchange earnings were 7.7 percent lower as a consequence of the terms of trade, which had deteriorated by 13 percent to 18 percent.[16] The surplus in trade in convertible currencies diminished from $608 million in 1984 to $114 million in 1985. However, when Janos Hoos blamed developments on the world market and international tensions for Hungary's difficult economic situation, he found no support among the majority in the discussion, who believed that it was not so much objective conditions that were responsible for stagnation of the economy and incomes, as the existing economic system, which, despite the modernized steering mechanisms, had basically remained unchanged. Robert Hoch expressed this view the most trenchantly of all: "We have never thought about how the future economic system should be shaped so as to be able to integrate the reformed steering mechanisms," he wrote. It was this lack of congruence between economic mechanisms, which in some areas were quite well developed, and the central power structures, which had remained almost untouched, that seemed to be at the root of current reform problems. Carrying his argument further, Hoch observed: "The reformed economic mechanisms will be worthless if the system overall remains unchanged." The discussants have had no answer to the key economic questions, namely: what is the place of the state enterprise in a planned economy, what criteria determine its performance, should profit be the only evaluative criterion, etc?

Some of the discussants, including Lukacs, Pirityi, and Osman, see the main cause of malaise, unrelieved by the half-hearted economic reform measures since 1968, to lie in the unclear relationship between the state economy and the state enterprises: "We have been attempting for fifteen years to steer Hungary's economy by using a symbiosis of plan and market. But we still do not know what we should do with enterprises that cannot make the grade in the face of modern production methods," they say. In a market economy, a declaration of bankruptcy is a normal consequence of mistakes and poor performance, but not in Hungary. At least 120,000 people are employed in unprofitable enterprises and no less than one-third of the products in the machine-building industry no longer meet present-day standards.

An effective mechanism is therefore required to enable capital to be transferred from unprofitable to profitable activities: the state has shown itself willing to meet this requirement of the reformers through the issuance of bonds, but the progress that has been made is slight compared to the restructuring actually required. The reformers demand a radical restructuring of the banking system with the establishment of commercial banks on the Western model.

Stagnation of real wages is considered a threat to social tranquility

What disturbs economists most is the stagnation or decline in the real incomes of the population. Laszlo Antal can scarcely imagine that the living standard of the Hungarian people could stay at the 1978 level until the mid-1980s. Otto Lukacs adds that real wages have hardly moved in the last few years and that some layers of the population have already begun to feel the freeze on wages and salaries. Peter Hankiss discusses the problem of equality and social justice in this context and concludes that the criteria of justice and utility by no means coincide, at least in periods of great social transformations. There are considerable differences in living standard among the different social layers in Hungary, but it has not been demonstrated, writes Hankiss, that the poorest are also those who perform poorly as well. He therefore suggests that the advantages and disadvantages of the reform measures be assessed in terms of the material interests of individual social layers. "Those who under the given conditions profit the most are those who desire the traditional steering system, the present status quo, or, at the very least only most, very modest changes," says Hankiss. Hankiss's opinion is reflected in the summary of the discussion. Material aid is recommended for those who have fallen into hard times materially at no fault of their own.

Creeping inflation, introduced by reclassifying existing products rather than by direct price rises, is also a matter of great concern. This practice raises profits or prevents losses without, however, giving better satisfaction to consumer demands. As another party to the debate, A. Pirityi, stresses, Hungary's inflation differs from the inflation in the market economies in that it does not produce an excess supply of goods and services but rather repudiates this possibility. However, a shortage in supply weakens the incentive potential of wages. The existing price-setting practices have also been severely criticized. Tibor Erdos declared his disappointment with the practice of "free" prices, one of the pillars of the reform, since in his opinion they have not fulfilled their function. Prices are set without state interference for 40 percent of foods and luxuries, 75 percent of chemical products, 65 percent of building materials, and 73 percent of services.[17] The president of the Central Price Office, Bela Csikos-Nagy, even said that "free" prices were a necessary precondition for dynamic growth in the manufacture of foods in large farms and, hence, for overcoming supply problems. But Erdos says that the practice of free price formation is often manipulated because there is no competition among sellers. He is especially disturbed with the often-abused practice of price subsidies. In his opinion, subsidy should be applied only in extreme cases. Although there is no free competition in Hungary's economy, the competent authorities of the Central Price Commission always raise prices when demand is greater than supply. Corresponding means are used to combat unjustified price rises. An intention to raise prices must be reported to the Price Commission with reasons given to justify such a measure. If the request seems unjustified, the Price Commission can postpone it for three to six months. An unjustifiable price rise results in transferring the concerned product to the category of official prices.

More plan or more market?

It is clear that previous incentive factors have been considerably weakened, but there seem to be no other factors to replace them. Laszlo Antal says: "Stable prices and stable jobs, universally accessible state services financed with state subsidies, and a rapid rise in consumption cannot continue to be guaranteed in the future." He can find no answer to the question of how people's creative initiative can continue to be motivated. An editorial in the weekly, *Heti Világgazdaság*, concluding the discussion announces that the rise in standard of living has come to a halt, that a large number of the employed will even experience a decline, and that what is attainable will not be satisfactory. There is a consensus in the evaluation of the economic situation and the effect of the half-hearted reform, but disagreement on the therapy required: whereas Marton Tardos pleads unambiguously for broadening the use of market mechanisms and proclaims the slogans, "market, demand, supply, competition, and commercial banks," his opponents demand that the market be held within acceptable limits. R. Hoch thinks that the oft-repeated view that a perceptible improvement in performance can be achieved by expanding market mechanisms is naive. In his opinion, primacy in economic policy belongs to planning. Economic mechanisms, economic administration, economic policy, and an institutionalized system that could integrate these steering instruments are an organically interrelated whole and no part of the system should grow more intensively than any other. Hoos has a similar opinion: "The way out of the difficult situation is to be sought not just in an increasing reliance on market mechanisms, but also in the perfecting of central planning and administration."

The farsighted discussants are convinced that the economic reform can be successful only if it is accompanied by a reform in the political regime. Mihaly Bihari, Department Head in the Ministry of Culture, shared these opinions in an interview with the American magazine *Forbes*.[18] "Many economic reforms, but no political reform, have been undertaken since 1957." He continues to say that "A pure economic reform cannot be successful" and that democratic socialism is a contradiction in terms in its practical application. In his opinion, you can have either "socialism or democracy but not both."[19]

The Party leadership has no intention of undoing what has already been achieved. The established state institutions are not subject to debate. Although Janos Kadar called the Hungarian Parliament one of the most fundamental institutions of the democratic regime of his country in an interview with the newspaper *Helsingen Sanomat*, during his state visit to Finland in October 1983, the Central Committee Secretary of the Hungarian Socialist Workers' Party, Mihaly Korom, justly calls to mind that the Parliament and the Councils have become retreats for retired Party officials who have done their service.[20]

Of course, the Party would like to make the Parliament more efficient. The new electoral system is said to go no further than to stipulate that two candidates must be nominated for every seat in Parliament. This novelty, which has been in force in Poland for twenty-five years, causes the ruling party no problems whatsoever in the exercising its leading role in this real socialist state.

Not only does the Parliament have no influence on events, the Party always makes sure it has a majority in the government. Reszö Nyers, member of the Central Committee and one of the major architects of the 1968 economic reform, had the following to say in his speech to the 22nd Congress of Hungarian Economists in June 1983: "The concept of an 'administrative government' must be replaced by a concept which also implies political activities."[21] A one-party regime permits no ideological pluralism. The chief ideologue, György Aczel, does not deny symptoms of crisis in some of the socialist countries (in the capitalist system he sees "a new deep and total structural crisis") but is unable to imagine a socialist society without a leading ideology.[22] The monopoly on ideology is indispensable for Aczel even if he does concede that there is no such thing as perfect and complete Marxism. Further, the sole and leading party will permit no pluralism in the economy.

Limits of the reform

Hungary's reform is the most radical in the history of the Eastern bloc. It loosened the organizational structures of the centrally administered economy more, and gave more free play to traditional economic mechanisms than any attempts heretofore in the Eastern countries. Hungary's reform set the standard for liberal reform in the economic system in the East. More social differentiation rather than more equality, more private initiative rather than more nationalization; and more decision-making powers to production units and more free play for traditional market mechanisms rather than more planning and administration are the preconditions it laid down for greater efficiency.

But the reformers are not satisfied with the way the modernization process has gone, not only because the economy and incomes are stagnating (Hungary is no exception to the way things have been going across the world) but because the reformed steering mechanisms have been unable to bring about the restructuring of the economic system. The reformers feel that the country's economic system has reached a crossroads which, as Jozsef Veress put it, has reduced the options to but two of the three existing possibilities, either a return to a centralized steering system, standing pat on what has been achieved so far, or a fundamental reform in economic policy, with the second totally ruled out. If the decision were to remain at the status quo, this would inevitably entail a swift return to the status quo ante, says Veress.

But with the leading party's monopoly on power, decentralization of economic policy can go no further without jeopardizing that monopoly. A monopoly on power may have been institutionalized by the rules of a one-party regime, but the mechanisms introduced by the reform certainly do not require it. The reformers stress that the reforms are very often thwarted by counter-measures. There is powerful opposition in the ruling party against the reform. The Party leadership does not wish to turn back the clock on the reform movement, but it is not particularly keen on going forward either.

Faced with the alternative of allowing the economic reform to escalate into a reform in economic policy, the country's political leadership will certainly not dare to violate the geopolitical constraints. The limits of liberalization of the economic system have been preprogrammed into the real socialist system.

Notes

1. Bela Csikos-Nagy, "Die ungarische Wirtschaftspolitik," *Europäische Rundschau*, 80/3, p. 54.

2. Rezsö Nyers, Interview in the newspaper *Trybuna Ludu* (Warsaw), 1 August 1983. 1983.

3. *Financial Times*, 10 May 1983.

4. David Buchan, "Taking steps to improve the quality of life," *Financial Times*, 10 May 5 1983; *Trybuna Ludu* interview, p. 8.

5. Jozsef Bognar, introduction to *Handbuch der ungarischen Aussenwirtschaft*, Budapest, 1972, p. 17.

6. David Buchan, "Flexible rules for trading," *Financial Times*, 10 May 1983.

7. K. E. Wädekin, "Sonderbare Systemveränderungen," *Neue Zürcher Zeitung*, 26 August 1983.

8. Leslie Colitt, "Private plot farmers prove their worth," *Financial Times*, 10 May 1983.

9. C. A. Dzewanowski, "Ungarn—Das Geheimnis eines Agrarsystems," *Trybuna Ludu*, 28 September 1983.

10. Colitt, op. cit.

11. *Nepszabadsag*, 30 July 1983.

12. "Bulgaria: Small is beautiful," *The Economist*, May 1983.

13. The description of the discussion is based on the report in the Polish Economic Newspaper *Zycie gospodarcze*, 13 February 1983.

14. Bela Csikos-Nagy, "Die ungarische Wirtschaftspolitik," *Europäische Rundschau*, 1980/3.

15. *Nepszabadsag*, 29 January 1983.

16. Ibid.

17. *Trybuna Ludu*, 16 November 1983.

18. 4 July 1983.

19. Ibid.

20. "Hungary," *The Economist*, 1 October 1983.

21. *Muszaki Elet*, 16 June 1983.

22. György Aczel, "Für eine aktivere ideologische Tätigkeit," *Nepszabadsag*, 15 January 1983.

7. Economic problems as a symptom of dysfunctions in both systems

A thorough analysis shows clearly that it is not only an economic crisis—the inability of the market economies steered by the traditional invisible hand, or of the centrally steered planned economies, to adapt to the extremely complicated conditions of the national and international market and the requirements of the new stage of industrialization—that is at issue, but that the growing economic problems are a consequence of the ever-growing inadequacies of the social system. Incentives to improve performance, to improve the ability of economic management to serve society, to encourage the definition of goals and the finding of solutions to the ever-growing conflicts, have diminished in both economic systems. In both East and West, the gap between intellectual input and reality is steadily growing wider. The influence of the great religions and secular ideologies on how people behave and on their performance is declining precipitously.

The organic link between the ethos and the creative deed has been broken. The intellectual revolution that has always preceded any social change has not taken place. There is no infallible guide to point the way out of the darkness. Faced with the dreaded arms race and the prospect of total destruction, as well as growing pollution of the environment, the uneasy citizen in both East and West asks "Quo vadis, domine?" and receives no answer.

The Reformation, the Enlightenment, and the French encyclopedists paved the way for the transition from feudalism to capitalism and to the great French Revolution of 1789; the German philosophers of the first half of the nineteenth century paved the way to the "Spring of Nations" of 1848. The minds of men, freed from the shackles of the Middle Ages, prepared the way for the transition from absolute to enlightened monarchies and to a parliamentary democracy.

In the seventeenth century, Descartes, Pascal, Leibniz, and Newton set forth the principles and methods of the exact sciences, while the philosophers of the Enlightenment posed a question which Voltaire formulated quite cogently: "Why should we not attempt to employ rational thinking in the science of government?" The reinterpretation of the course of world history had begun: henceforth, the rational and comprehensible deeds of men would replace the mystical powers of providence. The British historian, Arnold Toynbee, writes: "The emergence of lay ideas gave the modern epoch one of its most important meanings . . . Reason became a revolutionary principle for philosophers and economists . . . ; the anti-Christ aspirations that had accompanied the evolution of individualism since the days of humanism contributed to making man the measure and lord of all things.''[1] The eighteenth century philosophers still accepted the existing world order; they wanted to enlighten monarchy, not to abolish it. For them it was no longer a divine institution, although it was still an irreplaceable one provided it was enlightened by reason. ''Reason is to philosophers what grace is to Christians,'' wrote Diderot. For rationalist thought, service to the state, rather than service to the king, was paramount.

Each of the great minds of the Enlightenment would have liked to rest his reformed monarchy on another social layer; however, the rational idea of the influence of a growing consciousness on the course of human history was alien to all of them. In his famed work *Esprit des lois*, written in 1748, Montesquieu based his liberal monarchy on the aristocracy and gave its citizens a guarantee that they had nothing to fear as long as they observed the law; but citizens must also have the right to express their opinion on all important matters without having the state prescribe what they should think. Voltaire (1694–1778) desired that ''great minds'' should have a powerful influence on political life but did not want to include the ''dangerously wavering masses in political life.'' Jean-Jacques Rousseau (1712–1788) regarded himself as a thorough democrat. In his *Contrat sociale* (1782) he developed a theory of civil liberty and popular sovereignty by which he meant that if the people obeyed the state, they actually were only obeying themselves. But even Rousseau wanted to restrict democratic principles to the bourgeoisie; in his *Lettres de la montagne*, he described the ''baser people'' as a ''crude and stupid popular mass and the cause of all misfortune.''

But the following observation of Jacques Adelbert, historian of the eighteenth century Revolution, is very pertinent to the ideas of the great minds of the Enlightenment and the encyclopedists, who published their great work—*Encyclopedie et dictionnaire raisonné des sciences, des arts et des metiers*—under the direction of Diderot between 1751 and 1772:[2] ''The eighteenth century was without a doubt revolutionary in the domain of ideas, but it was much clearer about what it wanted to destroy than what it wanted to put in its place.'' But this observation applies just as fully to the legacy of the French and German philosophy of the eighteenth century and the first half of the nineteenth century, namely, Marxism. The minds of the Enlightenment and of Marxism began two of the great revolutions of modern times without knowing what to put in the place of what they had overthrown.

The mentality of nations is just as responsible for mass actions as the development of the productive forces

The forces of production, caught up in a veritable revolution and the changing class structure, were, of course, crucial to the progressive revolution in human civilization. But social and political developments in different countries have also been influenced by tradition and by the popular mind, so misunderstood by Marxism. The population of Europe increased from 118 million people to 187 million people in the course of the eighteenth century, with youth making up the majority, especially in France. On the eve of the great French Revolution of 1789, three-fourths of all Frenchmen were less than forty years old.[3] The reason for the rapid demographic growth, which even at that time had led a number of intellectuals such as Malthus to conclude that the earth was not capable of feeding its growing population, was first and foremost the progress in agriculture and the considerable improvements in nutrition. Industry as well, especially in Great Britain, showed a radical progress. The enclosures, which expelled the smaller landowners and transformed large cultivated areas into pastureland for sheep, freed cheap labor and produced cheap wool for the dynamically expanding textile factories throughout the country. Aided financially and technically by Boulton, a manufacturer, James Watt invented the first steam engine in Birmingham. Great Britain became the fortress of capitalism, providing Marx with so much material for his monumental work *Das Kapital*.

But the agrarian and industrial revolution spread extremely unevenly. It extended into only a few areas of Great Britain and to an even lesser extent the countries of the Atlantic coast such as France. Central and Eastern Europe remained remote from these developments; there the feudal economy and the hegemony of the aristocracy over the hidebound peasants remained intact. Even in the United States, in 1776, about 90 percent of the total population were employed in agriculture, forestry or the fishing industry. Nevertheless, events in America served as a model for France, which by that time was already quite far along both socially and politically.

Every revolution has its Thermidor

It is a peculiar fact of history that it was economically backward France and not Great Britain, already quite advanced, that became the breeding ground of the revolutionary movement in the second half of the eighteenth century; this should have given Marx pause as he was developing his philosophy, not to mention his epigones who surely were unable to explain why economically and politically backward semifeudal Russia and not progressive Western Europe became the breeding grounds of the "proletarian" revolution in the twentieth century. Developments in France and Great Britain in the last two decades of the eighteenth century demonstrate just as clearly how fateful the underestimation of the popular mind can be in attempts to interpret the driving forces of human history. It was not so much the level of economic development as the different psychologies of the British and the French that was decisive for the social momentum of these nations. As the historian, Jacques Aldeberg, writes, at the time, France was more open to theories—it was here that the physiocrats developed their ideas of economic freedom—in contrast to the pragmatic turn of events in Great Britain which was then just on the verge of effecting a thorough restructuring of agriculture and industry. These developments also showed that a revolution is not an inevitable consequence of sharpening contradictions in the distribution of the national product, but in fact takes place more readily where suppression becomes more intolerable and the gap between the rulers and the ruled more unbridgeable. Repression in France at the end of the eighteenth century, as in Russia in the early twentieth century, was fiercer than anywhere else in Europe, and the revolutionary leaders were also more primed to battle; and it was these factors that gave the revolutionary movement its decisive turn. The French Revolution of 1789 and the Russian Revolution of 1917 also showed clearly that social transformations can take a course totally different from that originally intended, quite independently of the situation at the outset or the political program of the revolutionary leaders. Every revolution has its Thermidor.

The evolutionary development of economics and politics has been more beneficial than revolution

Developments in the eighteenth and twentieth centuries yield valuable clues regarding the solution of social conflicts. France, more prepared intellectually than industrially for a radical transformation of traditional social structures, embarked upon a clearly revolutionary path. Great Britain, more developed socially and economically, instituted and carried through intensive reforms, without venturing into revolutionary extravagance. Oliver Cromwell's revolution, the genuine English Reformation, was the last in Great Britain's history and the country was "beside itself with joy" as Michael Freund, Cromwell's biographer writes, when the old monarchy was restored. But Cromwell had not altered the country's social order; this was radically restructured later by evolutionary developments in the eighteenth and nineteenth centuries. The British grand bourgeoisie invested more and more of its capital in the country and the landed nobility was unafraid to embark upon enterprising ventures traditionally regarded as bourgeois. The paths of the nobility and the grand bourgeoisie converged. Wealth rather than birth determined social status and the distinction between rich and poor rather than between nobility and bourgeoisie shaped Great Britain's social landscape. Class structure and power relations adapted progressively to the evolution of the productive forces without major turbulence, which also favorably influenced the dynamic development of the society and its economy.

The evolution in France was totally different: the gap between the privileged nobility and the rising bourgeoisie was as unbridgeable as that between the possessing social classes and the *sans culottes*. The nobility had control of the most important political, military and intellectual functions; the bourgeoisie controlled the money and exercised a decisive influence on industry, which was developing rapidly in the cities; the peasants were still deeply immersed in feudal structures, while the workers were organized in guilds. France's absolute monarchy was hardly willing to give up its unlimited dominion. No compromise was in the making, and a wave of anarchy and violence spread over the land.

The course of the French Revolution of 1789, and later, that of the 1917 October Revolution, shows unequivocally how not only the psychology of a nation, underestimated by Marxism, but also the psychology of the revolutionary leaders can be crucial for the success or failure of a revolution. For without the small but violent group of Jacobins headed by Robespierre, Danton, and St. Just, the French Revolution would have been impossible, just as the Russian October Revolution would certainly not have attained the same dimensions without the Bolsheviks, Lenin, Trotsky, Stalin and a few others. Further, neither the French nor the Russian Thermidors would have taken the course they did, contrary to the very spirit of the revolution, without the iron wills of Napoleon and Stalin.

"A violent revolution first falls into the hands of narrow-minded fanatics and tyrannical hypocrites," wrote Joseph Conrad in *Under Western Eyes*. "Afterwards comes the turn of all the pretentious intellectual failures of the time." [4] And Franz Kafka observed, "The further a flood spreads, the more turbid and pestilent becomes the water; the revolution dissipates, and the mud of a new bureaucracy remains." These statements retain their validity independent of time and place.

No revolutionary movement in the modern history of Europe has been able to "maintain order in the midst of change" to use Joseph Schumpeter's phrase. The costs of revolutions in terms of human life and economic loss have become prohibitively high and the political and social results increasingly more problematic, and not only the French and Russian revolutions but also the mass movements in Eastern Europe in the last decades are cases in point.

The changes introduced by the nobility in the late 1870s in France, so weighty in their consequences, had the rather limited objective of allowing the king to reign but not to rule. But events soon got out of control. Leadership was assumed by the bourgeoisie, which inadvertently found itself relying more and more on the *sans culottes* of Paris and on the peasants, until finally in 1791 it fell to the dictatorship of the Jacobins. Napoleon's *coup d'état* on the 18th Brumaire, November 9, 1799, restored the monarchy after years of mass terror, the beheading of the king, and the destruction of wealth. After victories and defeats costing hundreds of thousands of human lives, France finally achieved the 1814 charter, on the British model which had evolved over the course of time through a series of permanent adaptations of the superstructure to the radical transformations taking place in the forces of production without placing the social order at risk. The Russian Revolution of 1917 was also denied "order in change." Once again, it seemed that the mass movement, once set in motion, would bring the country a social and political system appropriate to its level of development. The February 1917 revolution, led by the enlightened nobility, the bourgeoisie, and the intellectuals, and supported by the broad popular masses, enabled the most backward regime of Europe to be overthrown and a system of government, quite advanced for that time, to be established.

Who could have suspected that this representative democracy, which was achieved much too belatedly in Tsarist Russia (although it had existed for decades already in the other countries of Europe and would continue to exist for decades more), would function for no more than a half a year, and moreover that this regime, legitimated by the course of history and in step with the march of civilization, would be overthrown by a party that defined itself as Marxist, i.e., by an organization of professional revolutionaries so devoutly wished by Lenin, that would "lift Russia out of the swamp" as he put it? How indeed should this arbitrary act of conspirators fit in with Marxist theory, which holds that the determining influence on the course of human history is exercised by the forces of production, when it was after all their intention to overthrow a regime that met the country's needs and to begin a "proletarian revolution" in a country in which the peasants made up as much of the total population as farmers did in the United States in 1776? It is not surprising that this heroic and voluntaristic deed of the Russian Jacobins should end in a situation as chaotic as that existing in France at the end of the eighteenth century. It was no more than logical that the dictatorship of the proletariat should degenerate into a dictatorship over the proletariat, that the "expropriation of the expropriators" should be followed by the expropriation of the direct producers by the state, and that after the brief experiments with war communism (which saw labor productivity decline to a fourth of its former level) and with the mixed economy (NEP), a terrorist regime and a total nationalization of social life in Stalinist real socialism should necessarily ensue.

Productivity is no higher but there is less freedom

A comparison of statistics in post-Revolutionary Russia with those in other countries of the world raises the same question as a comparison of France with Great Britain after the 1789 French Revolution, i.e., the perennial question of revolution versus evolution. No one can say with certainty that the history of Russia would have taken a turn for the better or for the worse after the February revolution if the October Revolution of 1917 had not occurred. But statistics show that the per capita national product of the Soviet Union is on a par with that of underdeveloped countries of Europe such as Greece or Ireland and that the dream of overtaking the United States has been forgotten: the U.S. per capita national income in 1980 (11,360 dollars) is still two and a half times higher than in the Soviet Union (4,550 dollars). Further, while the Soviet Union has been unable to surpass the level of the economically underdeveloped countries of Europe, the economies of the industrial countries of Eastern Europe, such as the GDR and Czechoslovakia, show a considerable decline compared with those economies with which they were on a par before World War II. Whatever one's final judgment of the steering system in the Eastern countries, it seems certain that a centrally administered economy fits the needs of a developing country more than those of a modern industrial society. But economic growth is not the most important criterion in evaluating the path of progress chosen; that a profit-oriented market economy is more successful than an administered economy is beyond question. But it has also been shown that a profit-oriented market economy is able to give workers a greater share in the national product than a real socialistic planned economy. Nowhere does the burden of economic progress weigh so heavily on working people and nowhere is meeting the needs of the population so clearly subordinated to other goals as in the countries of really existing socialism.

But the purpose of the Revolution was not only to raise the living standard, but also to free working people from alienation, to implement the eternal ideals of liberty, equality, and fraternity. Yet here as well the countries of the East are far behind the traditional democracies of the West. The voice of the Soviet people swells in the defense of human rights—but only where there are already sufficient native defenders, and not in the Soviet Union. Many Russian writers and artists found themselves in exile or in Siberia, even before the Revolution. Certainly no one could have imagined that, after so many had been murdered, suppressed, and persecuted, so many Russian writers would still be found in exile today. East German writers too are often given the choice of writing obediently within the system or emigrating to West Germany, and a similar fate is met by prominent artists and writers of other countries of Eastern Europe.

As Churchill once put it, democracy is surely the worst form of government with the exception of all the others. And just as surely it may be said that pluralism benefits organized social groups more than individuals and that the members of democratically elected parliaments very seldom represent, and then often not very well, the interests of the voters. It is no surprise then that the disillusionment of those who vote with their feet is growing perceptibly: the most successful victors in the most recent elections, Ronald Reagan and Margaret Thatcher, won no more than 29.7 percent and 32 percent of the electorate of their respective countries. But the 99.9 percent votes for unknown personages—the traditional election result in the unanimous elections to the parliaments of the East—are clear enough evidence of the reduction of *Homo sapiens* to a mute ballot-wielder who, in the words of the Italian sociologist Gaetano Mosca (1858–1941), "is determined to elect the popular representatives that have already been elected."[5]

From utopia to a science—a long but uncertain path

The history of ideas is not always logically consistent: intellectual continuity is often broken, and the internal coherence of even far-sighted theories often leaves gaping lacunae. The coherence of Marxist theory fell victim to its messianic vision. Marx wanted not only to explain human history but also to change it, unlike Hegel, who formulated his historical determinism in the maxim: "All that is is rational, and all that is rational is." But Marx wished to abolish what existed, not to justify it. His aim was to be able to predict "the fate of mankind from the entrails of the economy." Since he was convinced that he had demonstrated the injustice of the capitalist mode of production and distribution, he passionately worked for the overthrow of the traditional society and the establishment of a classless society which, in his view, had to be the product of a struggle as necessary as a law of nature.

But Marxism is not only a contribution to political economy, a furtherance, at times brilliant, of Smith's and Ricardo's theories of value and surplus value, a prediction of a falling rate of profit and an unavoidable absolute and relative immiseration of the proletariat, etc., and an impressive contribution to Hegel's and Feuerbach's philosophy on the driving forces of world history; it also contains a vision of a future socialist society free of alienation and suppression. One of Marx's innumerable biographers writes: "No German of modern times has had a greater effect on the world than Karl Marx. Through his works the German intellect almost dominated the world for a whole historical period . . . The Bolshevik Revolution, the genesis and rise of the Soviet state—events of world historical significance almost beyond measure—took place in his name. . . ."[6] But sociologists were not inactive before or after Marx. Great thinkers and intellectual pioneers such as Smith and Ricardo, Max Weber and Keynes, Hegel and Feuerbach, Jaspers and Adorno, have left their telling marks on economic theory, historiography, and philosophy. Minds disagree on the scientific value of Marx's theory. Usually Marx's work is very highly esteemed, but no one has a monopoly on absolute truth and perspicuity, provided theory is not lifted to the rank of a taboo and a dogma. No one has understood this danger better than the Marxists themselves. In a speech on the occasion of the "Year of the Heroic Partisans," Fidel Castro said on January 12, 1968, "Nothing is more anti-Marxist than dogma, nothing more anti-Marxist than an ossification of ideas." But, nevertheless, no theory either before or after it has become so dogmatized and tabooed as Marxism itself.

But even Marx, always self-assured and egocentric, the "godless god unto himself," as Heinrich Heine called him, understood this danger when he uttered his astute *bon mot*: "As for me, I'm not a Marxist." The fact remains, however, that it was not his *Kapital* and other innumerable works which brought him mass recognition—workers don't read them. Nor does Marx owe much to his activity as a working class leader. He came from a prosperous bourgeois family and led a thoroughly bourgeois life, although usually with the aid of support and inheritances. He knew the proletariat from descriptions and was interested not in the suffering proletariat, but a proletariat that he had selected to be the executor of history's death sentence, as he saw it, on a deeply hated capitalism, a capitalism which in its period of primitive accumulation had to suffer the ill repute of an alienating social order, "covered with blood and filth," in order to fulfill its role. The great workers' movement of the nineteenth century, Chartism, arose before Marx; the movement in which he participated in 1862 lasted only eight years. It dissolved because of lack of followers and because of disputes between its leaders, Marx and Bakunin. The Gotha Program of the German Social Democracy of 1875, in which he had no hand, was criticized by him for its illusions about the "national state" and its exaggeration of the role of the proletariat in Germany, which at that time was populated mainly by peasants.

Marx owes his renown and worldwide recognition to the missionary component of his thought, his heralding of a classless society, in which liberty, equality and fraternity and many other virtues so coveted by a tormented mankind would reign. But Marx was not the first great thinker who had dreamed of a fabulous future for mankind. The great religions of this world and the great utopian world reformers had also dreamed of equality and fraternity: in 1516, Sir Thomas More (1480–1535), who dreamed of an ideal egalitarian society in his famed work, *Utopia*, in which collective property and communist production relationships would reign, which used "gold for chamber pots" and despised war as something bestial; Charles Fourier (1770–1837), who not only bitterly assailed parasitism in commerce and anarchy as the cause of the economic crisis, but also proposed an ideal utopian social system in which there would be no constraint, men would realize their good passions, and live in concord with their passions in absolute harmony with others; and Robert Owen (1771–1858), who was not only the author of many works in which he attempted to link socialist ideas with the then nascent labor movement, but also conceived of a communist society without authority and alienation and without private property and class conflicts, in which equality and social justice would reign.

But none of the greatest utopians had presented his vision of an ideal society of the future as a scientifically based world theory. Robert Owen had to accept the failure of his social experiment carried out in his own textile factories. Thomas More—who certainly did not learn the gallows-shadowed history of his country by reading Shakespeare's royal plays, but experienced it firsthand—doubted whether a "wise man" could be a counsel to the king since "wisdom" is inaccessible to the world's mighty because "war and profits" were their concern, and they tolerated only those who gave them their applause. Henry VIII had condemned his Lord Chancellor to death, to disembowelment, the burning of his entrails, and the exhibition of his quartered body on the four gates to the old city and his head on London Bridge, but then allowed him to die peacefully on the gallows, not because of his harmless *Utopia* but because of his resistance to the king, who had appointed himself "the supreme leader of the English Church under God."

Marx was the great thinker of modern times who attempted to scientifically ground his vision of a just future society; he firmly believed that he had discovered the path into a happy future and that he understood how to address those social forces which would bring about the overthrow of a dying system and would erect a classless society free of alienation to protect itself from ruin, otherwise inevitable.

Marx achieved worldwide recognition because he and his epigones were able to persuade underprivileged social classes that a social order worth fighting for need not be a utopia as the dream of a just society had been reformulated in a scientifically grounded theory, and that this idea could now be carried through with the necessity of a natural law. Thus did Marx rank his socialism, as a scientifically grounded antithesis, among the necessary phases of world history along with antiquity, feudalism, and capitalism.

German philosophy and the proletariat, the head and the heart of the liberation of mankind from alienation and repression, were to lead man into a glowing future. The intellectual and material weapons of inevitable revolution, which was to be the last in human history, were at hand. The path from utopian imagination to a real society of free men seemed open.

Today we are a few experiences richer and a few illusions poorer: the Marxist method shows better than any other that Marx's analysis of capitalism with minor qualifications can be applied only to the early capitalism of the first half of the nineteenth century and that late capitalism, with all its contradictions and flaws, offers a higher standard of living, a more moderate exploitation of the workers, and, above all, a more humane social life in democracy than does real socialism, a system that defines itself as Marxist. Further, the alternative socialist society, which has existed for almost seven decades now, has demonstrated graphically that the distance between a utopia raised to the status of a science and reality is great indeed. A third human generation has now experienced this socialism, and Horace's statement is still valid: "Our fathers, baser than our grandfathers, engendered us and we are more miserable than they were and we will bring progeny into the world who are more degenerate than ourselves" (*Ode* 3.6).

From a utopia replete with promises
to the grim realities of daily life

No lay ideology has had a stronger influence on the spirit and course of world history than Marxism. No ideology has understood better how to activate such destructive powers and vital forces and develop a vision of the promised land than Marx and his theory. Marxism is still an official state ideology. A third of the world's inhabitants and ninety communist parties throughout the globe are pursuing their militant mission under its red banner yet today. But it is only nostalgic old Communists who still believe in the fine-sounding utopia. The bureaucratic elites of Western Communist parties have only one relevant argument capable of retaining a hold on their disillusioned members, namely, the increasingly more serious flaws in the traditional system and the reassuring averral that Marxism was meant for the West and not for the economically and socially backward East and that it is the universally coveted vision and not the real practice encountered in the East that the future holds in store.[7]

The ideological crisis is therefore first and foremost a crisis of Marxism as a state ideology and antithesis to the traditional social system. It is hardly able to stimulate any creative activity where it has degenerated from a utopia promising bliss to a state religion, and it is even less capable of initiating changes where the situation has developed in a diametrically opposite direction to what the biblical interpreters of Marxism had imagined.

Sartre's statement that "Marxism thus remains the philosophy of our times" is being increasingly questioned, and indeed toward the end of his life he himself came to reject the practice of real socialism and even the more recent Eurocommunist interpretation just as categorically as earlier he had welcomed it. The late Lucio Lombardo Radice, theoretician and leader of Italy's Communist party, did not attempt to conceal his indignation when he wrote: "In the past phase Marxism emanated a true political, cultural, philosophical, and pedagogical *Sturm und Drang* movement. But in the authoritarian centralist phase of real socialism, the Marxist-Leninist doctrine has become a genuine 'state religion.'"[8]

The intellectual elite of France, at one time the fire and the flame of the Communist movement, writers such as André Malraux, Romain Rolland, Henri Barbusse, and Albert Camus, the world-famous painter, Pablo Picasso, the Nobel Prize laureate Joliot-Curie, the film director, Renoir, etc., had once waxed enthusiastic about communism, but later turned their backs on the French Communist Party. As the internationally esteemed Marxist interpreter, Henri Lefevre, observed contemptuously of the zealots of the French Communist Party, "Now the only Party members left are those who honestly and hedonistically abandon their intelligence."

Marx's epigones have changed a great part of this world, but they have not changed the fundamental principles of his theory. Nor were any changes necessary. The utopian components, the promise of an ideal and unrealizable social order, have become a dogma ossified into a state religion to be believed or not, just like other fantastic promises of this world, but with one difference—those who are still believers dream of a paradise on earth and not in heaven.

Real socialism vs. democratic socialism

Far from enjoying an uninterrupted progress, the socialist movement has suffered splits and setbacks that have led to the division of the world into two antagonistic systems. The first international workers' association, founded by Marx and Engels in 1864, was officially dissolved in 1876 (although it had already ceased its activities by 1872) owing to disparity of views among the leadership and its relatively tiny membership.

The Second Socialist International, founded in 1889, functioned for only fourteen years as a unified movement. Lenin's dissent in 1903 split first the Socialist Labor Party of Russia, then the world, into two world systems in 1917 and two years later the movement split into the communist and socialist parties. It would be a futile undertaking to endeavor to determine which, the Second or the Third International, represented the true legacy of Marxist theory. Whether Lenin or Martov, Kautsky, Hilferding, and Consortes were the true epigones of the great teacher, the fact is that it was Lenin who applied the epithet renegade to Karl Kautsky, then leader of the Socialist International.[9] But it is an undeniable fact that Marx projected the overthrow of capitalism through the use of force and had spoken of a political period of transition in which the state had of necessity to be a "revolutionary dictatorship of the proletariat."[10]

In this sense, Lenin was the authentic executor of the Marxist legacy, notwithstanding the fact that the dictatorship of professional revolutionaries with Lenin at its head was established not only over the Russian proletariat, small and backward as it was, as Kautsky had claimed, but over the 160 million inhabitants of Great Russia. Lenin's true successor was Stalin, whose character, of all the Bolshevik leadership, was perfectly tailored to the task of giving final form to the inevitable Russian Thermidor and replacing the dictatorship of the collective leadership with his own one-man dictatorship. In the recent dispute of Serbian theoreticians, Slobodan Inic was certainly right when he said that the quadrumvirate (Marx, Engels, Lenin, and Stalin) symbolized the intellectual continuum of Marxism down to 1953, and not a triumvirate, excluding Stalin, as his opponent Alexander Djukanovic insisted in his defense of the official version.[11] This is true not only because Stalin had molded the history of the country for thirty years, but also because he shaped the basic principles of the Soviet state; the power, production and distribution relations governing it, its class structure, and its military industrial complex, were fashioned by his hand, and it was he who annexed Eastern Europe. The Soviet state has remained basically unchanged to this day, although Stalin's reign of terror is a thing of the past. There is indeed an unbridgeable gap between real and democratic socialism, just as there are unmistakable differences in the production and distribution relations among countries calling themselves Marxist, and, above all, between the industrialization concept of the Soviet Union and the Chinese policy of maintaining healthy proportions, or between the latter and the Yugoslav mixed economy; nevertheless, it is of relatively little use to compare the Socialist model with the Marxist paradigm. As Kurt Schumacher correctly observed just before World War II: "It is without a doubt a serious flaw that Karl Marx left no coherent theory of the state and society behind him and that Marxism has only been able to develop such theories fragmentarily."

As regards the relationship between democratic socialism and Marxism, developments after World War II tended more toward a definitive break than a convergence. While the SPD Chairman, Erich Ollenhauer, has still been able to reiterate his often-cited opinion: "If we surrender Marxism, we surrender ourselves, and the keystone of our politics," the term "Marxism" is no longer even mentioned in the SPD basic program of 1959. In the section "Basic Values of Socialism," it states: "Democratic socialism, which in Europe is rooted in Christian ethics, humanism, and classical philosophy, wishes to proclaim no ultimate truths—not because it lacks understanding and not because it is indifferent to philosophical outlooks or religious truths, but out of respect for the beliefs of mankind, over which neither a political party nor the state has the right to decide."[12]

The controversy over the SPD program as it is (and it is not a party program committed to orthodox Marxism) becomes even clearer in the chapter "Basic Values of Socialism" where we find the following sentence: "The Social Democratic Party of Germany is the party of intellectual freedom, it is a community of men, who come from diverse currents of belief and thought." The party program of the Austrian Social Democratic Party of May 20, 1978, implies that the relevance of Marxism to the international socialist movement is limited to its value as a tool of social analysis: in the section entitled "Socialism and Religion" it states that socialism is an international movement in which "people work together for a better society on the basis of humanistic values, Marxist or other types of social analyses, or religious belief."

However, political parties' activities provide a more accurate assessment of them than do their party programs. The socialist and social democratic parties function both as opposition and governing parties, sometimes with an absolute parliamentary majority as in Austria until April 24, 1983, or currently in France and Spain. Whether in government or opposition they struggle to consolidate traditional pluralistic democracy and to improve the working conditions and participation of the working class. But they make no serious encroachments on the existing property relations. The sweeping nationalizations undertaken under the Labour government in Great Britain or the Socialist government of Mitterand in France were intended more as a measure to curb the power of the large corporations than as a precursory stage on the way toward a centrally administered state economy. Mitterand's nationalizations were on a much more modest scale than those undertaken by de Gaulle's post-war government. Social Democracy has made a major contribution to the progressive evolution of Western Europe into a community of welfare states and to aggrandizing the workers' piece of the national pie. But it has also abandoned "a belief in a fundamental transformation of production or of politics," as Thomas Novotny put it. Rather it has endeavored—and with noteworthy success—to be the "bedside doctor" of the industrial capitalist system. It has reformed the system to make it more acceptable and agreeable even for the previously disadvantaged classes.[13] Because of the lingering economic crisis the Social Democratic governments, like conservative governments, have felt it necessary to take measures to ensure the survival of the capitalist system and to reduce the growth in wages and social services without, however, being able to guarantee full employment. The German and Austrian

Social Democratic Parties and the British Labour Party therefore lost votes in the last elections; the SPD had to retreat into opposition and the Austrian Social Democratic Party was forced to form a coalition government. But Spain's Socialist Workers Party gained an absolute majority in the parliamentary elections of October 28, 1982, with 202 deputies compared with 121 in the previous parliament, while the number of Communist deputies decreased from 23 to 4.

Symptoms of crisis are especially visible in international cooperation: the Communist International founded in 1919 was dissolved in 1943, although the Soviet Union was never prepared to surrender its hegemony over the international communist movement. The Communist Information Bureau (Cominform), founded in 1947, which comprised the Communist Parties of the Soviet Union, Eastern Europe, Italy and France, was unable to maintain the executive powers of the Comintern. The progressive emancipation of the Italian Communist Party, by far the largest communist party of Western Europe, became ever more apparent. In a declaration of the Central Committee of the CPI at the end of 1981, it is stated literally: "The Communist Party of Italy intends to maintain normal relations with all communist parties in the same way as with every other socialist revolutionary and progressive force, without special or privileged relations to anyone, on the basis of an absolute autonomy in theory and political action, without any ideological, political, and organizational conditions."[14] The leader of Sweden's Communist Party, Lars Werner, observed[15] that a "complete break with Moscow is superfluous since no firm relationships had been maintained for about ten years with the Soviet Party." The international conferences of the communist parties, which have been convoked only with extreme difficulty, have been unable to hammer out a common international policy. The resolutions have been restricted to innocuous empty formulas, such as "consolidating peace" or "limiting the arms race," etc., which each party could accept.

The socialist movement "consolidated itself internationally" for the first time through the COMISCO (Committee of the International Socialist Conference), founded in 1947, and later at the Frankfurt Congress of 1951. The Socialist International currently comprises 75 national organizations with about 15 million members, including about 900,000 in Sweden and only 5,000 in the United States. The Socialist International has, however, never regarded itself as an executive organ, but rather as an ideological and information center.

The ruling communist parties have introduced important modifications in the social system derived from the Soviet model, without, however, detracting from the principles of this system. The Western communist parties, and especially the Italian CP, have distanced themselves from the Soviet and East European models although their oft-proclaimed "third way" has never become a reality. The socialist and social democratic parties have made essential contributions to the "socialization" of capitalism, while leaving the system itself unchallenged. The following opinion of Francois Fejtö, Professor at the Institut d'Etudes Politiques in Paris, is not without its relevance here: "The social democracy is not blameless in the abandonment of the great dream called socialism. But its uniqueness resides in its hidebound mistrust of eschatological solutions and radical cures that merely make the illness worse . . . and it is its historical merit to have conveyed the humanistic rationalistic anti-fanatic traditions of the Enlightenment and the nineteenth century belief in progress to generations of workers, and to have educated them in a democratic and antitotalitarian spirit.''[16]

Ideology is unable to explain contemporary class structure

The Russian Revolution ineluctably found its way back to the mainstream of Russian tradition. Of course, given the extremely difficult conditions of the time, the Russian revolutionaries were even less able to implement the eternal human dream of liberty, equality and fraternity than the like-minded thinkers elsewhere in the world. And today we are just as far away from it, now that ''the pioneers of yesterday have become the besotted of today,'' as Wilfredo Pareto (1848–1943) so trenchantly put it. The October Revolution was antifeudal and anticapitalist, but it was by no means socialist, as its humane social and democratic slogans might have indicated. Russia leapt over one social formation, namely, fully developed democratic pluralism, but the civilizing phase of development, i.e., industrialization, was an inevitability. Since the new property relations were less suited to industrialization than the traditional capitalist production relations, and since industrialization took place at a more rapid pace than elsewhere, much harsher work conditions and a significantly higher rate of investment, ergo exploitation, were necessary than was the case in the traditional competitive market economies. The results were impressive indeed, but the workers of the first socialist empire have not had it any easier.

One of the greatest Russian thinkers, the philosopher, Nikolai Berdyaev, expressed this unique confrontation between West European thought and the modernizing mania of Russia in a trenchant aphorism: ''Soviet communism is a mixture of Marx and Ivan the Terrible, not a mixture of Marx and Montaigne.''

Private capitalist ownership of the means of production was replaced by state ownership, not by social ownership, and industrial enterprises were not placed under the management of factory councils, as the revolutionary slogans proclaimed, but handed over to the state bureaucracy. The class structure of the country took shape in accordance with its property and organizational structures. Of course, the very thin stratum of land and factory owners was eliminated and usually physically annihilated as well. The working class remained that and no more, and nothing has changed in its status as an underprivileged social layer. Workers are ''wage slaves,'' even in the state which legitimates itself as a proletarian state, and Arnold Toynbee's statement retains its validity and will continue to do so as long as a working class exists: ''Seen from the standpoint of the worker, it is in practical terms becoming less and less important what the official ideology of his country is or whether he happens to be working for a government or for a large economic enterprise."[17]

In comparison with his colleagues in the classical class society, the worker in a state enterprise would seem to have less rather than more advantages. In really existing socialism he is not treated as an employee of a private enterprise, but as a member of the state; the workers' instruments of defense, acquired through hard struggle and now an integral part of a democratic system, i.e., strikes, and independent trade unions, are denied to the workers in these countries.

The Revolution was no sooner achieved than a careful distinction was drawn between the proletariat as co-owners of the means of production, as proclaimed in the revolutionary slogans, and the workers, degraded to the status of mere wage earners by the Russian Thermidor. In 1921, the "workers' opposition," led by Shliapnikov, was still able to demand that Soviet industry be built up on a syndicalist basis, i.e., that the means of production should be under the control of the trade unions, organized according to the structure of the country; management of industrial enterprises would be the responsibility of the democratically elected factory councils; and officials would be democratically elected, not appointed. Alexandra Kollontai, a general's daughter converted to communism, pleaded in vain with the delegates of the Tenth Party Congress (1921) to heed the communist ideal of workers' control of the factories. She argued that the bureaucracy had already extended its stranglehold to embrace the whole of social life and that the Party had been taken over by petty bourgeois elements while the number of workers in top level functions amounted to no more than 17 percent;[18] very few, however, were persuaded. Indeed, her words were addressed to precisely those who had carved a place for themselves in the political bureaucracy.

Even earlier, the Ninth Party Congress of March 1920 had resolved to introduce unrestricted one-man management, putting the final seal once and for all on the hierarchical steering system. The trade unions were downgraded to instruments of Party and the state and their functions remained limited to promoting labor productivity and labor discipline. The traditional function of the trade unions was never again restored. In our day, the heroic struggle of the Polish workers for an independent trade union that would have protected them from abuses of power by the state encountered the stubborn resistance not only of the Polish government, but of the entire alliance.

The class structure is recognizable; there are no capitalists in the Eastern bloc, and, with the exception of Poland, neither are there private peasants. But there is without a doubt a hierarchically structured society. The ruling elite is no less greedy for and conscious of power than it is in the traditional class societies of this world. In the East the fall of a member of the elite into the abyss of the underprivileged is regarded no less as a stroke of destiny than the fall of a capitalist into the abyss of the unpropertied. The dignitaries under real socialism are perhaps more poorly remunerated than those in capitalism, but they are no less demanding and no less ingenious in satisfying their relatively extravagant needs. Of course, no socialist dignitary will reject the aristocratic privileges officially granted him: a car of a make worthy of his rank, medical care in exclusive and special institutions set up for the privileged, etc. But he will also know how to utilize his special position in the state hierarchy to improve his by no means modest status. One need only recall the greed that became evident amongst Poland's powerful through the revelations of the Inspection Office in 1981. Eighteen Ministers, fifty-six Vice-Ministers, and almost half of Party and top state officials in the forty-nine regions had acquired luxury villas through the misuse of power.[19]

The class structure is perpetuated in real socialism, not because the son of a worker or peasant finds it more difficult than his materially better off Western colleague to find his own niche in the social hierarchy, but because a person who already enjoys privileged status is not prepared to step down even for his successors.

Oskar Lange, the world famous economist and reformist, once published a conversation he had had with a worker who asked him the following purely theoretical question: "Can you imagine a general's son who does poorly in school and descends to the status of a manual worker on that account?" The worker answered his own question: "Of course the general's son will remain among the elite and be promoted from one school class to the next even if he is a donkey. Special tutoring, and occasionally even protection will be resorted to until he gets to the university after all. And this only because it is not fitting for a general's son in this society to spend his life as a common worker."[20]

There is also no lack of statistics demonstrating the perpetuation of the class structure in the Eastern countries. Surveys made in the Tatar Autonomous Republic of the Soviet Union in 1967 are representative. The findings show that 56.3 percent of the children of manual workers remained in their fathers' professions and only 14.9 percent acquired the position of manager or some other prestigious occupation; on the other hand, 47.3 percent of children of highly trained persons such as managers and other elite professions remained in the social stratum of their fathers, and only 20 percent fell to the level of a worker.[21]

Professor Michael Voslensky shows how great the difference is between the social classes in a quotation from a comparison presented by the conformist Soviet writer, Sergei Mikhalkov: "The simple Soviet citizen is portrayed as a beast of burden carrying his oats and bearing away the manure!; those in the nomenclature, on the other hand, are described as racing stallions and thoroughbreds who have all that befits their status."[22]

Of course, even in the countries of real socialism a class struggle is going on, although it takes an unorganized form, since the trade unions represent the interests of the state and the interests of the workers are equated with the interests of the state. The dissatisfaction of the underprivileged, usually as a consequence of the raising of the norms of performance (no extra pay for more work) or as a result of price rises for which no compensation is offered, is expressed in mass explosions that erupt from time to time with unparalleled vehemence, as for example the June Days of 1953 in the GDR, October 1956 in Hungary, or 1956, 1970, 1976 and 1980 to 1982 in Poland.

In the Western industrial countries farm labor is converging with industrial labor, and the latter with intellectual labor, more rapidly than in the Eastern countries

The machine has taken over the work of revolution, says the well-known U.S. sociologist, Charles Reich.[23] Marx implied the same in stressing the development of the forces of production as a basis for progress in the relations of production and distribution. The relation between the social superstructure and the forces of production has assumed forms different from those Marx imagined in the nineteenth century. The relations of production have ceased being capitalist precisely in Russia, where industrialization was least advanced among the countries of Europe. Further, productivity has increased at a slower pace in the noncapitalist countries than in the competitive market economies. Accordingly, the class structure has developed diversely, and differently than had been surmised. Not the revolutionary slogans and good intentions of revolutionaries, but the progress of the scientific and technical revolution has been the decisive force in the evolution of the class structure in the two social systems. But the scientific and technical revolution has made much greater progress in the competitive market economies than in the planned economies. In traditional class society, farm labor has converged with industrial labor and the latter with intellectual labor much more rapidly than in the planned economies: in 1776 90 percent of the gainfully employed American population were working in agriculture and forestry, but by 1980 this figure was no more than 3.7 percent. In 1917, the rural population of Russia was 82 percent of the total population, and in 1980 it was still 37 percent, while the share of farm laborers in the total number of employed was 20 percent.

The advance of industrial technology, automation and the use of robots has brought about a true revolution in economic structure. Just as a mass immigration of peasants into industry took place in the initial stages of industrialization, today the scientific and technical revolution is driving industrial workers out of industry into other economic sectors, especially the information sector. This far-reaching revolution, which is transforming every aspect of social life, is proceeding at a much more dynamic pace in the industrial countries of the West than in the East. The following table shows this difference clearly.

These data show more clearly than any other arguments how the economic and class structures have developed along far different lines from what was foreseen in the nineteenth century. They refute the view stated in 1848: Society as a whole is more and more splitting into two hostile camps, into two great classes directly facing one another: bourgeoisie and proletariat.[24] In the Western industrially

Breakdown of employed population by economic sector in West and East (percentages in 1980)

	Number of employed	Agriculture and forestry	Industry	Construction and transport	Other	Trade sectors
Western industrial nations						
France	20,921	9.1	25.1	13.8	14.7	37.3
FRG	24,679	6.5	36.3	13.0	14.2	30.0
Italy	19,332	15.5	25.1	14.0	16.8	28.6
Japan	54,080	11.7	23.9	13.1	23.0	28.3
Great Britain	24,610	2.7	30.2	12.3	16.3	38.5
USA	94,373	3.7	24.3	13.4	19.8	38.8
Austria	3,015	10.9	31.6	15.2	17.3	25.0
Eastern countries						
Bulgaria	4,448	24.5	35.0	15.1	8.1	17.7
GDR	8,683	10.5	43.2	15.2	10.7	20.4
Czechoslovakia	7,455	14.2	37.9	16.5	10.6	20.8
Poland	17,962	30.2	29.7	14.2	7.6	18.5
Romania	10,350	29.8	35.5	15.4	6.0	13.3
Hungary	5,074	22.0	33.4	16.0	9.6	21.0
USSR	134,860	20.2	29.5	18.1	8.0	24.2

Sources: The OECD Member Countries 1980; *Rocznik Statystyczny* (Poland, 1982), p. 500.

developed countries, industry seldom employs more than one-third of all gainfully employed persons and the share of workers in the total number of employed is
certainly no greater than 15 to 20 percent. As automation and the use of robots
progress, the number of blue-collar workers decreases in favor of white-collar
workers, whose work scarcely differs from intellectual labor.

The proportion of workers in agriculture is greater than 10 percent only in
Japan and Italy. Commerce, services and the information sector employ almost
half and in the United States as high as 60 percent of the gainfully employed.

These data also confirm the view that an economic and technical revolution
rather than a violent social revolution has played the decisive role in the progress
of the economic and class structures. In the Eastern countries, the proportion of
persons employed in agriculture is at least twice as high and the proportion of
persons employed in industry at least one-fifth higher than in the industrial
countries of the West. Labor productivity, however, is significantly lower. Although only 3.7 percent of the work force is employed in agriculture, the United
States is still able to supply grain to the Soviet Union, whose agricultural sector
employs six times more persons proportionally than in the United States. Further,
Soviet industry produces at least one-fifth less than the United States although it
employs 36.4 million persons; in the United States only 21.9 million are employed in industry.[25]

In both social systems a revolutionary process is taking place that is claiming
its victims. In the industrial countries of the West, those expelled from the
production process must sometimes wait quite a long time for a new job. Relatively often, they must be retrained and live on their unemployment insurance.
The planned economies prefer to keep underemployment behind the factory
walls. Often this is done as a conscious preventive measure on the part of a
factory manager who is concerned with obtaining favorable conditions for plan
fulfillment. The higher-ups in the hierarchy as well as the Party continue to attach
greater importance to quantitative than to qualitative indicators of enterprise
performance.

The unmistakeable progress of the class structure in modern society, and the
clear reduction in the size of the underprivileged social layers deprive Marxist
thought of one of its most important supporting pillars, namely, the inherent role
of the proletariat as the demiurge of the progress of human civilization and the
leader of the revolutionary movement. The liberation of this underprivileged
social layer has taken place in accordance with a scenario fundamentally different
from that Marx imagined, i.e., by means of a considerable reduction in the
number of industrial workers relative to the total number of employed and by a
rise in the number of white-collar workers at the expense of blue-collar workers.
Since the scientific and technical revolution is progressing at a more dynamic
pace in the West than in the East, the liberation of the proletariat is also a more
rapid process in the West. Competition, the use of modern technology, and free
trade unions have had a more favorable influence on the social progress of the

proletariat than all the lofty slogans of state ideology.

The dictatorship of the proletariat was undemocratic as a call to battle at the time of the 1917 October Revolution when the proletariat, which had been promised absolute dominion over the people and the country, still had to be created. The proletariat did not gain power then, nor even later, when it had become the largest social layer. Power is wielded in its name. It is no more representative of the people now than in the first years after the Revolution when workers needed 25,000 votes but the peasants 125,000 votes for a mandate and the "exploiting class" (land and factory owners, merchants, priests and monks) did not have the right to vote at all and were barred from public office. Today all social layers are constitutionally guaranteed equal rights, although they are by no means equal. The social revolution, rolling relentlessly onward, has had no influence on the state ideology of the Eastern countries because that ideology has had nothing to do with reality for some time. It does, however, have an influence on the ideology of Western communists. At the Milan meeting of the Communist Party of Italy in February 1983, the Party ideologue, Giuseppe Vacca, stressed that white-collar workers and technicians, students and unemployed, make up almost half of the CP members. But there are just as few workers in the Party apparatus of the CPI as in the ruling party apparatuses in the Eastern bloc. The communist parties of Italy and Spain have expunged the slogans "Dictatorship of the proletariat" from the Party program. Recently, Nicolae Ceauşescu, head of state and of the Party in Romania, also called this slogan obsolete. But this changed nothing, since the proletarians in the East have never felt that they were a ruling class, unless in some mythological sense or, as Raymond Aron so tersely put it, "in the same way that God ruled in France in 1700, over the person of Louis XIV."[26]

Of course, not much will be changed by striking the slogan "dictatorship of the proletariat" from the program of the communist parties both in and out of government. But the same cannot be said of the Marxist intellectual tradition; according to Marx the proletariat is the heart of the emancipation of mankind and philosophy is its head. Since 1848, when Marx wrote, "All movements heretofore have been movements of minorities or in the interests of minorities. The proletariat movement is the independent movement of the vast majority in the interests of the vast majority," the class structure of the class societies of East and West have changed radically. The proletariat neither constitutes the majority nor has it only its "chains" to lose, and this is no less emphatically true in the East than in the West.

Vaclav Machajski, Poland's revolutionary theoretician of the founding period, doubted the independence of the proletariat as a leader of revolution and maintained that the messianism of the socialist movement expressed the ideology of "dissatisfied intellectuals." With the perspicacity of a farsighted prophet he correctly predicted (1899) the future: "The new socialist society will replace one ruling class by another so that workers will still be exploited, but this time by a new class of professional leaders."[27]

Lenin too reiterated time and time again that revolutionary consciousness had to be brought to the proletariat from without. But if Marx's thesis on the emancipatory mission of the proletariat is correct, the following statement from the *Communist Manifesto* refers in equal degree to proletarians in the East and in the West: "The proletarians, the lowest layer of present-day society, cannot rise up, not stand alone, without destroying the entire superstructure of the strata constituting official society." This is how Poland's proletariat understood its mission although it was not able, for well-known reasons, to fulfill it.

The Western proletariat is now struggling to improve its conditions of existence, and for codetermination and for a better future for its successors. But it surely has no reason to want to overthrow a social order in which it has made some impressive gains.

The class struggle no longer aims at overthrowing the social order but at improving conditions under the existing system. Even the trade unions controlled by communists no longer venture into a class struggle that would destroy the existing order.

The Western communist parties have moderated their program of struggle. Torn between loyalties to antiquated Party ideals and the existing realities in their own countries and the paradigmatic system of yesteryear, from time to time they divest themselves of a few fragments of their obsolete ideological ballast—such as "the dictatorship of the proletariat" or the one-party system—without, however, being able to enrich the Party program with new, creative and desirable alternate objectives. The Polish proletariat, deprived of its national and social ideals, continued to struggle with a classical enthusiasm for battle for the elementary material and political conditions of existence. But the interest of the world at large waned. "Poland," wrote Friedrich Engels on February 10, 1882, "was abandoned to itself when it fell to a tenfold stronger Russian superpower in 1863."[28] History has repeated itself. As always, Poland is an exception. In Europe and in North America there is no classical proletariat in the Marxist sense and no classical class struggle. The socialist revolution has shifted to the precapitalist areas of the world, i.e., where industrialization is still taking place with the early capitalist methods of exploitation.

In every social system, the rate of investment reflects the degree of exploitation

Marx portrayed a terrible picture in 1848: "The accumulation of wealth at one pole is thus at the same time an accumulation of misery, toil, slavery, ignorance, brutalization and moral degradation at the opposite pole, i.e., on the side of the class which produces its own product as capital.'' When this grim picture is accompanied by the assertion that ''the rich become richer and the poor become poorer,'' conscience demands passage of the death sentence on such a corrupt system, and with the class it mercilessly exploits serving as the executioner.

Marx was not the only nineteenth century thinker to paint such a grim picture of early capitalism. In 1839, nine years before the publication of the *Communist Manifesto,* Thomas Carlyle (1795–1883) published his book *Chartism,* in which he described the situation in England at that time in terms even gloomier than Marx's. Writes his biographer Michael Freund: "Early capitalist England is nowhere shown more terribly and grippingly. . . A symphony of horrors emerges before our eyes as Carlyle describes brandy consumption as the barometer of social decay in England and paints the dreadful portrait of social need as the strength of an entire nation is dissipated in liquid madness.''[29]

Unlike Marx, who wanted to overthrow this system because, as he wrote in the *Manifesto,* bourgeois relations had become too narrow to do justice to the wealth created through them (and this was in 1848), Carlyle augured no land of bliss but wished only to restore to the state its lost power. With Carlyle, the state "in the fullness of its great and awesome power returned to the centerpoint of political thought.'' Bismarck (in a letter of December 2, 1875) called Carlyle a writer whose ''noble nature compelled him to speak the truth,'' while Goethe referred to him as one of Europe's ''moral forces.'' Yet even such laudations were not enough to spare him from oblivion.

Carlyle was right nonetheless. Russia emerged from the rubble and ruins of World War I to become a great power, not because of the realization of the utopian slogans of the October Revolution but by virtue of an omnipotent state, which very early in industrialization succeeded in making cardinal virtues out of labor discipline, consciousness of duty, and care and concern without even commensurate reward. The interests of the workers and the peasants were equated with the interests of the state without an authentic representation of those interests even being deemed necessary.

The achievements of its five-year plans, the building of a modern industry and a broad base in energy and raw materials are in the Soviet Union owed not to the slogans of equality, which have never been realized, but to the might of a totalitarian state. Erich Honecker, who had personally experienced and admired this pioneer period as a German Young Communist, maintains his esteem for these achievements even today, as evidenced in his speech on the occasion of the sixtieth anniversary of the Soviet Union: "During the brief period of peace, and, in particular, during the first five-year plans, that tremendous economic potential which proved its mettle so outstandingly in the great patriotic war, was created under the leadership of the Bolshevik Party and Josef Stalin.''[30] So does Honecker praise the founder of the Soviet Union and autocrat of the first half of the country's six decades even as the present Soviet rulers would prefer to be silent about him.

No miracle was accomplished; the rate of accumulation was extremely high and consumption extremely low. Just as in early capitalism, in early socialism as well, capital came into the world "dripping blood and dirt from head to toe from all pores," as Ernst Fischer graphically described it: in the years 1928 to 1932, when the first and most ambitious of the five-year plans was implemented, the forcibly collectivized agricultural enterprises supplied agrarian products at prices below cost and the supply situation was so precarious that basic foods had to be rationed; the wages fund grew by a factor of 3.5-fold, but domestic trade increased by only 35 percent and prices by a mere 2.5-fold.[31] The distress caused by the British enclosures system, the transformation of farmland into pasturelands for sheep, was a bagatelle in comparison with the millions of victims of forced collectivization.

To paraphrase Toynbee, it is not only a matter of indifference to the worker what the official ideology of his country is and who he has for an employer, it is just as unimportant who controls accumulation, despite his tangible contribution to it: what is important to him is the size of the worker's share in the national product. And in the Soviet Union, this is much lower than in the industrial countries of the West, as is evident from the table that follows.

	1960	1976
Soviet Union	53.4	48.6
USA	63.7	64.7
France	61.9	62.3
West Germany	56.8	55.8
Great Britain	66.2	59.7
Italy	64.2	64.3
Japan	58.3	57.9

Source: *Consumption in the USSR: An International Comparison*, a study prepared for the use of the Joint Economic Committee, Congress of the United States, August 17, 1981.

The Soviet Union is in last place on this list. Consumption has a smaller share of the national product, not only compared with the United States and France, but also Japan, where the rate of accumulation is above average. Moreover, in the period covered by the table, the proportion of consumption has even declined perceptibly in the Soviet Union. Furthermore, the backwardness is reflected in the most important items in the consumer shopping basket, as is evident from the following comparison with the United States:

	Total consumption	Foods, beverages, & tobacco	Consumer durables	Household services	Communal services	Public education
USSR in percentage of USA	34.4	53.7	13.3	17.8	49.4	76.6

*A geometric average of the ruble and dollar values.
Source: Ibid., p. 6.

The Soviet Union is ahead of the United States (by only 3.7 percent) in sugar consumption; for bread and potatoes it is slightly behind (4.5 percent and 10 percent respectively), but far behind in the consumption of vegetables and fruits (19.3 percent and 19.7 percent of the U.S. level). Alcohol consumption in the Soviet Union is extremely high, exceeding American consumption by 19.1 percent. The accumulation rate is almost twice as high as in the United States, but labor and capital productivity are at least 50 percent lower.

In the official lexicon, forced industrialization on the basis of an extremely high investment rate measured in Western terms is described as "preparing the preconditions for the establishment of a communist society." But three generations have already had to pay a heavy price for this in reduced consumption and chronic supply problems. The effect of the extremely high costs of forced industrialization, referred to officially as the building of communism, on the wellbeing of Soviet citizens is depicted most graphically by the Romanian writer and director of the Party academy, Dimitru Popescu: "The people are grey, with over-fatigued, prematurely aged figures, a hobbled gait, caused perhaps by long hours on their feet or exhausting physical work."[32]

Of course, the present generation is committed to passing on to future generations a clean environment and a sound economic and cultural basis and to avoiding conflicts which could lead to renewed destruction. But it is unreasonable to expect the present generation to accept meager incomes and even more meager consumption potential for the sake of super high investment and economic growth rates, regardless of what such forced industrialization is called for propaganda reasons. The famous Russian writer and philosopher of the nineteenth century, Alexander Herzen, expressed as much in a letter to his friend: ". . . Do you really want to sentence all people now living to the sad role of karyatides who hold steady the floor on which others will someday dance . . . ?" He continues even more directly: "A remote goal is no goal at all, but a trap. . . . Every age, every generation, every life has its own gratifications. . . ." Thomas Jefferson said as much: "The present belongs to those living in it." And Leszek Kolakowski wrote, "I will never believe that if we save more today we will have more tomorrow."

A dynamic growth policy that saps the strength of the present generation to the benefit basically of the military industrial complex is neither just nor committed to the future; nor is the economic policy of those Western countries that enable the present generation to live beyond its means at the expense of a disproportionate burden of budget deficits, credits and interest on future generations.

Under real socialism, the blame for this fatal economic policy lies with an obsolete notion of growth that persists in giving absolute priority to heavy industry and with an antiquated steering system that makes capital investments the cheapest, and hence for factory managers the most attractive, way to fulfill the plan. In the West, on the other hand, the causes of the unjust economic policy lie with the infamous democracy of convenience in which the politician "who is thinking of the next election" is often more conspicuous than the statesman "who is thinking of the next generation," as the great British politician and statesman William Gladstone trenchantly put it.

The cultural revolution that had no sequel

Blok and Esenin, Mayakovsky and Mandelstam, and many other writers, musicians, and painters began a genuine cultural revolution after the October Revolution in 1917. They aroused courage and inspired confidence throughout the entire world that culture was not necessarily "a thin covering over an abyss" (Jacob Burkhardt) which threatened to break through at any moment, but that this abyss could diminish, and that mutual understanding and mutual interaction between the intellectual elite and the broad layers of the population were a real possibility. Within a dazzlingly short time illiteracy, the lot of almost three-fourths of the population of Great Russia, was eliminated.

But the enthusiasm of the great Revolution soon waned. None of the poets named above died a natural death. As the Russian revolutionary Stepnyak Kravchinskii once wrote, "The plague kills without discrimination, but the present regime seeks its victims from amongst the very flower of the nation." The best of the best were physically annihilated in prisons and exile camps. The greatest talents were dissipated in inane portrayals of positive heroes of a daily life that was becoming steadily grimmer, of "socialist realism," utterly remote from reality and forcibly imposed, which no one dared denounce lest the bureaucrats of the mind use the usual well-tested means to return them to the procrustean bed of realism. An almost unbridgeable gap opened up between the ideology, with its many promises, and an ever gloomier present. The positive heroes described in books became more and more unrecognizable in the people encountered in everyday life, who were utterly unable to understand a poetry and prose as remote from the world as the moon.

Russian literature, once the realm of giants, such as Tolstoy, Dostoevsky, Gogol, and Gorky, declined to a level which no longer could meet even the relatively low requirements of the wielders of power. The talented Russian people were no longer able to nurture talents befitting their own intellectual grandeur.

The utopian dreams of a superman created by socialist society have vanished without a trace. Marx believed that the contradiction between asceticism and morals would cease in a classless future society because every person would experience the spontaneous need to act in a way both useful to himself and to his fellow man; Engels thought that in communist society men would achieve a maximum and optimal morality, which would make all external constraint superfluous. But one of the greatest martyrs of the future communist society, Leo Trotsky, described the greatness of man in that society much more passionately than the fathers of scientific socialism: "Man will make it his mission to become lord of his feelings, raise his instincts to the level of consciousness, and thereby bring himself to a higher state, i.e., a superior social and biological type, or if you will, a superman. . . . The human average will be raised to the level of Aristotle, Goethe or Marx. But new peaks will arise over this range. . . ." Man, said Nietzsche, can be both an *Übermensch* and an *Untermensch*. He certainly has not become an *Übermensch* in the new society—indeed such a creature cannot be made in the test tube of society. The anticapitalist social system has not changed consumer habits; the people are just less able to satisfy them than the citizens of Western Europe or North America. He who can does, emulating the Party and state elite. No one in these countries venerates asceticism or a vegetarian model of consumption. A car, summer house, and trips abroad are just as much status symbols in the East as in the West. But the average citizen in the East must usually wait longer for them than his Western counterpart. He pursues the consumer values of the West, but drinks more. Driven between the "pleasure principle" and "reality principle," he must yield to realities that are, however, much harsher than in the West.

The people under real socialism display more of the character traits described by Thomas Hobbes than the sublime qualities of a superman, dreamed by the dreamers of all times.

Commercialized and mummified cultural behavior

Henry Miller, the famous American writer and author of the well-known trilogy *The Rose Crucifixion* (1960), coined the aphorism: "Culture is a piece of luck, a series of cases of good luck or favorable opportunities which a people creates for its own use or the use of others; their purpose is to offer the crowd a human existence in which everyone can better develop his humanity. . . ."

It is surely fortuitous that geniuses such as Tolstoy or Victor Hugo have had such a tremendous influence on the literature and on the readers of Russia and France as well as the entire civilized world. Yet on the whole, the classical literature of Russia or France in the nineteenth century cannot have been pure chance, just as it cannot be by pure chance that the culture of our time is in a serious crisis. "An abundance of ponderous events have accumulated," says the esteemed French cultural historian Georges Rodier. "World War I, the profound malaise of the 1930s, World War II, conflicts, ideologies laden with sharp contrasts about man and his fate . . . the great fear of annihilation by the atomic bomb . . . ,"[33] have altogether had a negative influence on our common culture.

Manes Sperber, the well-known French author of Austrian origin, saw the cause of the cultural crisis in the effects of the world wars and totalitarian regimes and in the ideological fashions which no one has the courage to oppose: "We have been witnesses for years now of ideological fashions and the paralyzing inability of broad layers of the middle class and petty bourgeois intellectuals to oppose them or indeed oppose any current in politics, art and literature provided they are extremist enough." Sperber continues, "This is the psychological legacy of world wars and the effects of totalitarian regimes."[34] The organizational weight of omnipotent intellectual bureaucracies that attempt to organize and control all areas of cultural life also has a negative effect on the general culture of our time. Culture is transformed into a marketplace that manipulates man's cultural behavior and gradually becomes a seller's market. The electronic mass media have been perfect instruments to this end. Their managers are bearers not of culture but of subculture. What is conveyed is what makes a hit and is easily marketed, just as in the East the media convey what is useful to narrowly conceived purposes of the government. The world market is glutted with cultural goods of negligible worth that are then distributed by the strict rules of the market, and the electronic culture industry ensures that the market swells to unprecedented dimensions.

Alvin Gouldner, author of *The Dialectic of Ideology and Technology* (1982), saw a feedback mechanism operating among ideology, the cultural apparatus, and the consciousness industry. The spread of television worldwide marks the end, he claims, of one and the beginning of a new phase in the revolution in communication, to wit, the development of computerized information systems. This thesis, popular in the 1950s, that the triumph of technological, scientific, and rationalistic pragmatic consciousness implied a higher stage of development of the human mind, beyond "ideology," is false according to Gouldner. The end of ideology, he felt, is far more regressive than progressive. "The creation and consumption of ideological values for and by the elite of society is intensified; but at the same time mass culture for those whose consciousness is formed by the radio, i.e., 'the consciousness industry' and much less by the products of the 'cultural machinery,' increases."[35] A similiar thought is, in fact, reflected in the party program of the Austrian Social Democrat Party of May 20, 1978: "The capitalist system has led to a strong differentiation of the society in terms of consumption potential and education, but it has also led to a levelling out and impoverishment of cultural needs and to uniformity and commercialization of cultural behavior." The program goes on to raise objections to a course of development that "divides the whole of cultural life into luxuries and trivia, while at the same time the culture industry reduces it to a flatland."

Whatever the reasons, whether for purposes of commercialization and profit or for subordination to the narrowly conceived pragmatics of state policy, the technical consciousness industry under the dominion of an omipresent intellectual bureaucracy represents a not to be underestimated peril, both for those who make culture and for man's cultural life in general. The American sociologist Richard Reich wrote in *The Greening of America*, "All cultural values are offered for sale, those from which nothing can be gained are abandoned." Manes Sperber says that anyone who writes in our times must cope not only with the opposition of the dreadful simplifiers, but also with the hostility of the dehumanizing reducers who invoke the ideologies of yesteryear, the violence of the present, and the paradises of tomorrow.

The Plenary Session of the Central Committee of the CPSU of June 15, 1983, which dealt with ideological problems, is an utterly clear demonstration of how extensively state ideology is subordinated to pragmatic goals. The Party leaders were more intent than ever on using ideology and propaganda to implement economic and political planning goals. In Chernenko's words, "A perfecting of developed socialism should be the focus not only of theoretical research, but also of Party propaganda and education." He wanted, however, to soften the contradiction between propaganda and reality somewhat, and therefore mounted a criticism whose anonymous target was unmistakably Khrushchev. In the past, said Chernenko, a simplistic view prevailed of the path of transition to the higher stage of communist development and of the time required to achieve it, a view in which twenty years of history have shown to be wrong. In 1963 Khrushchev announced that by 1980 the per capita national income of the Soviet Union would be greater than that of the United States. Yet, the gap remains. Chernenko was clear that the intent had been to "fire our dreams and to make the rough path ahead easier going." Still, what was actually achieved was that the gap between propaganda and reality grew. Having been chief ideologist of the CPSU as well as its General Secretary, Chernenko understood that "The formation of a new man is a continuous and complicated process, as complicated as life itself." Therefore the Party and the people had to focus on the tasks of everyday life: "If we are able to mobilize the intellectual energies of our people and promote work and social activity, we will also be able to fulfill the five-year plan, accelerate the pace of our progress, and strengthen our country's defenses."

What is noteworthy here is the unrelieved hostility of Soviet leaders to Western ideologies—in Andropov's words, "the unprecedented intensity and bitterness of the rivalry between the two world outlooks and the two contesting political currents, socialism and imperialism." "At stake," said Andropov, "are the minds and the hearts of billions of people of this world. The future of mankind will depend on the outcome of this ideological struggle."

In the new version of the Third Party Program, adopted by the 27th Party Congress in March 1986, the "capitalist" world is characterized with the same formulations as in the formal programs of 1903 and 1919 and in the first version of 1961. This formulation also differs little from the terms used in the *Communist Manifesto* of Marx and Engels. Contemporary Western industrial countries, with their relatively high living standards, extensive social security systems, powerful trade unions, and pluralistic, *ergo* democratic, political systems, are castigated again and again as enemies of the working class. The imperialism of today, now minus the colonies, seems to remain as depicted by V. I. Lenin in his 1916 work *Imperialism: The Highest Stage of Capitalism*. And the proletariat of today, depicted with the same features as in the *Communist Manifesto* of 1848, is equipped with the same historical mission to fulfill, namely an overthrow of the capitalist system. All this as if the quasiproletariat of the contemporary Western world, declining in numbers, had not solved its material social problems better than the real proletariat in the real socialist world of today, and as if the gap between physical and intellectual work in Western industrialized society (entering the information society stage) is not being closed faster than in the Eastern countries.

This resolve to create a shield from the outside world and protect domestic ideology from Western onslaughts has a long history. Is the intention really to protect the delicate ideological blossoms of Marxism, long since ossified into a state ideology, from Western attack? Hardly, since true believers in Marxism as the theory and ideology of struggle are greater in number in the West than in the East. Marxism was born in the West, and in the East, where it became a state ideology, it drove out all other ideologies and religions. The point, therefore, is not to protect Marxism Soviet-style, but to create a shield against libertarian ideologies and Western Marxism. The influence of Western libertarian ideologies has been a traditional Russian fear. It can only be regretted that isolation from the West, and obstacles to establishing and maintaining the contacts that could be so beneficial for mutual understanding and detente, has grown rather than diminished. As early as 1589, the English traveller Giles Fletcher observed that people "from the civilized countries are permitted entry into [Russia] only when this is necessary in the interests of imports and exports." ". . . There is a fear of contamination with alien morals and with qualities that distinguish foreigners," noted Fletcher's countryman William Cox in 1792. His observations led him to the sad conclusion that "A real change in national customs and mores is impossible if the people cannot enjoy absolute personal or material freedom."

Customs and habits molded over centuries cannot be expected to change radically within only a few decades. Indeed why should the abolition of private property and its transfer to an omnipotent state bureaucracy change the customs and morals of a whole people if the majority of these people as workers must face off against the state as collective employer in a new but no less evident type of alienation? What was most feared happened: the people regard the nationalized means of production as anonymous property and, accordingly, nowhere is theft and corruption so widespread and lack of discipline so egregious as in state enterprises. Party resolutions throughout the Eastern bloc now openly say as much. As was noted in a resolution of the sixteenth Party Congress of the Communist Party of Czechoslovakia: "It is no secret that there are people who live at the expense of society, who obtain wages not for work done, but merely because they show up."

There is no lack of awareness of the impending decay and the ever-growing gap between officially proclaimed ideology and grim reality. But since changing the realities of everyday life is an impossibility, efforts are concentrated on perfecting the propaganda of an ideology now ossified into a dogma. Proudhon had warned of this unsalubrious practice of stuffing mankind with dogma and adjured Karl Marx, "For God's sake, let us not try to pump our own dogmas into mankind after we have destroyed all the other dogmas!" And somewhat later he wrote, "Let us give the world an example of wise and far-seeing tolerance." But at that time Marxism was just one abstract ideology among many others. Today, however, we must cope with a world system which differs radically from others yet one in which man has not become the measure of all things as Marx had hoped, nor has mounted the throne that God had abandoned, as Marx's intellectual father, Ludwig Feuerbach, had proclaimed. Instead, man has been subordinated to a form of domination in which each is under someone else's sway, and in which the ruling elite is much more demanding the more inconspicuous it is. For these people, Saint-Simon's dictum applies: "Man is the lord of all things, but not lord of himself."

This system attempts not only to justify itself internally by invoking "the ideologies of yesteryear, the violence of today, and the paradise of tomorrow," as Manes Sperber put it, but also attempts, in the words of Yuri Andropov, "to win the hearts and minds of millions of people throughout the world." There is no cost too great to this end; what is lacking is provided by the communist parties of the West. The socialist fatherland must be shielded from the outside world and for this no means are too dear. "The Soviet Union alone has 3,000 jamming stations that are in operation round the clock and have about 5,000 employees. The cost is about 150 million dollars. To this must be yet added the expenses of Czechoslovakia and Bulgaria, which have their own jamming."[36] But in Hungary foreign broadcasts are not jammed; since the Hungarians make a genuine effort domestically to provide thorough information so that there is little demand for more.

But the gap between ideology and reality continues to vex even the new Kremlin leadership. Yuri Andropov spoke of problems in the communication between Party leaders and the people and proclaimed a bitter struggle against "intellectual inertia, and the cramming or rote repetition of theses known to everyone already from sheets prepared beforehand."

But writers and artists have already sensed a fresh wind blowing and are putting the opportunity to "portray realistic socialism somewhat more realistically" to good advantage. A most recent Soviet film, *Railroad Station for Two*, for example, made by the Moscow director Eldar Riazanov, is especially interesting. Nothing is embellished, neither the grim life in work camps nor the daily life of a normal Soviet citizen, burdened by intolerable problems of making a livelihood. The film is not the official "socialist realism," with the obligatory positive heroes seldom to be found in real life, but the actual life of the man in the street as it takes place: in a restaurant, the food is inedible—because the staff skims off the best for itself; in a bar, the cognac is diluted with water. Typical speculators are shown, who actually perform the role of benefactors in the film since "the people have to get their vitamins." Speculators will not soon disappear, as Andropov acknowledged clearly enough to the Plenary Session of the Central Committee on June 15, 1983: "People prefer to pay more for better quality goods, rarely to be found in the state stores."

A determined campaign against corruption and poor-quality production of consumer goods was started by Mikhail Gorbachev. In his marathon speech during the Twenty-seventh Party Congress, he stated that a new law giving citizens the right of legal redress against officials was in preparation. "We will not progress unless we work in a new way. . . . Servility toward officials must be eradicated . . . ," stated the new leader. Quality, rather than quantity, is the main postulated target of the Soviet economy. Of course, Gorbachev's predecessors had the same goal, but were confronted with the stubbornness and inertia of the mighty party and state apparatus. The near future will show whether Gorbachev will be more successful than his predecessors in his fight against corruption—the eternal enemy of his land, whether he will turn out to be stronger than the bureaucrats, and whether his determination will not falter.

There are a number of encouraging signs that the culture makers are trying much more conscientiously to draw a realistic picture of life, if for no other reason than that the propaganda of official ideology is falling on deaf ears, the intellectual vacuum is becoming ever more conspicuous, and the godless are slowly, or even dynamically as in Poland, returning to religion.

The Soviet Union continues to proclaim itself the source of communist ideology in its purest form, although some qualifications are now heard. Yuri Andropov seemed to face up to the discouraging experiences of the last twenty year when he told the June (1983) Session of the Central Committee that the period had enriched people's notions of the world of socialism, a world more differentiated and more complicated than might have been assumed. "There were differences in the economy, in the culture, and even in the methods of coping with socialist tasks," he said before going on to end this passage with a somewhat more self-critical note: "These differences are self-evident, even though it may once have appeared that the socialist world would be unified."

The once one-and-only communist church is now split. The Chinese are not at all inclined to subordinate their version of Marxism to the Soviet one, even though they have dethroned Mao as the church father of pure Marxism. The

Eurocommunist parties regularly toss overboard formerly sacrosanct doctrines—"the violent seizure of power through a proletarian revolution," then the "monopoly of power of the Communist Party," and recently "the dictatorship of the proletariat." The debacle of Communist rule in Poland has been of special concern to the Kremlin leadership. "A bill has been presented for the errors in policy; the Party has lost its rapport with the people, and self-proclaimed representatives of the interests of the workers and of all-embracing nationalism are creeping into this vacuum. If we are unable to overcome these nationalist moods, conflicts which should have no reason to exist in the socialist world will become inevitable between states," he reported to the June (1983) meeting of the CPSU.

Unfortunately, the Soviet Union still sees itself as the home base of a universal and total ideology proclaimed to be the be all and end all of human civilization. But that ideology has been used as a means to conceal territorial conquests and to enable the Soviet Union to operate according to the medieval principle of the German princes, *Cuius regio eius religio*. The unarmed prophets of the starving peoples of Africa, Asia, and South America, oppressed by the military and feudal lords, readily accept the aid of foreign bayonets to establish a social order that is within the realm of possibility under the circumstances. But the net result is more hunger and more human victims than was the case under the regime they overthrew. New aid is sought, this time urgently needed economic aid, but now in the only place it can be found, namely, in the West.

Ideology has also been used as a kind of spiritual massage. But the "final solution," communism, is continually postponed as, in fact, was proclaimed at the Plenary Session of the Central Committee of the CPSU on June 15, 1983 (it was not even mentioned at the Plenary session of the United Polish Workers' Party of that same month; there were, after all, more important problems to deal with there). And the new edition of the Third Party Program of the CPSU, adopted by the Twenty-seventh Party Congress, replaced Khrushchev's vision of 1961 of a communist society to be realized twenty years later with the formulation that the next historical phase will be "developed socialism."

Forward-looking reforms are not concerned with reinforcing the collective components of the state religion. Quite to the contrary, more market, more independence, more self-determination, more reliance on the traditional market mechanisms (such as prices, money, and credit), less planning and less state *dirigisme* are demanded and, in fact, in some cases have even been introduced. The Soviet government itself seems to have embarked upon this path in its resolution of July 26, 1983, and in the resolutions of the Twenty-seventh Party Congress, and certainly the reforms in Hungary since 1968 point in this direction.

Of course, Soviet cultural life has not stood still. Relativity theory is no longer an evil invention of the imperialists, as it was in Stalin's times. The charlatan Lysenko (former member of the Academy of Sciences and for a quarter-century the tsar of Soviet biology) is not around to destroy what remains of the wreckage of Soviet agriculture. Artists no longer need fear the sad fates of Babel, Mandel-stam, or Pilniak. But these changes are not enough to give birth to a new cosmopolitan spirit, and so numerous Soviet writers, musicians, and sculptors have emigrated to the capitalist West. There is no reverse emigration of Western artists seeking to pursue their creative activities in the East.

It would, of course, be naive to compare a rather abstract paradigm that is more utopian than scientific with a real social system. But this, in fact, was the great mistake of the ideologues of yesteryear who attempted to fashion a blueprint for an extremely complicated social mechanism at their writing desks or to conjure it from their test tubes.

It would be foolish to deny the importance of Marx's theory. But it can by no means be regarded as a paradigm for an exemplary model of a just society, freed of alienation. It lacks the "head" which, according to Marx, German philosophy was to have provided. It would be impossible to bring together a task force of philosophers under real socialism who are still among the ideologically faithful or of the few thinkers who have remained true to communist ideology that could rank with the minds of mid-nineteenth century Germany, headed by Hegel, Feuerbach, and Marx.[37]

But the ideology also lacks the heart, namely the proletariat, elected by Marx to carry out the anticapitalist revolution. The workers of today bear little resem-blance to the proletariat Marx observed from the window of the British Museum, the proletariat that who inspired his monumental work *Kapital*.

The twentieth century has taken a completely different course from that which could have been predicted in the middle of the last century. At that time, when the steam engine and the firing pin weapon marked the heights of man's creative and destructive potential and misery was the ineluctable fate of the majority of the population, it was correct to conclude that the social system had exhausted its progressive potential and sooner or later would be overthrown by the oppressed of the earth. However, despite setbacks, the capitalist system has proven to be more efficient than any other alternative society. The proletariat did not accept its sentence to a life of impoverishment, especially where it was able to organize itself into free trade unions to defend its interests. The greatest scientific and technical progress has occurred not in the society established in Marx's name, but in traditional society, as a consequence of the greatest progress ever made in transforming a traditional social structure: i.e., the absolute and relative reduc-tion in the working class.

Dysfunctions occur in both societies. But economic crises occur not only as a consequence of the "anarchy" of the market, but just as much as a consequence of the anarchistic conditions existing in the planned economies.

The convergence theory so avidly discussed in the early 1970s can no longer be sustained. Peaceful coexistence of the two world systems and a lively exchange of goods and services must be secured at any price. The heavy costs of East-West confrontation must be eliminated. Arms entail not only the risk of war. They are a hazard to human civilization even without war. It is not just the cost, which is especially prohibitive for the East, but the decay of the structures of the economy and society and the growing influence of the military on world events, which may have devastating consequences for the state, which are cause for concern. Arms negotiations have never ever cooled the arms race for any lengthy period of time. A mass movement must therefore be created to defend the cause of peace. But the *sine qua non* for success is equal rights in both world systems and the right to free passage across borders for those struggling for peace. But above all, our youth must be educated to the cause of peace, rather than to the cause of war.

Notes

1. Quoted from Michel Billerey, "Ideen, die die Welt verändern," in *Das menschliche Wagnis (Enzyklopädie des Geistes und Sozialwissenschaften),* (Verlag Kister: Geneva, 1971), p. 97.

2. Jacques Adelbert in ibid., p. 186.

3. Ibid., p. 188.

4. Quoted by Paul Johnson in *Modern Times: The World from the Twenties to the Eighties* (New York: Harper & Row, 1983).

5. *Pareto and Mosca* (Englewood Cliffs, N.J.: Prentice-Hall, Inc., 1965).

6. Quoted in Michael Freund, *Propheten der Revolution* (Bremen, 1970), p. 163.

7. Marx did not have much use for the ideal of equality, as he straightforwardly confirmed in a conversation with the wife of his intimate friend Ludwig Kugelmann: she: "I can't imagine them in a time of levelling since they have thoroughly aristocratic inclinations and habits"; he: "Nor can I; these times will come, but we must then no longer be around" (Franziska Kugelmann, April/May 1867), in *Gespräche mit Marx und Engels,* ed. Hans Magnus Enzensberger (Frankfurt, 1973), p. 319.

8. "Der italiänische KP-Führer Lucio Lombardo Radice über Bahros System-Kritik," *Der Spiegel,* 42/1978.

9. In his article in *Pravda* on October 11, 1918, "The proletarian revolution and the renegade Kautsky," Lenin described Kautsky's *The Dictatorship of the Proletariat* as "a hundred times more full of indignation and bears a hundred times more deeply the stamp of the renegade than do Bernstein's conditions for socialism. Kautsky has become a true renegade and a lackey of the bourgeoisie—a whole brochure would be necessary to describe in full this debased renegade Kautsky and every pearl of his renegade condition. . . ."

10. Karl Marx, *Randglossen zum Programm der deutschen Arbeiterpartei (Gotha Programm),* April-May 1875.

11. *Vecernje Novosti,* 16 June 1983.

12. *Grundsatzprogramm,* op. cit. p. 7.

13. Quoted in Thomas Novotny: "Arbeiterselbstverwaltung und Dezentalisierung— Ein realistischer Weg zum Sozialismus?" in *Der Europäischen Rundschau,* 2 March 1983.

14. Quoted in *Neue Zürcher Zeitung,* 9 January 1982.

15. In interview for *Svenska Dagblatet,* 5 January 1982.

16. Francois Fejtö, "Trotz allem Sozialdemokratie," *Europäische Rundschau,* January 1981, p. 105.

17. Arnold J. Toynbee, *Harvard Business Review,* September-October 1958.

18. Leonard Shapiro, *The Origin of the Communist Autocracy,* London, 1955, pp. 254–255.

19. *Polityka*, 19 July 1981.

20. *Polityka*, 11 October 1980.

21. Murray Yanowitch, *Social and Economic Inequality in the Soviet Union* (New York: M.E. Sharpe, 1977), p. 124.

22. Michael Voslensky, *Nomenklatura, Moskaus Macht-Elite* (quoted from *Der Spiegel*, 6/1980, p. 176).

23. Charles Reich, *The Greening of America* (p. 150 in the German edition).

24. Communist Party Manifesto, p. 32.

25. National Foreign Assessment Center, *Handbook of Economic Statistics 1980*, p. 50, and *Narodnoe khoziaistvo SSSR 1978*, p. 49.

26. Raymond Aron, *Demokratie und Totalitarismus* (Christian Wegner Verlag, 1965), p. 218.

27. Vaclav Machajski, "The Revolution of Social Democracy," quoted in Bell, op. cit., pp. 335–36.

28. In the preface to the third Polish edition of the Communist Party Manifesto, p. 25.

29. Freund, op. cit., p. 153.

30. Quoted from "Es ist zu früh einen Sieg zu feiern," *Der Spiegel*, 28/1983, p. 80.

31. J. Konnik, *Dengi v period stroitel'stva kommunisticheskogo obshchestva*, Moscow, 148, pp. 148–149.

32. This sentence from Popescu's novel *The Fist and the Hand* was subjected to harsh criticism in the Soviet literary periodical *Literaturnaia Gazeta*, 4 May 1983; the Romanian counterpart *Romana Literara* responded with an article "Scissors against Truth."

33. Georges Rodier: "Der Begriff Kultur" in *Das menschliche Wagnis*, op. cit., p. 112.

34. Manes Sperber, "Schreiben dieser Zeit," *Wiener Journal*, 3 April 1983.

35. Alvin Gouldner, *The Dialectic of Ideology and Technology* (New York: Oxford University Press, 1982).

36. From "Report of the Director of the Munich U.S. Radio Station for Eastern Europe, James D. Buckley," *Die Press*, 18 July 1983.

37. Mikhail Bakunin, Marx's contemporary and opponent, saw in Marx the debasement of the greatness of German philosophy and, above all, the expression of German chauvinism in the following passage: "Because then as now (1871), he, the great German patriot, did not acknowledge the right of the Slavs to free themselves from the German yoke, because now as then he thinks that it is the mission of the Germans to civilize them, i.e., to Germanize them peacefully or by force." See *Gespräche mit Marx und Engels*, op. cit., p. 95.

Index

Absenteeism, 39–40, 57
Academy of Sciences (USSR), 93, 99
Aczel, György, 149
Adorno, 158
Afferica, Joan, 13
Afghanistan, 85
Africa, 183
Agriculture: crisis in Soviet Union, 35; development, 168–172
Ahlen program, 111
Alcoholism, 12–13, 53
Aldeberg, Jacques, 153
Aliev, Geydar, 96
Andropov, Yuri, 12, 43, 52, 76, 77, 90, 93, 94, 95, 96–97, 98, 100, 179, 181, 182
Antal, Laszlo, 144, 146
Anti-Corn Law League, 103
Aron, Raymond, 171
Asia, 183; mass production, 48
Aspen Institute, 53
Association of Employers, 121
Attlee, Clement, 114
Austria, 7, 15, 55, 163; comparison of economic structure, 22; competitiveness, 34; economic growth, capital investments, and productivity, 73; economic performance, 71; employed population breakdown, 169; employee-employer relations, 39; foreign trade, 71–72; nationalization, 114–115; per capita income, 58; private initiative, 141; proportion of tax revenues and social security pay-

ments, 25; share of state sector, 115, 116; status of state sector, 126; taxes and social security payments, 83; unemployment, 14; wage levels, 83; work hours, 37
Austrian National Bank, 115
Austrian School, 103
Austrian Social Democratic Party, 178
Austro-Hungarian monarchy, 15

Bad Godesberg program, 24, 106, 110, 111, 117, 118, 124, 125
Baibakov, Nikolai, 95–96
Bakunin, Mikhail, 159
Bank of england, 106, 114
Banque de France, 112, 113
Banque Nationale de Paris, 112
Banque Nationale pour la Commerce et l'Industrie (BNCI), 112
Barbusse, Henri, 161
Belgium: comparison of economic structure, 22; proportion of tax revenues and social security payments, 25; public expenditures in percent of GNP, 24, 25; wage levels, 83; work hours, 37
Bell, Daniel, 102
Berdyaev, Nikolai, 76, 165
Bernstein, Eduard, 107
Besançon, Alain, 76
Beveridge, William, 87
Bialer, Seweryn, 13
Bibo, Istvan, 132
Bihari, Mihaly, 148

187

About the Author

Adam Zwass for many years held managerial positions in the central banking systems of Poland and the USSR. From 1963 to 1968 he was Counsellor in the Secretariat of the Council for Mutual Economic Assistance in Moscow, where he was responsible for financial settlements and the work of the International Bank for Economic Cooperation.

Since his emigration to Western Europe in 1969, Dr. Zwass has been affiliated with the German Institute of Economic Research (West Berlin), the Austrian Institute of Economic Research (Vienna), and the Viennese Institute for Comparative Economic Studies. He is currently active as a bank advisor.

Dr. Zwass is the author of numerous articles on monetary questions, banking, and problems of integration, which have been published in Europe and in the United States. His books published in English by M. E. Sharpe include *Monetary Cooperation Between East and West* (1975), *Money, Banking and Credit in the Soviet Union and Eastern Europe* (1979), and *The Economies of Eastern Europe in a Time of Change* (1983).